The Small
Community

The Small Community

Foundation of Democratic Life

Arthur E. Morgan

With forewords by **Baker Brownell** *and* **Donald Szantho Harrington**

Transaction Publishers
New Brunswick (U.S.A.) and London (U.K.)

Published in 2013 by Transaction Publishers, New Brunswick, New Jersey.
Originally published in 1942 by Harper & Brothers Publishers. Copyright
© 1942 by Arthur E. Morgan. Foreword copyright © 1984 by Community
Service, Inc.

WH, 36⁰⁰ Feb 5, 2013

This book is printed on acid-free paper that meets the American National
Standard for Permanence of Paper for Printed Library Materials.

Library of Congress Catalog Number: 2011035573
ISBN: 978-1-4128-4746-9
Printed in the United States of America

Library of Congress Cataloging-in-Publication Data

Morgan, Arthur E. (Arthur Ernest), 1878-1975.
   The small community : foundation of democratic life / Arthur E.
   Morgan; with a foreword by Baker Brownell and a foreword by Donald
   Szantho Harrington.
       p. cm.
   Originally published: New York : Harper & Brothers Publishers,
   c1942.
   ISBN 978-1-4128-4746-9
      1. Community life. 2. Villages. 3. Sociology, Rural. I. Brownell,
   Baker, 1887-1965. II. Title.
HT431.M6 2012
307.76'2—dc23
                                                      2011035573

CONTENTS

PART THREE

SPECIFIC COMMUNITY INTERESTS

PART FOUR

CONCLUDING OBSERVATIONS

FOREWORD

Arthur E. Morgan was one of the truly great men of our age. He had the ability to distinguish what was really important from what seemed important to most of the world. He had a knack for going directly to the heart of any matter which concerned him, and there was no area of human knowledge or skill that did not concern him. In dealing with problems of engineering or human engineering, he went below the symptoms to the causes, and, from their careful analysis, onto imaginative and holistic solutions. He was not interested in shortcuts or quick fixes which would bring about the appearance of solutions, but in the fundamental changes involving individual human growth which would guarantee lasting individual and social progress.

Out of a lifetime of experience and reflection over many affairs, great and small, he came to the conclusion that the crucial element in the building of a better society is the improvement of the quality of individual character. His philosophy was honed out of such far-flung pioneering ventures as the rebuilding of Antioch College in Yellow Springs, Ohio, with its innovative work-study program and concept of a well-rounded education for each student, to his many extensive flood control assignments and his becoming the first Chairman and Chief Administrative Officer of the Tennessee Valley Authority. The TVA construction camps on his big engineering jobs were in most cases set up as model communities. These attracted—and held—a quality of work force that greatly enhanced the efficiency of the projects, though that was not his chief motive.

As a member of the Indian Commission on Higher Education he was directly responsible for the creation of India's system of rural universities, designed to enhance the viability and quality of life in India's 500,000 villages. He was also an advisor to governments in Africa, Asia, Europe and America and had a hand in bringing about the League of Nations after World War I.

Writing to his editor forty years ago, he said:

Various persons have wondered why, after years of association with extensive affairs, I should come to center my attention on those seemingly insignificant elements of our society, the small villages and other primary groups. This centering of attention has not been capricious or accidental, but is a normal and essential conclusion of a long process of inquiry.

From the time I was a high school student I was impressed with the slow and halting course of human progress, and constantly asked myself, What are the controls of human character and personality? What are the keys to the direction of those influences which would lead to the fulfillment of the possibilities of human life? No matter what I did, that question remained near the forefront of my mind, and so my varied experiences became data to be used in trying to answer that question.

In a little gem of a book written in the 1930's, *The Long Road*, he had likened the building of a good society to the building of longer and longer suspension bridges. There comes a point in the lengthening of a span, he wrote, when no amount of increasing resources and no improvement of design can make up for poor or uneven quality of material, for the weight gathers faster than the holding power, and beyond that point the bridge will fall. Today we have in America a wealthy society, capable of supporting a much higher standard of life for all. We have in our democratic institutions a reasonably good design. The missing element is a general improvement of the quality of the material, of the human character of the people who make up the society. The long way round of building human character, he wrote, will prove to be the short way home to a better social order.

And how are we to build better human character? Where is it that character is formed? He found the answer to these questions in the primary human groups, the family and the small community. To build a better society, therefore, one needs to find ways to strengthen precisely these areas in which our society has largely failed. Our small communities have been permitted to become run down and impoverished while society concentrates upon huge, impersonal cities where family life is difficult to sustain and increasingly large numbers of our most gifted people find it impossible to raise families. Thus, Morgan concluded, if we want to have a better society with more rounded and competent human beings, we must concentrate on preserving and perfecting the small community.

This concern is what led to his writing *The Small Community: Foundation of Democratic Life – What It Is and How to Achieve It* just forty years ago. Much has changed since this book was written. The references and statistics reflect a world less self-conscious, even less in need of Morgan's message than it is today. The problems and the solutions remain, however, as critical and as valid as they were in 1942.

The book is a classic in its field and is distinctive in that it combines a discussion of the significance of the small community with social theory guidelines for specific activities. It looks at the small community as neither a panacea nor an isolated phenomenon but as an integral part of the larger human society. Morgan discusses the significance of the small community, how communities can be organized, the development of economic enterprise, cooperative expression and community services, the recreation and development of a sense of ethics and morality, and finally concludes with observations concerning the importance of maintaining freedom within the community and motivating in young people a desire for community pioneering.

"In the long run," Morgan says, "the basic culture of human society can maintain itself on no higher level than the culture of the small community." This is the area which today needs attention more than any other. If I were the newly elected governor of one of our fifty American states, I believe my first act would be to set in motion a study of the health of my state's small communities. I would organize small teams of experts trained to go into small communities to meet with their people on home ground, face to face, to help them study themselves. They would discover ways in which their economic life could be strengthened, providing more income for families, more opportunities for young people while staying at home in the community. They would learn how to create new cultural opportunities to lend interest to life, new possibilities for health services, music, art, drama and the like, using their own home grown talents. I would experiment with these, trying to evaluate and improve them by experience, thus prompting the slow growth of human character and quality which within a generation would begin to bear fruit in a better society and a more satisfying way of life.

A good many years ago Arthur Morgan visited with me in New York and we discussed his long life experience as it was drawing toward its close. I asked him if he considered his work as chairman of the Tennessee Valley Authority as the high point of his career. His response, as I recall it, was that he believed his work with the TVA to have been an important contribution, especially because of the concept of regional, multi-purpose water development which was designed and carried out in a way that paid full attention to the development of human beings and human community in the process, making it a kind of model of the right way to undertake such developments, as contrasted with the human-disregarding methods followed by most large construction engineering firms. However, he said his years with the TVA were precisely the years when he should have been out around the country arousing interest in America's small communities and raising the endowment necessary to fund a great national effort at small community renewal. By the time he had finished with the TVA and its aftermath, he felt that he was too old to undertake this on the scale required and no longer able to interest those who would have been necessary for the undergirding of such an effort. So deep was his commitment to the cause of the small community development and what he felt would be its immediate consequence, the strengthening of family life and individual human character, that from the point of view of his long-range life goals, he felt he may have made the wrong choice in accepting the chairmanship of the TVA.

Yellow Springs, Ohio, is a living testament to the reality of Morgan's vision. In many respects it has realized his dream of a vital, neighborly, creative and productive small community. The organization he founded in 1940 to try to spark this development is located in Yellow Springs. This organization, Community Service, Inc., continues to give advice and counsel to individuals, groups and communities seeking to enrich and enhance their living. We owe a debt of gratitude to Community Service, Inc., for this reprinting of Arthur Morgan's practical, yet visionary study and manual for action for the improvement of small community life.

DONALD SZANTHO HARRINGTON
Minister Emeritus,
    The Community Church of New York
State Chairman,
    The Liberal Party of New York

New York
September, 1983

This material first appeared in the 1984 edition by Raven Rocks Press.
Copyright © 1984 by Community Services, Inc.

EDITOR'S FOREWORD

This book is in its way a manual of human survival. It is a study of the small, primary community where more than anywhere else, men can find the way to live well. It points out how the good community may be attained.

In this era of great cities, megalopolitan culture and massive events we are likely to forget the human measure. The human scale, the quiet integrity of our finite powers, is ignored; and because we can pile events on events in mountainous accumulations by the use of mechanized energy, we assume that the human scope and range of life can expand to include them. But this is not true. Neither is it desirable.

Life now is no bigger than it was four generations ago. A man today has no more ability to comprehend in his thought the experience of living or to appreciate its values than had his grandfathers. He has no more control over his affairs. Men have increased their control of the natural environment, it is true, but in so doing they have created a social and mechanical environment so out of scale with man that it is overwhelming. The struggle now is less with Nature than with man. To maintain human integrity against the mass of our own creations is the main problem.

This book points the way, and the only way in my opinion, not only to the good life but to the very survival of our Western world. Other books, other people through the ages have pointed out this road to human welfare. But with each

age, with each new technology, with each birth of a new culture, it becomes necessary to point the way again. Modern
men are bluffed by the prestige of bigness, by the so-called
efficiencies of centralized control and mass production. In
some fields production and control of this sort are efficient
and effective, it is true, but by no means in all. The small community, the intimate group within the scope of a man's acquaintance, remains the primary pattern in which men must
live if they would have good life. Their moral sensibility and
devotion, their appreciative integrity and natural art depend
on it. They must live in small communities, it would seem,
to maintain even their reproductive vitality and racial existence.

If Arthur Morgan, the author of this book, were more
limited in his social interests and sympathies he would be an
appropriate symbol of that American type and legend called
the dynamic man. As a man of action his career might well
be the envy of any two-fisted but one-minded go-getter,
whose stereotype dominates the advertisements, the mass
literature and the sentiments of so many modern people. An
engineer of national repute, perhaps the foremost figure in
the United States in the reclamation of wet lands and flood
control, he has ranged through the fields of action from
helping a neighbor clean a pond to projects involving many
millions of dollars over ten or fifteen states. In fifty or more
co-operative engineering projects, in the Dayton flood-control work, in the Pueblo flood-control work, in the Arkansas
drainage project, in the reclamation works in the Southern
States, in the early work and development of the Tennessee
Valley Authority he has been the main factor in dynamics
and design. For twenty years he was an engineer by profession, president of his company, prominent in the American

Society of Civil Engineers and a member of the governing board. As a man of action, not merely on paper but in the field, he is one of the forces that have made America powerful.

But Mr. Morgan is also a man sensitive to human needs and values. He is an educator nationally known, president for many years of Antioch College and originator of the "Antioch idea," first president of the Progressive Education Association, member of the executive committee of the League to Enforce Peace which initiated the plan for the League of Nations, and a philosopher who never went to college. In these generous interests and sympathies he is decidedly more than that American stereotype, the man of action.

For behind these variegated interests and activities there is a unity of life that is at once intellectual, dynamic and moral. It is a deliberate and organic unity. Its main interest is human beings, their motivations, their controls. In his engineering activities, his educational work, his business, his administrative, political, financial and managerial affairs, the study of the human being was central. Mr. Morgan tells of this interest in a letter to me from which I quote:

"Various persons have wondered why, after years of association with extensive affairs, I should come to center my attention on those seemingly insignificant elements of our society, the small villages and other primary groups. This centering of attention has not been capricious or accidental, but is a normal and essential conclusion of a long process of inquiry.

"From the time I was a high-school student I was impressed with the slow and halting course of human progress, and constantly asked myself, What are the controls of human character and personality? What are the keys to the direction of those influences which would lead to the fulfillment of the possibilities of human life? No matter what I did, that question remained near the forefront of my mind, and so my varied experiences became data to be used in trying to answer that question."

Mr. Morgan has worked primarily with men throughout a life of action and varied interests that have taken him to every part of America. He has been not only an engineer working with materials but, in the best sense of the word, an engineer of human destinies. His boyhood was spent in a small frontier town. His early work as a land surveyor took him into small communities where he lived for a few days at a time in many families deriving from almost every stock in Europe and representing every culture. As a reclamation engineer, he lived for years in the field in close contact with the workers on the job and with small communities and the families of the region where the work was done. He employed during this period more than two thousand engineers as well as many other men, and he worked out careful plans for the selection of personnel. He personally examined the records of thousands of these assistants. He interviewed thousands of prospective employees. He supervised the work of more than two hundred contractors in various fields of construction. He handled large projects by "force account," by direct purchase of equipment and employment of men, and he carried through the legal phases of these undertakings with scores of lawyers.

In his educational work, as college president and chairman of the board, he adopted new methods of selection of students, searching their backgrounds almost as closely as those of prospective faculty members. In financing the college he became acquainted with hundreds of leaders of American life in business and the professions. Many of those persons became close personal friends.

As administrative head of the Tennessee Valley Authority a hundred million dollars worth of construction was under his direction. He assembled his staff and selected his employees by a thoroughgoing process of examination never before attempted in a great public agency. The savings in turn-over and general efficiency were great. He has worked for more than fifteen years with labor leaders and their followers, and in 1918 and 1933 co-operated with them to develop uniform overall labor codes. He has worked with manufacturers and has had close contacts with numerous persons in public life, including the President and his wife, cabinet members, senators, congressmen, governors. In the Tennessee Valley Authority he accomplished a great work by his ability to understand and to co-operate with diverse sorts of people. When the movement of the TVA seemed no longer in his direction there was a break. He left the TVA with a great work done.

Through the long years of life and work in all parts of America Mr. Morgan's continuing interest has been the observation of the drives and incentives of men. In fields seemingly remote from his main professions, as vice-president of the American Unitarian Association, as trustee of a theological seminary, as originator and director of a small but successful technical industry, as charter member of the American Eugenics Society, his interest has been always in people. He studied over the origin of personal traits and in his youth wished to become a physician so that he could examine the sources of personality in his patients. This hope was never fulfilled in himself. After years of discussion with his friends, however, he finally found in Samuel S. Fels a person who responded to this interest. The Fels Fund laboratories at Antioch College were founded for carefully planned studies and records of the development of children, beginning at an early prenatal period and extending into maturity. For about ten years the development of one hundred fifty children has been carefully followed by a professional research staff.

From this lifetime of experience, from extensive travel and observation here and in Europe, there gradually has emerged in Dr. Morgan's thought a conviction of the significance of the small, primary social group in the determination of human culture. That conviction he says, "does not go to the extent of a belief that other elements of social and personal environment are not also vital. A conviction has been reached, however, that the significance of the primary group has been so greatly overlooked that the oversight is coming to menace the continuity of our basic culture. Just as concern over nutrition does not imply that no other element of personal care is important, but only that nutrition cannot safely be ignored; so concern for community development does not imply lack of regard for other elements.

"In social as in personal economy, it is wise to give attention to vital concerns that have been overlooked or neglected. It would be very unwise to see those neglected elements as the only important ones. Significant as is the primary group, its usefulness has limitations. It is the source of social order, good will, and personal and economic security, but not of the ranging, inquiring mind, or of the free personality. The very process by which I became convinced of the importance of the primary group was that of transcending such groups and having a wide range of experience which enabled me to see them objectively. A good society demands a far higher regard for the importance of the small community, but it demands that all elements of social organization, of which the small community is but one, shall be kept in good proportion."

So important to Mr. Morgan is his belief in the primary significance of the small community that he has formed an organization called Community Service, Inc., designed to give professional assistance, counsel and managerial aid in the rehabilitation of small communities or the formation of new ones. To the small community and its development in the United States he intends to devote the rest of his life.

But Mr. Morgan is no fanatic. He recognizes the need for large-scale organization, for mass production and mass power in their proper places. But he rejects their domination over human life. He insists on the primary place of the small community in human welfare. This alone would involve a deep and wholesome change in modern affairs of revolutionary significance.

BAKER BROWNELL

INTRODUCTION

Several years ago I went to visit a man in the southwest of France. The village street on which he lived was lined by a high, solid brick wall which sheltered the houses from the passers-by. At each house was an iron gate, above which hung a bell. When the bell was rung a servant would come and open the gate. Each house was separated from its neighbor by a similar wall, while to the rear was a steep rocky hillside covered with an almost impenetrable thicket of wild plum and blackberry brambles. Thus, each house was a sort of walled castle.

I arrived at the village in the morning, and since my host did not expect me until afternoon, I decided to spend the intervening time in exploring a nearby forest. After walking for two or three hours I was absent-mindedly making my way when the rough going brought me to my senses. I found myself in a tumble of boulders in a thicket of thorn trees and briers. The path had entirely disappeared. The time of my engagement was approaching, but it seemed better to push ahead to the other side of the forest, rather than to retrace my course. Shortly I came to a place where the waste from a household was dumped, and following the path leading to it through the thicket, I soon found myself at the entrance of an enclosed garden.

As I walked up the garden path, whom should I meet but my host! When he saw me emerge from the thicket and enter the garden he raised his hands in almost frightened astonishment and exclaimed, "But, Monsieur, it cannot be! There is no path! One does not come from America by that way." He would not be at ease until I had explained the manner of my arrival.

Is it not similarly necessary that I explain my apparently sudden if not forcible entry into a field commonly included in the domain of Rural Sociology? Why should a person whose life has been spent as engineer, educator, and administrator essay entrance into so different an area, one already so well occupied by able men? To indicate how such a course came to be taken is to disclose the major theme of this book.

Archimedes is said to have remarked, "Give me a fulcrum on which to place my lever, and I can move the world." Every person who is trying to make his life yield enduring results is on that same quest. He is trying to discover the situation and the conditions in which the limited powers and abilities which are his can be used most effectively to produce enduring values.

During the course of twenty years the writer sought to use the profession of engineering as his fulcrum. He would carry through public works with economy, efficiency, and integrity. People would see that work being done, he reasoned to himself, and would come to respect the philosophy of life which produced it. Also, certain necessary work would be accomplished.

Such a course yields great satisfactions. It brings one close to reality. Structures of earth, concrete, and steel are not sustained by propaganda or by wishful thinking. Engineering is excellent discipline. Yet it has its shortcomings. If one has paid a great price to achieve a philosophy of life he will wish to express that philosophy with clearness and definiteness. A dam or a bridge or a river-control work may perfectly serve its purpose, and yet as a medium for expressing a philosophy of life it may be inadequate.

Also, the practice of engineering seemed to the writer not to provide full opportunity for communicating to others the view of life he had worked out for himself. With the public for whom the engineer works, this is especially true. People see the engineer in his specialized capacity. What they want from him is engineering judgment and action. Most of his contacts with his clients are so specialized, so limited, and so infrequent that they do not provide effective opportunity for exchange of views on general aims and purposes, much less for achieving unity of fundamental outlook. In large measure the same holds true for the relations of the executive engineer with his staff. Such contacts usually are specialized, brief, and related to the work immediately at hand. Most of the persons involved already have matured and definite views of life which are but slightly subject to modification by such contacts. Pleasant and satisfying as are the professional associations of an engineer, they perhaps do not provide a most effective fulcrum for the lever of one whose chief interest is in achieving for himself and in co-operating with others who are striving to acquire a total view of life in good proportion and perspective.

It was for this reason that, after twenty years of professional practice, the writer changed his field of work from engineering to education. In association with college faculty members, and with students during that nascent period when learning by imitation may be replaced in some degree by critical, reflective thinking, would there not be greater opportunity for maturing and for giving expression to one's philosophy of life? The years spent in that field were most interesting and, let us hope, not wholly unprofitable. But they taught a lesson which was further emphasized by several years of public administration.

That lesson is that the fundamental traits of personality are fixed earlier in life than is generally supposed. College students may greatly extend their intellectual outlooks; philosophy and religion may be revolutionized, political views may be changed as greatly; yet the basic habits of action may be but slightly modified by such intellectual and emotional transformations.

It is not that this period of training is unimportant from the standpoint of character-building. The environment of the earlier years may be far from unified. Parents may give one direction to the lives of their children, while the influence of friends and playmates may be quite different. Church and school, books, newspapers, movies and radio, may add yet other, perhaps discordant, elements. The young man or woman of college age, therefore, may not be a unified, integrated personality, but may reflect a great range of discordant influences. The college years may be a period of adding to that confusion of personality; or they may be a period of clarification, unification, and integration. Those years may provide opportunity for wise appraisals, for elimination of disintegrating influences, and for the strengthening of those which give clarity, strength, and consistency to character. The period when physical and intellectual life are maturing is very important.

Yet only occasionally do college years change the basic personal reactions, and when such change does take place it represents great personal achievement at great effort. Even when there is sincere intellectual and emotional conversion, the early habits of life may continue to control. The brilliant medical student may continue to be careless of his own health. The deeply convinced pacifist may continue to be aggressive and unkindly in his temper. The man who is consumed by a sincere urge for public service, through lack of early training in thrift may be very wasteful of public funds. The research scientist may be far from eliminating prejudice in his general views. The person who by great effort has achieved a satisfying philosophy of life for himself may find his early conditioning leading him to dictatorial habits, to trouble-making, and to inconsiderate actions. During all his life his early training may be a drag upon his actions, and may partly neutralize his usefulness. Many men endeavor to influence others, not because they wish others to be like themselves, but because they hope that others may escape the personality-handicaps under which they themselves live and work.

Where there is fine quality, it, too, has come largely from the early environment. Little by little the impression has deepened that the early years are of controlling significance. By and large it is those years that make character.

Then comes the necessary conclusion, which is the main theme of the first part of this book, that to a very large degree it is the family and the small community that determine the influence of the early years. Observation makes it clear that the small primary group or community which has this profound influence is being greatly neglected, and in America is tending rapidly to disappear. Yet need for it is not disappearing.

From these experiences it has become the conviction of the writer that of all major factors which enter into the determination of our national life, few if any are receiving so inadequate attention as is the welfare of the community or primary group. It was by this course of experience that he came to feel that the preservation and the perfecting of the small community is one of the greatest issues facing our times, and also that for many a person a life-career in such a group may be the best possible fulcrum on which to use the lever of his capacity for social usefulness. This book is in brief a survey of the field, and a guide to work within the small community.

The treatment of the subject differs markedly from those which record case studies of technical social anthropologists. Such studies are necessary and valuable; but to a considerable degree it is not necessary or desirable to use their methods in pointing out some of the major difficulties facing communities, and the grave dangers to society resulting therefrom, or before pointing to some obvious means for meeting the situation. Sometimes what is most needed is to emphasize to the layman what to the sociologist is common knowledge. Even in sociology many men are laymen in branches outside their own specialties.

There are certain obvious lacks of balance in the book. Aside from the treatment of community councils, methods of community organization are insufficiently described. Education, aside from adult education, is passed over almost entirely, as being too vast and varied a field to be effectively treated within the limits of this book. Particularly, agriculture receives almost no attention. Many rural sociologists have thought of small-community life and farm life as almost synonymous. Fundamentally, however, the nature of a community does not depend on the callings of its members. A fishing, mining, or college town will be found to have the same fundamental traits as a farming community. It is the underlying characteristics of community life with which this book is concerned, rather than their application to any particular calling.

The writer is greatly indebted to those men in the field of rural sociology who have read and criticized the manuscript, especially to Edmund deS. Brunner and Arthur Dunham for their many valuable suggestions, and to Lowry Nelson, Robert A. Polson, and Thomas D. Eliot for their helpful comments and criticisms. Many other persons have offered comments and proposals. His secretary, Eleanor Switzer, has carried the burden of typing and putting the manuscript in order. Lucy Morgan and Griscom Morgan also read and criticized the manuscript. Acknowledgments to publishers for permission to make quotations, with identifying notes for all quotations used, are given at the end of the book.

ARTHUR E. MORGAN

Yellow Springs, Ohio
June 1, 1942.

Part One

THE SIGNIFICANCE OF THE COMMUNITY

CHAPTER I

THE SIGNIFICANCE OF THE SMALL COMMUNITY*

IN MODERN times the small community has played the part of an orphan in an unfriendly world. It has been despised, neglected, exploited, and robbed. The cities have skimmed off the cream of its young population. Yet the small community has supplied the lifeblood of civilization, and neglect of it has been one of the primary reasons for the slowness and the interrupted course of human progress. It is high time that the fundamental significance of the small community be recognized.

Over most of the world the village is an ancient institution, often with a history extending into the dim past, sometimes thousands of years, outlasting kingdoms and dynasties. Modern and ancient ways exist there side by side. Often existing informal democratic village government, well adapted to its purpose, differs little from that of the dawn of history.

The village has played a dominant part in the destinies of men. Anthropologists ascribe a million to four million years to the life of mankind. So far as we know, most of

* This introductory chapter is taken, with slight changes, from an article, "The Community—The Seed Bed of Society," by Arthur E. Morgan, in the *Atlantic Monthly*, Vol. 169, No. 2 (February, 1942).

our ancestors during this long period lived in small groups of from a few dozen to a few hundred persons. Only when necessity compelled did they resort to isolated dwellings. The city and the separate farm home, so important in American life, have had a relatively small part in human affairs. Sims, in *The Rural Community*, wrote:

> The great outstanding fact of all the evidence is, however, that throughout the ages man has been a communal dweller. And such for the most part he still remains. The isolated family, when the world at large is held in view, is the exception and not the rule. Isolated homesteads certainly made their first appearance on a large scale in the New World. Here in America, where land was free and relatively unlimited, they came to dominate the rural order.[1]

Cities have existed only during the past ten or twenty thousand years—for perhaps one per cent of the life of the race—and many of them were but overgrown villages. During the Middle Ages most "cities" of Europe were self-sustaining agricultural villages. Even Rome was then a town of about ten thousand, and for centuries scarcely a city in all Europe had a greater population.*

Even today most city dwellers are children or grandchildren of rural people. When the writer's grandfather was born, only six American cities had as many as eight thousand

[1] See p. 304 for references.

* Various medieval European cities were reported to have populations of 60,000. Concerning such reports Edwin F. Gay writes, "During the early part of the medieval period '60,000' was evidently a round number, meaning 'a great many.' There were 60,000 students at Oxford, 60,000 students at Paris, 60,000 parishes in England, etc. At the close of the fourteenth century Parliament imposed a tax on the 60,000 parishes, and was surprised to find that in fact there were only about 9,000. And by the fourteenth century they had become sophisticated enough to alter the 60,000 to a more precise figure, like '61,349,' or '59,495.' London, Paris, Rome, Venice, Genoa, Florence, and perhaps Barcelona had populations of more than 10,000 in the fifteenth century, but for the most part the other cities ran about 5,000 or less." (From a letter to the author.)

inhabitants. Even now probably three quarters of the human race live in villages. There are estimated to be two million villages in Asia, while probably more than half of all Europeans are villagers.

Small communities are the sources of city population. Large cities have such low birth-rates that if their population were not renewed from outside they would almost disappear in four or five generations. Latest census reports indicate that American city families have less than three quarters as many children as would be necessary to maintain their population. The rural fertility rate is more than twice as great as that of cities of more than one hundred thousand.

The community also is the chief source of leadership. A leader is a person of unusual native vigor, intelligence, or personality, who uses that superiority to give expression to the character he acquired from family and community. Great men may make history, but the kind of history they make is determined chiefly by their childhood environment. Napoleon as a boy on the faction-ridden, brigand-infested island of Corsica learned the local ways of intrigue, feud, and ambition. When he was well nigh master of Europe, enthroning and dethroning kings, the ways of the Corsican village ruled his life. A similar story might be told of nearly every present-day European dictator.

The ancient village was not just a collection of families, each going its own way, as is so common in America. Except where blighted by war and conquest, it was a closely organized association of people who lived and worked together for common ends, with mutual good will, respect, and tolerance, sharing dangers and hopes. Since the members all knew each other intimately, dishonesty did not succeed. The villagers had common standards, a common background, a community of memory and association. They helped each other and shared the common lot, not as charity, but as the natural course of community life. That is what we mean by community. Ancient villages varied greatly, and not all had all those characteristics. Yet by and large they justified this description, just as the family is properly referred to as a unit of unselfish co-operation, though not all families exemplify that trait.

Controlling factors of civilization are not art, business, science, government. These are its fruits. The roots of civilization are elemental traits—good will, neighborliness, fair play, courage, tolerance, open-minded inquiry, patience. A people rich in these qualities will develop a great civilization, with great art, science, industry, government. If the basic qualities fade, then no matter how great the wealth, how brilliant the learning, how polished the culture, that civilization will crumble.

These finer underlying traits, which we recognize as the essence of civilization, are not inborn; neither are they best acquired in rough-and-tumble business or political life. They are learned in the intimate, friendly world of the family and the small community, usually by the age of ten or twelve, and by unconscious imitation, as we learn the mother tongue. Only as such traits have opportunity to grow in the kindly, protective shelter of family and small community, or in other groups where there is intimate acquaintance and mutual confidence, do they become vigorous and mature enough to survive. Unless supported by the surrounding community, the single family is too small a unit to maintain fine standards.

When we say that human nature does not change, what we generally mean is that this chain of teaching or conditioning seldom is broken from generation to generation. Each generation acquires while very young the elemental incentives which preceding generations learned in the same way. This basic human culture is of very slow growth. Apparently simple attitudes such as honesty or courtesy have required thousands of years to originate and to be refined and established. Those from whom we learned them, be they parents, neighbors, teachers or companions, did not originate them, but caught them from others, and so on, from time immemorial. If the social threads of community, by which they are preserved and transmitted, should be broken, equally long periods might be necessary to re-create them. The traits of refined culture can be passed by contagion from one individual to another, but that does not mean that they can be quickly originated. The displacement of a lower culture by a higher, such as took place when European culture replaced that of the bushmen in Australia, does not mean that a new culture has been created, but only that an existing culture has been transferred or diffused. That the dandelion has spread all over North America from Europe in a very short time does not nullify the fact that millions of years were necessary for its evolution. If we eliminate a type of plant or animal or of human culture, thousands of years might be necessary for the re-creation of its equivalent.

Even after some of the most precious human qualities have been developed through long-time living together in communities, they have often been nearly destroyed by changing conditions. The idea of continuous, uninterrupted progress of human society—"onward and upward forever"— expresses an ideal to be pursued, rather than a reality which has been achieved. No characteristic of human cultures has been more obvious than their uneven, interrupted course. Advances alternate with regression; great promise is followed by collapse and sometimes by complete disappearance. Many fine achievements of culture have died out in a hostile environment.

The doctrine of the "survival of the fittest" means only that what survives is that which is fittest under the particular existing circumstances. In a crude society fine qualities may be under great handicaps, just as in a refined society crudeness tends to be eliminated. Christianity bears the name of a civilized man who was so "unfit" for the crude environment in which he found himself, that he did not survive. His contribution was that in undertaking to live by a fine pattern he helped to create conditions in which such a pattern of living could survive.

Today the English-speaking world is convinced that extension of the Nazi or Communist program would result in a deterioration of life and society. Yet today is not the first time that more excellent human cultures have been threatened with submergence by crude violence on the part of less excellent societies. During the very long periods when the prevailing type of social organization was the small community, a high degree and fine quality of social adjustment was achieved within the limits of the ancient village.

The age of force and strategy, of conquest, of empire, and of feudalism, swept over and submerged this ancient community life. The democratic equality, the good will and co-operativeness, of communities the world over were largely displaced by dictatorship and serfdom. Men's minds were subjected to indoctrination and propaganda. The common man became the tool of his master, bound to the soil. Deceit, intrigue, and shrewdness—the spirit of Machiavelli—

often prevailed over simple honesty. Yet the ancient spirit of community was not killed. Nearly everywhere it survived in small groups and close to the soil. Feudal society could exploit that quality, but could not live without it. Community traits of good will and mutual confidence constituted the very life-principle of society. Without them society would disintegrate.

There were, it is true, serious limitations to that old community culture. Good will often did not extend to other communities; village life tended to be provincial; men were burdened by superstitions and taboos. The village was too small a unit to fulfill the destinies of human society. Yet that old village culture produced some of the finest qualities the race has known.

Many of the ideals which the Western world holds as most precious are survivals from the ancient community way of life. The burden of the Hebrew prophet's message, good will and brotherhood, which flowered in Christian teaching, was not a new revelation, but a resurgence and extension of ancient community ways in the hills of Palestine. The democracy of Switzerland, which became a beacon light to the modern world, did not originate when men of the forest cantons tore down the baron's castle six hundred and fifty years ago. Those Swiss communities were fighting to preserve their ancient democratic way of life, which in their mountain retreats never had succumbed to feudalism. Religious democracy, which has been a potent school for political democracy, has a similar history. The pre-Reformation reformers did not start a new kind of church government or a new way of life. They chiefly persisted in ancient community ways which they found strikingly in accord with primitive Christianity. When we trace democratically governed religious groups to their origins we find that in most cases they lead back to small communities where the traditions of political and religious democracy had never been wholly extinguished.

Today, as in the ancient past, the small community is the home, the refuge, the seed bed, of some of the finest qualities of civilization. But just as the precious values of the ancient community were submerged and largely destroyed by empire and feudalism, so the present-day community with its invaluable cultural tradition is being dissolved, diluted, and submerged by modern technology, commercialism, mass production, propaganda, and centralized government. Should that process not be checked, a great cultural tradition may be largely lost.

Statesmen and warriors seldom create issues. More often they seize upon those that are becoming dominant, and precariously hang on to them or ride them, guide or misguide them, through their later stages. There are few more alluring myths in all history than that social wrongs can be set right in one mighty effort directed by great organizing genius at the top. Neither the size and complexity of the task, nor the record of failure, has ended that romantic dream. The will to believe in sudden, general social progress, organized from above, is forever exploited by those who seek to control the loyalties and resources of men. The evil results of this myth appear not only in the rise of an Alexander, a Napoleon, a Hitler, but also in competition for power and prominence the world over. The mass of people are influenced to hold in low regard the self-mastery of their own lives, and to focus attention on great programs initiated in centers of government and industry. How often have the seemingly colossal achievements of such programs crumbled away by subsidence of the foundations!

World events of today and tomorrow took their determining directions further back in the past than we realize; and the work of today, if in accord with fundamental realities, will come to full fruition further in the future than we supposed. When events are full grown, herculean effort may change them but slightly. How little change in the current of human affairs, except in spiritual disorganization and exhaustion, was made by the prodigious efforts of the first World War!

Yet very moderate powers, wisely used in harmony with the nature of things, may have profound effect on the more distant future. The free men in obscure Swiss valleys who kept alive the ancient tradition of democratic life may have had more enduring influence than the heads of the Holy Roman Empire. Excellence may be more significant than bigness.

Should people of serious purpose realize the extent to which the local community is the seed bed of civilization, the source of basic character and culture, as well as the medium for their preservation and transmission, then, within their communities, they might be sowing the seeds and cultivating the growth of a better future. The slowness of this process may seem discouraging, yet to expect quicker results may be wishful dreaming—a common cause of cynical despair. One sees everywhere frustration and disillusionment among young people as they measure their small individual powers against vast world currents. Could they see clearly the process by which the future is made and the opportunities they have to share in the making, they would have compelling reasons for a sense of significance and validity for their lives.

Great civilizations rise and fall, and when they fall it is to the level of the small rural communities. In England about the year 1500 a brilliant group of Oxford reformers seemed to usher in a new day of free, liberal thought. There were Erasmus, the counselor of kings; Thomas More, High Chancellor of England; Colet, leader of the group, and dean of St. Paul's; and Lilly, head of St. Paul's School. Yet in less than a generation their movement had faded away, almost as though it had never been. The great tradition of political and religious freedom survived in England largely because Wyclif, one of the greatest spirits England ever knew, had sent his Lollard preachers through the villages, arousing the old democratic community spirit as the essence of a new vision.

Many times in history urban civilizations have broken down, leaving society to rebuild, largely from the village level. Should there be a breakdown in the present social order, the small community is the seed bed from which a new order would have to grow. If it now deteriorates by neglect and by being robbed of its best quality, the new order will not be excellent. Whoever increases the excellence and stability of small communities sets limits to social retrogression.

Though the art and practice of community life are vital to social progress, during historic times the small community nearly always has been neglected. All rural America has been skimmed of its material wealth and of its human quality to feed the insatiable city. The small community has been despised as something to escape from to the larger, better life of the city. The typical American farm village has become little more than a local market, and a location for church and school. The mining town has been drearier still—rows of shacks along the sides of a gully; and the usual factory town, or quarry, fishing, or lumbering village, has been little better. That is an epitome of the old story of neglect and exploitation of the small community, the killing of the goose that lays the golden egg. Do we not have here one of the major causes of the slow progress of humanity in civilization?

Many an American small town or village is no longer a community. Too often it is only a small city, the citizens largely going their individual ways. This progressive disappearance of the community in present-day life is one of the most disturbing phenomena of modern history. It constitutes an historic crisis.

The community need not disappear. The very changes which are destroying it have put into our hands means for re-creating it in a finer pattern. Seldom in modern times has the small community caught a glimpse of its possibilities. Today for the first time it can be abreast or ahead of the city in convenience of living. If we use the present time of social and economic transition as an opportunity, the disappearance of the old community need be no disaster. But there is little time to lose, for with its passing some fine cultural traditions are being broken; and with human culture as with the human breed, if we have no children we cannot transmit our inheritance to grandchildren.

If many young people, searching for careers of significance and adventure, should see the small community as the place where basic human culture is preserved and transmitted, and should seek careers there, the results might be more important than failure or success of any present political or economic movement; and enduring satisfactions along the way might be very real. Many rural callings provide economic footholds for such careers.

In every phase of community life there is room for research, invention, discovery, and for the patient development of community spirit. There one deals with basic realities. There, as a rule, no false appearance of success blinds one to the necessity and the difficulty of the elemental process of developing good will, mutual respect, fair play, co-operation, thrift, and competence.

Suppose a man or woman living in a small community wishes to work for its development. What can he or she do? First it is necessary to get a clear vision of the new community as an all-round, well-proportioned society in which human relations are fine and sound, and where all the elemental needs of men can be met, together with a vision of the place of such communities in larger societies. The poverty of the average small American town or village is not wholly due to shortcomings of economic and political systems. In large part it results from lack of such a vision.

There are many opportunities for community service. Much work is needed in community economics. Fine culture does not thrive best amid starvation or squalor. The community needs help to appraise its economic needs and resources, to plan through the years to achieve sound economic balance. There are unfilled needs for community services, the supplying of which would provide community careers. There are similar opportunities in vocational guidance, in recreation, in developing community libraries, in musical and dramatic programs, in working out recognized community ethics and standards, in promoting community health, and in improving public administration.

America is waking to the meaning of the community, and to its present danger. During the last decade about three hundred communities in the United States, nearly half of

them in California, have established "community councils."
Each socially-minded organization in a community—such as
the Parent-Teachers Association, the Chamber of Commerce,
the service clubs, the trades and labor council, the Y.M.C.A.,
the several churches, the juvenile court, and the school board
—appoints one member to a central council. Through suitable committees this organization keeps in touch with all
vital community interests, brings neglected issues to the attention of those responsible or to the public, or directly
undertakes the necessary service. This new invention of
democracy promises to be a powerful instrument for community welfare, though as yet its workings are often crude,
superficial, and restricted.

Two or three years ago one of the larger American
foundations sent a man through Europe to discover ways to
vitalize community life. On his return he stated that the
Neighborhood Advisory Councils of the Ohio Farm Bureau
are a more promising development of community spirit than
anything he found abroad. A dozen national organizations
see small community interests as among their most vital concerns, and sociologists are studying the small community as
never before.

But it is in American communities themselves that some
of the most encouraging developments are taking place.
Many country ministers are helping to build up their communities in health, housing, and income, and especially in
neighborly community spirit. The people of an Ohio village
of five hundred, together with surrounding farmers, found
community co-operation so interesting that in ten years theirs
has become a pioneer in American community life.

More than a score of Ohio communities have followed
the example of this village of Alexandria. In a town of two

thousand in a Nevada desert a community council is co-ordinating a wide variety of social projects. A farm village of thirty-five hundred in Oklahoma has made itself into a live, progressive community, not through formal organization, but by meeting its various problems as friends, neighbors, and fellow citizens. In a thousand towns and villages, individuals and small groups are doing what they can to make their communities interesting and productive. Perhaps with the small community it has been darkest just before dawn.

Edmund deS. Brunner, one of the foremost of American rural sociologists, who during the course of twenty years has made three successive studies of 140 villages, comments, "While there is much lacking in village life, the improvement in many aspects since my first study in 1923 is amazing." The writer, who has observed American small communities for forty years, confirms that statement, though improvement in some aspects has often accompanied retrogression in others.

Among interesting American communities are those that have a continuous tradition from ancient prefeudal democratic communities of Europe. At Valdese, North Carolina, is a community of Waldensians, that long-persecuted brotherhood of primitive, democratically governed Christians, who for nearly a thousand years have had a precarious survival in the high southern Alps. Tricked into buying some of the most worthless clay hills in North Carolina, they have by simple honesty, co-operation, and hard work, turned the barren hills into such an area of productiveness that they are now greatly outnumbered by people who have come to their community to share their stable prosperity.

Mennonite communities in America continue the ancient

tradition of political and religious democracy which they somewhat unconsciously took from Swiss and Dutch villages. After four hundred years of tenacious adherence to the democratic community ways of their fathers, they display a vigorous spirit of neighborliness and co-operation, which finds numberless expressions in informal friendly services as well as in formal co-operatives for life, fire, and storm insurance, for administration of orphans' estates, for banks and trust companies, for community elevators and stores, for registered breeding stock, and in various other ways. The Hutterite Brethren have continued in South Dakota the communal life which they maintained for centuries in Europe.

New England town government was a lineal descendant of close-to-the-soil political and religious democracy of England, Holland, and Switzerland. A curious offshoot of New England is Mormonism. Followers of Vermont-born Joseph Smith took New England democratic community tradition, and in the West, somewhat removed from machine-age compulsions, developed organized rural community living to a higher level than most of America has achieved.

In the Tennessee mountains a group of Swiss farmers, from Alpine communities that never had succumbed to feudalism, established a settlement seventy years ago, on land so poor that it was largely abandoned. Through intelligent, neighborly co-operation, after the manner of old Swiss democratic communities, they turned this into the most productive tract in the region. After three generations the community spirit still thrives, vigorous and strong enough to hold many of the best young people.

The community, by means of free inquiry and common

aspiration, must achieve a common view of a total way of life, and a common discipline. Only to the extent that it does so is it actually a community. That way of life must grow by the democratic process of voluntary general agreement. It will be influenced by leadership, both local and general, by knowledge of what other communities have done, by litera- ture, art, science, and religion, and by everyday experience. Never will a community be united on everything, yet it must be aware of the standards on which it is substantially united, and which its members can be expected to support. In the ancient community the common way of life was fully under- stood, deeply entrenched, and generally observed; so ques- tions arose in marginal cases only. The flux of modern life has largely erased these common values from the community mind. They must be re-established by conscious, intelligent, critical search, by example, and by teaching.

Community well-being requires a spirit of open, full, free inquiry, with no organization or sect claiming supreme merit, authority, or revelation, or plotting to capture community loyalty for its peculiar doctrines. Many an American com- munity has had its unity disrupted by the strategy of politi- cal or religious ideologies, some claiming to be sole reposi- tories of truth. A real community can emerge only when there is sincere recognition of the fact that ultimate truth or wis- dom is not given to any sect or class or organization, but that all alike should be open-minded seekers.

The new community can be something new under the sun. It can recover the precious qualities of the old, the fellow feeling, acquaintance, good will, mutual respect, planning and working together for common ends. But it need not lose the contributions of the new day. It can escape the narrowness and provincialism of the old village. It must have clear-inghouses for the exchange of ideas and experience.

The new community will not try to monopolize the whole life of its members, as did the ancient village. While it endeavors to satisfy those cravings for common purpose and united neighborly effort which modern life neglects, its members will use many other forms of association—national societies, trade unions, churches, universities, nation-wide industries, and the national government. While co-operating heartily with various federal agencies, it will firmly maintain its individuality and autonomy, and will not be swallowed up in grasping, characterless uniformity of far-flung, centralized government bureaucracy. The community, if it is wise and vigorous, need not be eclipsed, but can be richer, sounder, finer, for its contacts with the wide world. For thousands of young people who seek a way to leave their imprint on their own and on future times, there is room to take part in such adventures. But neither that vision, nor general interest in it, will come suddenly. It must be slowly won.

For the preservation and transmission of the fundamentals of civilization, vigorous, wholesome community life is imperative. Unless many people live and work in the intimate relationships of community life, there never can emerge a truly unified nation, or a community of mankind. If I do not love my neighbor whom I know, how can I love the human race, which is but an abstraction? If I have not learned to work with a few people, how can I be effective with many?

The following chapters undertake to supply a background of the history of the community, an appraisal of its place in present-day society, and suggestions for realizing its inherent possibilities.

CHAPTER II

WHAT IS A COMMUNITY?

A COMMUNITY is an association of individuals and families that, out of inclination, habit, custom, and mutual interest, act in concert as a unit in meeting their common needs. Always some action is reserved for individual or family initiative, and generally a part of life is formally and impersonally organized by legislation or other formal agreement. The extent and the manner in which action is common and unified, and the extent to which it is individual or family action, vary endlessly. Therefore the term "community" cannot be closely defined. To whatever extent common group needs are met by unified action in a spirit of common acquaintance and responsibility, to that extent a community exists.

Sir Henry Maine, whose studies of ancient villages in India and Europe did so much to clarify the nature of community living, made a distinction between *status* and *contract* in human relations. Under *status* he included those indigenous or "natural" relationships which are sustained by natural impulse, habit, custom, and tradition, so that they become second nature. He showed that in many old Indian villages of his day, half a century ago, there were no courts, no policemen, no written laws, but that the organization of society lay in these spontaneous and often deeply rooted folkways. This condition he called *status*. He found in India forms of village organization and land tenure which in his opinion are almost identical with forms which passed away centuries ago in western Europe, both being part of an ancient Aryan culture. In contrast he described the formal organization of society through legislation, with business organized by formal agreements and associations, as a condition of *contract.*

The German sociologist, Ferdinand Tönnies, influenced by Maine, made the central theme of his sociology the difference between *Gemeinschaft* and *Gesellschaft.* The former, like Maine's *status,* consists of the natural, spontaneous, organic relations of people as they develop in the course of living, growing out of mutual affection, acquaintance, custom, and tradition. The latter term he uses to describe the formal organization of society by contracts, legislation, and deliberately planned agreements. The natural, spontaneous kind of human relations based on *Gemeinschaft* he calls *community.* The conscious, deliberate, formal organization he calls *society.* Commonly the *Gesellschaft* or formal relations grow out of and rest on the spontaneous *Gemeinschaft,* and cannot thrive without it. That is, organized society grows out of community, and can thrive only so long as the spirit of community pervades and vitalizes it.

Cooley, in his *Social Organization,* published in 1906, was one of the first Americans to define the nature of the community. He used the term *primary group* to describe human associations in which relations are based on direct acquaintance, common standards, and mutual understanding.

The idea of community gradually has been taking definite form in the minds of American rural sociologists. Galpin, one of the earlier of them, saw the community as a group of families trying to satisfy together such common needs as education, clothing, religion, money. He considered the size of the community area as from sixteen to a hundred square miles, with a village center of from three hundred to three thousand population. Another early writer, MacIvor, gave a definition which, somewhat amplified by Arthur Dunham, reads, "A community is a group of human beings, settled in a fairly compact and contiguous geographical area, and having significant elements of common life, as evidenced by such factors as manners, customs, traditions, and modes of speech." Such a definition makes "community" almost synonymous with a local human society. There is a growing tendency to give more definite and specific meaning to the word. This chapter undertakes to reach and to express the concept of community toward which this tendency is moving; but it should be understood that definitions of community are many and varied, and that the word has also quite other meanings than that used here, as, for instance, when we speak of the "community of nations."

A neighborhood is a group of homes in which there are social relations between families and individuals. However, the neighborhood is not a community in the sense in which we use the term, unless the general and varied needs of the group are recognized as common needs, as the concerns of the group as a unit, planned for and worked for by the unified action of the group.

A community does not exist chiefly because of formal planning and organization, but through direct personal acquaintance and relationships, in a spirit of fellowship. Its members are people who to a considerable extent have cast their lots together, who share problems and prospects, who have a sense of mutual responsibility, and who actually plan and work together for common ends. There must be mutual understanding, respect, and confidence. There must be mutual aid—willingness to help in need, not as charity, but simply as the normal mode of community life. There must be a feeling on the part of each individual that he is responsible for the community welfare. There needs to be a common background of experience, a community of memory and association, and a common foreground of aims, hopes, and anticipations. There must be a considerable degree of unity of standards and purposes.

It is doubtful whether the term "community" should be applied to groups of people who act in common only in a routine impersonal manner in supplying the rudiments of economic needs, such as water supply, sewerage, fire protection, highways, and even schools. Yet if a group of people lacking these facilities should meet together and plan and work together in intimate personal co-operation to supply those needs, the working out of those problems together would be evidence of a real community.

What seems to be an unorganized neighborhood may in fact have the finest qualities of a community. In some small neighborhoods there is, in case of sickness, an informal but very effective distribution of co-operative effort in nursing and other assistance. There may be the same informal effectiveness of unified activity in transporting supplies, in buying, in entertaining visitors, in using farm machinery or other equipment, in carrying on the work of persons temporarily disabled. Quite commonly the competitive processes of buying and selling and bargaining are carried on in a spirit of mutual respect and good will, so that they constitute true community activity. The existence of a community is determined, not by the amount of organization and social machinery, but by the extent to which common needs and interests are worked out by unified planning and action, in a spirit of mutual interest. In such a community there is common acquaintance, and common purposes and standards are defined and maintained.

Negative illustrations of this fact are numerous. Sometimes where the machinery of producers' or consumers' cooperatives is set up, the members see the organization simply as a commercial concern from which they individually are to get as much as possible for as little as possible, just as they would from a private commercial firm dealing in the same spirit toward them. The inhabitants of a village may be having many of their needs supplied by tax-supported or publicly administered services, including schooling, water supply, electric power, sewerage, fire protection, sanitary inspection, and street maintenance; yet most of the inhabitants may know and care so little about their common affairs that they can scarcely tell whether any particular service is performed publicly or privately, or whether it is by the village, county, state, or national government. They may have little community feeling, and may be strangers to their next-door neighbors. As in many suburban towns and villages, their vital interests may be in a large city at some distance. There may be no more personal participation in the services they support by taxes than in the management of the corporately owned railroad on which they go to the city each day.

At municipal elections the inhabitants of such a suburb may not vote, or may vote after hurried inquiry about candidates who are total strangers. They may go their own ways as strangers, with no feeling of working together for common ends. Aside from the informal visiting of personal friends or limited associations such as golf or country clubs, the relations of the inhabitants may be quite impersonal and indifferent, or competitive. Many suburban villages and neighborhoods are of this character, and cannot be called communities, even though numerous services are provided by the municipality. Most suburban communities, however, have developed some elements of community spirit. The idea of the community implies personal acquaintance and direct person-to-person relationships between its members.

Vogt's statement, "A community consists of two or more persons who have one or more interests in common," is too abstract. Single-purpose associations do not constitute communities in themselves, though sometimes they develop definite community qualities. A stock breeders' organization, a co-operative creamery, a trade association, or a church, in which the association is for a single purpose with social relations only as a minor accessory, scarcely deserves the name of community. One may get many of the emotional satisfactions and some of the more material benefits of community living through belonging to and working with such groups, as in churches, lodges, social clubs, cultural societies, business and professional organizations. These specialized functions, however, give more of the emotional satisfactions of a community when they are supplemented by general community relationships. For nearly a century the temperance societies of Scandinavia have been among the chief agencies for social fellowship. Churches develop social life in addition to religious activities, as do literary and debating societies. The Neighborhood Advisory Councils of the Ohio Farm Bureau have done the same.

Some of the chief values of such special groups are in their generalized community functions. When, through the fading of religious faith or for other reasons, there is a general dissolving of such groups, in the absence of well-developed community life individual lives are not normal until some other community relationships are re-established. The influence of some purely social substitutes, such as bridge clubs, pool halls, or country clubs, suggest that to isolate such functions from purposeful activity is not normal. A community is most normal when it is concerned with a cross-section of life. Where community life is not well developed, people's purely social relations tend to be accessory to more purposeful relations, such as labor unions, churches, employment in a firm, temperance societies, nature study clubs, music associations, professional associations, or farm organizations. Otherwise there is effort to purchase social life on commercial terms, as at roadhouses, night clubs, or theaters.

Sometimes what are commonly thought of as single-purpose organizations develop the general characteristics of a community. For instance, a Mormon settlement, though primarily religious, tends to be a real community. The layout of farm lands, town lots, and streets sometimes is done through church agencies. The church officials sometimes do the selling of community produce and the buying of community supplies. Careful provision is made for recreation and social life. The poor of the community are cared for, education for vocations, including homemaking, is given careful attention, and in numerous other ways varied common needs are met by common planning and action. The spirit of being members of a community is present. With the Mormons community organization has the aim of serving the interests of life as a whole.

There is another type of single-purpose organization which develops some of the qualities of the community to a marked degree, and which illustrates the importance of first-hand acquaintance. An important part of American industry is occupied with producing goods, not for the general public, but for a small number of manufacturers. For instance, there are the firms which manufacture cement-mill equipment, paper-mill machinery, or electric-power-plant machinery. There may be only three or four firms in the country making equipment in such a field, and there may be not more than fifty or a hundred prospective customers for the product. The result is that a manufacturer of, say, paper-mill machinery, is well known to every possible customer and to every competitor. If the product is of high grade, every customer knows it. If it is poor in quality, no salesmanship or advertising can hide the fact. The customers are intelligent, well-informed and experienced men of keen judgment.

In such circumstances a high degree of integrity and co-operativeness comes to characterize the specialized industry. Quality can be counted on. Sharp practice tends to be eliminated. Large transactions are carried through on word of honor, without legal protection. Those who are in the habit of denouncing competition and private industry *in toto* should become acquainted with this unspectacular but very important phase of our economic life. That whole section of American industry which deals with producers' goods used by but few customers, in its standards of integrity, fair play, and co-operativeness is strikingly in contrast with some businesses which deal with the mass of the people. In dealing with the general public, sometimes the charlatan or the unscrupulous advertiser can take business away from the undramatic honest producer. Intimate personal acquaintance does not exist between the producer and the general public.

Another group which has some elements of community is

"Wall Street." One of the foremost bankers in the financial district recently remarked that, so far as banking is concerned, Wall Street is a small village, where every banker knows every other. There is a sort of village code of what constitutes fair play among themselves which is very clearly understood. For any banker to violate that code would result in definite loss of prestige, with danger of being eliminated from the informal, word-of-honor transactions which constitute no small part of interbanking business. Wherever in human associations there is a high degree of intimate, first-hand acquaintance, some of the characteristics of community will appear.

Sometimes the essential qualities of a local community are present even when there is no single unifying organization. If substantially the same group of people, in a spirit of working together for common ends, should use a variety of means for doing so, that fact would not prevent the group from constituting a community. Their education might be administered through a school district, their financial needs through a bank or credit union, their merchandising either through private merchants or co-operatives, their medical needs either through private practitioners or through a co-operative association. The essential character of a community is the spirit and the habit of meeting varied general needs by unified planning and action. However, for the same people to be seeking to gain their common ends through a multiplicity of organizations may be wasteful of effort and may tend to dissipate community spirit. Intelligent planning will tend to an optimum degree of integration of such efforts, including them in a general unified community program.

The term "community," describing the qualities which

lead people to act in common for common ends, cannot be limited to groups of any particular size, except by convention and usage. Many different-sized groups have this quality in some degree—the family in the highest degree. It is not called a community, simply because usage has given that particular kind of community another name to define it more specifically. Beyond the community, as the term is generally used, are other groups which have some of the characteristics of a community, such as the city and the nation. The ultimate social ideal of the *brotherhood of man* sees the entire race as one community.

While the characteristics of community—mutual respect, good will, living for and with each other by united effort for common ends, and mutual acquaintance—are not limited to groups of any certain size, there are groups of a certain range of size in which community of effort and interest finds fullest and most normal expression, and which seem most adapted to human nature and human capacity for intimate co-operation. Such groups range in size from a few dozen to a few hundred, or at most a very few thousand, persons. Cooley calls them "primary groups." Modern technical developments tend to make possible larger true communities. It is to such limited societies that the term "community" is here applied.

The use of the word "community" to describe such small groups does not imply that important community characteristics are not present in larger societies. Where found in cities, community attributes are enlargements and projections of traits originating in small communities.

Half the people of America live in cities. Can they also live in communities? To some degree they can. Men could scarcely continue to exist in cities if it were not possible for them to unite in smaller units, having some community characteristics. Also, the city as a whole provides a field for expression of community traits which commonly originated in smaller groups. Thus the city comes to have some of the unity and other characteristics of a true community. Without such traits a city cannot continue to exist.

CHAPTER III

MAN IS A COMMUNITY ANIMAL

B IOLOGICALLY man is a social creature. His throat and mouth are formed for delicately modulated speech, and that speech is a trait of social and not of solitary animals. A man is not a normal organism by himself, but only in relations with others.

In mental constitution men are more than social creatures, they are community animals. Cattle and horses, when living wild on the plains, may thrive in vast undifferentiated herds of thousands of individuals. They are social animals, but apparently not to any marked degree community animals. Men live best in integrated groups of limited size. They crave community life, not simply social life.

Men can become adjusted to almost any kind of life and may be so habituated to it that any change to a different mode is extremely unpleasant. New York slum dwellers on being transferred to rural communities often find the new life unendurable, and drift back to the city. On the other hand, the most isolated men in the Southern mountains come to prefer their relative loneliness to any more intimate community life. Even such men generally have community relationships. They may hunt and fish together, they take care of each other's sick, they maintain churches in common. Such relative isolation illustrates the fact that communities may vary much in the *spacing* of their members. Some spacing is essential in all cases. There seem to be normal degrees of association from which extremes of solitude or intimacy are variants. In that normal environment men best maintain their population and their basic culture, and the most normal traits of personality. Men who are not parts of some small community tend to be psychopathic or variants from a wholesome type. Men forced into too intimate and constant association become irritable or lose individuality.

Put a man among large masses of men and he will begin to gather a few of them together to build a small community. Such efforts take the forms of college fraternities, clubs, secret orders, church congregations, luncheon clubs, study clubs, and numberless other associations of limited numbers. We have here evidence of one of the most fundamental and universal of human traits—a craving of human nature which cannot safely be ignored. As a rule such specialized organizations, while they help to satisfy the craving for community life, take account of only a small part of the total interests of their members.

In modern America, the village, the neighborhood, the hamlet, or the city, often has become but an economic aggregation or only an incidental grouping, without the acquaintance, the personal relationships, and the common interests and activities, which are the essential characteristics of a community. Such aggregations do not fully satisfy the emotional cravings for fellowship, common interests, and unified planning and action. Neither do they provide the most wholesome environment. M. L. Wilson, formerly Under Secretary of Agriculture, writes in *Agriculture in Modern Life*:

There is a limit to the amount of cultural innovation and artificiality that the nervous system of man can endure. There is a limit to the degree of deviation from a natural physical environment in which humans can prosper. When these limits are exceeded, health and vitality depart. There is reason to believe that our complex urban culture has already exceeded these limits in many respects. City life as lived today alternately pampers, weakens, and denies basic desires and appetites. It removes the dangers and struggles for which we are prepared by nature, and substitutes others for which native endowment and accumulated human experience are unprepared. A few gifted or lucky individuals may prosper, but humanity as a whole cannot. The artificiality of this culture will be its own undoing.[2]

The idea that man is a small-community animal is supported by the science of anthropology. For the most part early man was a small-village dweller, and the villages in which he lived were not just accumulations of dwellings, but had well-developed social organization. In fact, the community may be older than mankind, for some of man's nearer relatives among the apes and monkeys also live in organized communities which have definite range of size, characteristic of the species.

Where men live on isolated farms, generally it is because some arbitrary circumstance has prevented action according to the tendencies of human nature. In Mexico the Aztec conquests, and after them the Spaniards, drove tribes from their villages into the hills for safety, where for centuries they have continued to live on isolated farms or in very small groups. In England the ancient villages with their common lands were broken up by the Norman conquerors, and by later enclosures of common lands by the nobility, so that through forcible means the character of English community life was largely destroyed. Brittany in France, where the people live on separate farms, was settled by a mass movement from Britain about ten centuries ago, with apparently

arbitrary division of lands. In the rough mountains of
Switzerland and Scandinavia many small valleys were settled
which were too small to support villages. Isolation occurred
because the only way for a young man to get a foothold was
to go beyond the confines of village ownership and make a
new clearing. Hamsun's novel *Growth of the Soil* is a picture
of the clearing of such an isolated farm in Norway. In
Russia the agrarian reform of 1906, which undertook to
break up villages and make separate farms, so disturbed
community ways that it constituted revolution. Recently
Manchuria has been settled largely by individual immigrants, many of whom have not yet matured a village organization.

In the United States the somewhat crudely drafted homestead laws, written with little thought of human nature, put
families far apart by giving each homesteader a tract of
land half a mile square. The resulting isolation left the craving for community unsatisfied. In the rich farming states of
the Middle West the more prosperous farmers sell or rent
their farms and move to town, leaving the less competent
and less independent people on the land. One finds fewest
farms abandoned by their owners among such people as the
Mennonites, the Amish, the Dunkards, and the Mormons,
where there is strong community feeling and where community life is most deeply rooted and best provided for.

In several other parts of the United States the tendency
to community life found expression. Most of New England
was settled by communities. At one time in Massachusetts
it was unlawful for a colonist to live more than a mile distant
from the community center. The Acadians of Louisiana live
in ribbon villages, farming the land back of their houses. In
New Mexico and Arizona the Mexicans live usually in fairly

compact villages, not on isolated farms. T. Lynn Smith, in his *Sociology of Rural Life,* has given a good description of American Alsation farm communities of "ribbon" type.

Thus it seems that where men live in isolated situations it usually is because circumstances beyond their control caused them to deny or to repress deep-seated community impulse. Whenever those compulsions to separation are removed, men tend again to congregate in communities. A large proportion of American farmers who lived on relatively isolated farms overcame that isolation to some degree and developed real community life among themselves. In the settling of new areas there is a constant tendency for men to organize themselves into communities, though human instincts are too vague to be fully effective without teaching. Unless some members of the new community have learned the arts of community making from older communities, the results may be very crude.

The modern town-planner, in trying to secure an impression of integration and unity in the physical planning of a village, tries to find an axis or a focus for his plan. Sometimes without fully realizing the significance of what he does, he tries to secure outward and visible evidence of an inward and spiritual condition which would characterize a true community.

Human nature in the raw is less dependable a guide to living than is animal nature. Subhuman animals rely largely on instinct or its equivalent, which generally is fixed in sharp detail. Human life has come to rely so greatly upon culture that specific instincts have largely faded away, leaving rather vague instinctive tendencies or trends, greatly subject to modification by culture—that is, by teaching and by imitation. Human instincts become little more than capacities, tendencies, potentialities for being conditioned or educated, rather than explicit impulsions to definite courses of action. The generalness and vagueness of these impulses serve human needs because men are intelligent and teachable. The exact expression which their impulses may have will be determined by tradition, experience, education, and reflection, and by the requirements of circumstances, rather than by the compulsion of nature, as in the lower animals.

A Baltimore oriole has a home-building instinct which is so specific that through the centuries it builds just the same kind of hanging nest. A man, it would seem, also has a home-making instinct, but it is so generalized that it may find expression in a sod house on a Dakota prairie, or in a suite in a New York hotel, or in a Buckingham Palace. The lack of specificness in the home-making instinct does not imply its absence, but only that it is fortunately adapted to the teachableness of men, just as the specific instinct of the Baltimore oriole is adjusted to its unteachableness. Whether a man lives in an adobe shelter in Arizona or in a Park Avenue apartment, the song "Home, Sweet Home" stirs something deep in his nature.

When we ask how far the specifically defined instincts of lower animals might be expected to disappear in the evolution of mankind, the answer would seem to be—far enough to take full advantage of the teachableness and intelligence of men, but not so completely as to leave necessary direction lacking. For instincts to have disappeared more completely would imply that the evolutionary process had overshot its mark. In the writer's opinion there is evidence of some innate impulses in men which, while vaguely defined, are nonetheless clearly existing. Among these is the impulse to community life.

Men have a strong impulse to imitation. This begins very early and lasts throughout life. There have been heated controversies among psychologists concerning the occurrence and nature of instincts. If we include inclinations which in a large proportion of young people seem ready to spring into vigorous being with a minimum of teaching or of other stimulus, we may hold that among possibly innate impulses are the inclination to hunt and to fish, to take exercise, perhaps to cultivate the soil, to mate, to create a home environment, and to create or to partake in community life. In the writer's opinion the impulse to create or to participate in community life is so deep-seated and so strong that where it finds no opportunity for expression, grave injury to personality may follow. In American pioneer farm life the isolation of farmers' wives on separate farms had tragic results, and in numberless cases isolated rural children have strong, though natural and untaught impulses to escape extreme isolation. There is evidence that in this respect man is biologically a community animal.

Mark Graubard sums up the issue as follows:

. . . man is a culture-making animal. Had Linnaeus lived today he probably would have named the human species *homo culturans* rather than *sapiens*. Man is a unique animal and his unique weapon, as well as his most puzzling and remarkable trait, is his social form of life and its concomitant, the formation of cultures. Man always led a communally organized life which he accepted as natural. His social behavior took on forms referred to as culture patterns which varied from group to group, from tribe to tribe. Hardly a human practice or belief, be it the kind of food or mode of eating, means of making fire or of burying the dead, prescribed conduct regarding sex and marriage, lullabies, rituals, wars, ceremonials, medicines, myths,

ornaments, art, tools, social organization, notions of gods, spirits, or
ghosts, hardly a minute activity or concept that failed to show
standardization within a group, and the most bewildering array of
variations even in erstwhile culturally related communities.

Yet in spite of all this diversification, the basic tendency to produce these beliefs and practices, the irrepressible drive to form a
specific culture, is universal and apparently innate in man. The only
conceivable reason for this tendency is the mode of action of our
central nervous system, producing mental and emotional responses
about which we know very little as yet. Their existence seems to be
as ubiquitous in human beings as the capacity to produce speech or
to grasp tools. Similarly their social expression is as varied as
sounds and language.[8]

There are present-day psychologists who hold that men have
no instincts, either for community or for other patterns of
action. The view presented here is not acceptable to them.

To summarize: Many lines of evidence point to the conclusion that men by natural craving and inclination are community creatures. Their subhuman relatives are largely community animals. The predominant evidence of anthropology
is that primitive men were community dwellers, and where
vestiges of primitive life remain in out-of-the-way parts of
the earth we find men living in true communities. The greater
part of the human race now, as in the past, lives in villages
or other small communities. Men are biologically and psycho-
logically adjusted to community life. Families die off in
cities, which would cease to exist but for being replenished
from small communities. Except where circumstances conflict
with natural tendencies, men almost never choose to live in
isolated farm homes, and there is a constant tendency to
abandon isolated homes unless they are tied together by
strong community bonds. People living in large cities or in
other large groups tend to form small communities within

those large groups. Where new lands are settled the natural community impulse finds expression by the development of community life. In general, the older and more mature the culture is, the more completely are the people united in vital, unified social organisms. Those communities which are most fully developed are limited in size to the numbers of people who can personally know each other and work together for common ends in a spirit of unity.

CHAPTER IV

HISTORY OF THE COMMUNITY

BY AND large, the story of mankind is the story of village or other small-community life. Through the centuries and through the millenniums cities have loomed large and then have disappeared, but the village has continued. Brilliant cultures have appeared and then have faded, but the continuing culture, through which the past has transmitted its basic heritage to the future, has been that of the village. After each great efflorescence of art and learning, the level at which culture could be perpetuated tended to sink to the level of the village. Ruins of great architecture might remain, immortal statuary might be thrown into wells or rubbish heaps to be found again, rare manuscripts might be hidden in brick walls or stored in monasteries, and refugees might carry culture to new centers. A great and brilliant civilization of thousands of years could so completely disappear that its language could not be read by a single man on earth until a key was supplied by the Rosetta Stone. In the meantime the only living part of a great culture which spanned the centuries was that which had its roots in the villages. (Under the term "village" we take the liberty of including all those varied forms of living together in small groups which characterized primitive men, including the shifting communities of nomads.)

It was through local community life that democracy survived the feudal period and re-emerged as a political ideal. Swiss democracy was a survival in the mountain communities of prefeudal life. In the Scandinavian countries, including Iceland, where feudalism never completely overran the ancient community life, democracy also survived.

New England democracy had a similar background. Herbert B. Adams, in *The Germanic Origins of New England Towns*, wrote: "The field meetings of Teutonic farmers for the distribution of lands and the regulation of crops were the germs of English parish meetings and of New England town meetings. The village elders, still so called in Russia . . . are the prototypes of the English reeve and four, and of the New England town constable and board of selectmen."[4] Close to the soil in many parts of the world local democracy persisted, though deformed and mutilated by feudalism.

Democracy in religion also is an ancient inheritance. Most democratic religious groups today—the Baptists, Congregationalists, Disciples, Quakers, Mennonites, Mormons, Unitarians, and others—arose, sometimes by curious turns of circumstance, in localities where there was an unbroken tradition from prefeudal communal religious life. We find records of these prefeudal democratic community groups, with democratic religious life, close to the soil in China, India, Palestine, Switzerland, Holland, England, and Scandinavia.

Embedded in common speech are hints that early prefeudal life was marked by good human relations. For instance, in the earliest recorded use of "kind" and "kindly" in English writing, in literature of more than a thousand years ago, as given in the Oxford Historical Dictionary, the words meant "innate," "implanted by nature." It is significant that in that primitive society kindliness was synonymous with what is innate and natural. The word "un-natural" was once a synonym for wicked and criminal.

Many of the social ideals which the Western world values most highly have been preserved from ancient times in small communities. The villages in which men have lived during most of their existence have not been mere hamlets—dwellings placed near each other by force of some circumstance. Rather, they have been social organisms in which men lived by unity of purpose and by community of effort.

These small communities have tended to be isolated. Cultural waves have passed over them, often leaving them largely untouched. They incline to be like the flywheel of an engine, which causes the old way to continue for a time and not to give way to sudden changes, and so to furnish gradual transition from the old to the new. The word "pagan" means rural person. When Christianity was sweeping the cities of the Roman Empire, the country districts held to the old ways for a time. That always has been characteristic of the village. It is true in Europe today. Some villages have carry-overs of arts and customs from thousands of years ago. Because the movement of population has always been from country to city, there has been little back-flow of culture. One of the characteristics of society is that it is continually recruiting its population—and its culture —from the *pagani*.

Village communities have not been immune to the ravages of time and circumstance. The English agricultural villages, after existing, apparently, for many thousands of years, were largely destroyed by the enclosure of common lands by men of wealth and power, and their inhabitants were set adrift. The capture of the Hebrew people by the Assyrians, and their long period of slavery, is a story almost accidentally preserved. Probably it had numberless counterparts in other conquests and enslavements whose stories have been lost. Genghis Khan, as he swept over Asia, wiped out entire populations. A broad strip through central China was once depopulated and its village life destroyed by the slaughter of the inhabitants during a military conquest. Northwest Africa, the region of ancient Carthage, was the location of a prosperous culture with many thriving villages, until breakdown of government and loss of security led to its devastation by robber bands, and its almost complete depopulation. The Spanish conquerors of Peru largely destroyed a highly developed village organization. The pioneer doctrine in the United States that "the only good Indian is a dead Indian" led to the wiping out of many native communities, and the disruption of many more. In Australia and Tasmania native communities were ruthlessly exterminated by white settlers. Rome slaughtered whole populations which rose in rebellion, while the barbarians in overrunning Rome did the same. In Polynesia, as among the Eskimos, disease, conquest, and "civilization" brought by white men have almost eliminated entire populations, and destroyed or disorganized community life.

In recent times economic forces have had disastrous effects on village communities. Both race suicide and emigration to cities have affected the village. Thus, the communities which have survived are not necessarily the best, but are the ones that did not happen to be in the path of some overwhelming force. In this destruction or disintegration of village communities there has been a vast loss of cultural values.

As an indication of similarities of primitive village organization the world over, we may compare a description of villages in Mediterranean regions with descriptions of village organization in China and India.

In *The Organization of the Early Christian Church*, by Edwin Hatch, we read concerning the patriarchal system in the Roman world of the time of early Christianity, in which the head of the family was administrator and judge: "Their tenure of office rested rather on general consent than upon formal appointment, and the limits of their authority were but loosely defined."[5] Out of this patriarchal organization grew groups of families with councils of elders. "The council of elders or presbyters had charge of administration and discipline. Discipline was very severe in order to maintain standards in a sodden environment."[5] It would seem that when some parts of the Protestant church adopted the presbyterian form of organization in an effort to get back to the inspired way of the New Testament they were, in fact, simply adopting the form of ancient primitive community government. The success of that general form of church government indicates the soundness of the type which was imitated.

Of those Chinese villages of the present day in which methods are loose, Arthur H. Smith wrote in *Village Life in China*: "The headmen are not formally chosen, nor formally deposed. They drop into their places—or perhaps climb into them—by a kind of natural selection. The qualities which fit a villager to act as headman are the same which contribute to success in any line of business. He must be a practical person who has some native ability, acquainted with the ways of the world,"[6] and able and willing to give time.

Liang and Tao, in their *Village and Town Life in China*, give an even clearer picture:

. . . the real China is not a centralized despotism, whether mon-
archical or republican in form, but a great aggregate of democratic
communities . . .

. . . the town is nothing more than an enlarged village or agglomera-
tion of villages, while the village itself is a state in miniature.

. . . in its actual working China is a huge republic within which
are myriads of petty republics. For the village in China is an
autonomous unit . . . with the exception of paying a nominal land-
tax and in a few other cases, the village is as independent of the
central government as any British self-governing colony is independent of the Imperial Government.[7]

The village has perfect freedom in industry and trade, in
religion, and in everything concerning the government, regulation, and protection of the locality. Whatever may be required for its well-being is supplied, not by Imperial edicts
or any other kind of governmental interference, but by
voluntary associations. Thus police, education, public repairs
on roads and canals, lighting, and innumerable other functions, are managed by the villagers themselves.

. . . the Chinese village folks are most capable of self-organization
and self-government. On the other hand, they are extremely jealous
of external influence. Reform, should any be needed, must come
from within, not from without.[8]

The village is organized around the family. Often all the
members of the village are a single large family. According
to Liang and Tao:

The earnings of all the members of the family are given to the
mother in a hotch-potch for the maintenance of the corporate whole.
The family . . . is a living organism which possesses a spirit quite
apart from the individuals who form it. Each member does not live
and work for himself, but for the family to which he belongs. Every
other member has a claim on his earnings.

It is in the villages, scattered over the cultivated land, that the great majority of the Chinese people live their quiet, uneventful lives in their homesteads.[9]

It would seem that there is a way of local leadership and government that is world-wide. That it is a spontaneous expression of human and social nature is indicated by its appearance in American communities in the form of the political boss.

Ancient village life in India was similar to that in China. A. S. Altekar describes the conditions there:

Dynasties have come and dynasties have gone, but it is the village communities that have preserved intact the culture and tradition of the old Bhavatavavsha through several revolutions.

The Aryan penetration in the Deccan took place . . . by the beginning of the 7th century B.C., and the authentic history of Western India practically begins at the same time. But to commence the history of our communities from that date would be unsound. For village communities founded in Western India by the Aryan settlers but continued the old tradition.

From the scanty data supplied by the Veda, it would appear that in the earliest times the village communities enjoyed a practically unlimited autonomy . . . the state was usually coterminous with the village.

Each village had its own council or Sabha. . . . The local disputes were settled by this council of the village elders.[10]

According to Altekar, village councils had come into being by the beginning of the sixth century A.D. During earlier times each village had a head man, who collected the revenue and defended the village with the help of local men.

Substantially the same pattern appears in most parts of the world. The primitive English village has been described by Harold Peake in *The English Village*:

We may picture the primitive village as consisting of ten or twelve small houses, rude dwellings, probably of wattle and daub, combining under one roof shelter for man and beast, as well as storage room for the produce of the soil. Near the village were a few small closes in which the plough oxen could be penned at night during the ploughing season, and perhaps a saddle-horse or two would be kept, and in favoured areas there were perhaps, as time grew on, small patches for the cultivation of vegetables and a few small orchards. The village must have been small and humble in its origin, though doubtless it grew larger and more complex as cultivation advanced; many rural villages have not advanced far beyond this stage to-day. In Saxon times the village seems to have been surrounded by a fence, or hedge, hence the name *tun* or *ton*, the predecessor of our modern *town*, which is said to be derived from the Saxon *tynan*, to hedge.

Beyond the village were large arable fields, which were held in common by the men of the Township, and beyond these again was the waste, either heath, down or wood, as the case might be, which extended till it met the waste of the next township. The woodland was valuable in many ways.

But the most distinctive feature of the Township, alike in this as in other countries, was the arable fields, the number of which varied in different townships and at different times. These were cultivated in common by the men of the Township according to certain well defined rules and regulations, which have been closely studied by many investigators.

The most striking feature in connection with these arable fields was that the lands were held in common by the men of the Township. The ploughing, sowing and harvesting of each strip was done by the community, each man undertaking his appointed task, but the crops were divided among the households, each man taking the produce of the acres allotted to him. That an equal number of acres was allotted to each in early times has been placed beyond doubt, and it has further been noted that the acres of each man did not lie contiguous to one another, but were interspersed among those of his neighbours; further, there is evidence that these acres were allotted in order.

What then was the reason for this somewhat strange arrangement? Only one answer is possible. The system was devised to promote equality among the men of the Township. By taking the strips in rotation the good land and the poor land were shared alike, by harvesting in the same order the good and bad weather fell equally to all, while by changing the strips yearly bad cultivation was discouraged . . .[11]

Examples might be multiplied from many parts of the world to illustrate the fact that the village community is a very ancient institution, and that it had common characteristics over vast areas. In some cases there has been continuous community existence for thousands of years. Peake mentions the discoveries of R. Pumpelly who, exploring southeast of the Caspian Sea, found the successive deposits of a village which he believed was first established more than ten thousand years ago.

All the information we have points to the conclusion that for long, long ages the only human social organizations were these small unified communities, and the families of which they were composed. Like anthills of a single species, they were much alike, but quite independent of each other.

Then began the process of uniting these small units into larger societies. Sometimes that union was voluntary, as in arid regions where it was necessary to build irrigation works larger than could be achieved by one community. Most ancient civilizations arose in irrigated areas. Probably more often the enlargement of societies was the result of the conquests of empire and feudalism. The records of that change for the most part are lost in the shadows of antiquity, yet here and there the process has been so recent that it can be followed. It will be interesting to trace one such case, as illustrating a course which, in some of its major elements, must have been repeated many times.

Half a century ago the British invaded and conquered

Burma, and annexed the country. Previously there had been a semblance of national government, with kings who waged war against nearby monarchs. Yet such central government, generally incompetent and corrupt, outside the large cities was little more than a shadow, and scarcely affected the lives of the masses of the people. More than ninety per cent of the population was in small communities, and of the remainder a considerable part were foreigners, most of them from India.

On the whole the Burmese had a high quality of simple village life. There were no castes, education was better developed than anywhere else in Asia, and women had a higher status than almost anywhere in the world outside of western Europe and English-speaking countries. The situation existing before the British conquest is described by H. Fielding, an English medical officer who went through the war of annexation from 1885 to 1889. In his book, *The Soul of a People*, he states:

. . . the central government was never very strong . . . beyond collecting a certain amount of taxes, and appointing governors to the different provinces, it hardly made itself felt outside Mandalay and the large river towns. The people to a great extent governed themselves. They had a very good system of village government, and managed nearly all their local affairs. But beyond the presence of a governor, there was but little to attach them to the central government. There was, and is, absolutely no aristocracy of any kind at all. The Burmese are a community of equals, in a sense that has probably never been known elsewhere. All their institutions are the very opposite to feudalism. Now, feudalism was instituted to be useful in war. The Burmese customs were instituted that men should live in comfort and ease during peace; they were useless in war. So the natural leaders of a people, as in other countries, were absent. There were no local great men; the governors were men appointed from time to time from Mandalay, and usually knew nothing of their charges; there were no rich men, no large landholders—not one.[12]

When the British began their conquest, the king and the weak central government surrendered after a few days' fighting. At first the people paid little attention to the change, for central governments had come and gone through the centuries without affecting the independence of the communities, and without touching their lives seriously beyond the imposition of moderate taxes. When it became apparent that the British really intended to govern and to interfere with local freedom, the people rebelled and fought for four years.

In respect to their religion the condition of the people differed from that in many primitive communities. Eighty-five per cent of the population was Buddhist, and Buddhism was fairly well organized—much better than the government—and was in touch with the whole people, revered and honored by every native of Burma. Buddhism had retained the high moral code of the ancient communities, but had given it greater range and universality, and a remarkable philosophy. English people coming to Burma at that time saw all this, the many monasteries with their monks, who taught all the schools, even in the smallest villages, and the people's attitude of reverence toward them. Yet the religious leaders were no help against invasion. According to Fielding, ". . . the explanation is, that the teachings of the Buddha forbid war. All killing is wrong, all war is hateful; nothing is more terrible than this destroying of your fellow-men . . . the country seething with strife, and the monks going about their business calmly as ever . . . preaching of peace, not war, of kindness, not hatred, of pity, not revenge, was to foreigners quite inexplicable."[13]

To the Buddhist teachers the unchangeable law was the same for all. "There is not one law for you and another for the foreigner; there is not one law to-day and another tomorrow." With all their influence the Buddhist monks never sought political power. They were teachers, not rulers or political strategists or intriguers. Buddhism in Burma never bent to popular opinion, as it never interfered in government. The monks particularly denied any divine status. They endeavored only to be reasonable men, trying to teach kindliness and reasonableness to the people.

Thus their religion gave the Burmese villagers no help in their rebellion against invasion. Since the village communities were independent of each other, and since there was no wealthy class and no aristocracy, the usual centers of unity for defense were lacking. They had no weapons but flintlocks and soft iron swords. Yet this spontaneous insurrection kept the British busy for four years. Where the people did fight, their leaders were outlaws and desperadoes. The resistance, however, had the typical character of the independent villagers. Fielding records, "The whole country was pervaded by bands of fifty or a hundred men, very rarely amounting to more than two hundred, never, I think, to five hundred, armed men, and no two bands ever acted in concert."[14]

The inefficiency of the independent village community in warfare was made evident. The relation of the central government to the people, and the reason why the conquest was undertaken, probably were typical of conditions that must have recurred many times in human history. (The ostensible reason for undertaking the conquest was that the central Burmese government had levied a heavy fine against a British trading company.) Fielding continues:

. . . in Burma it was only the supreme government, the high officials, that were very bad. It was only the management of state affairs that was feeble and corrupt; all the rest was very good. The land laws, the self-government, the social condition of the people, were admirable. It was so good that the rotten central government made but little difference to the people, and it would probably have lasted for a long while if not attacked from outside. A greater power came and upset the government of the king, and established itself in his place; and I may here say that the idea that the feebleness or wrong-doing of the Burmese government was the cause of the downfall is a mistake. If the Burmese government had been the best that ever existed, the annexation would have happened just the same. It was a political necessity for us.[15]

And so, in a small corner of the world—the population of Burma was about seven million—the world-wide process of the subordination of a land of independent village communities by empire and feudalism was re-enacted. And, as everywhere under the circumstances, the result had a tendency to the disintegration of that old community life. Writing ten years after the conquest, Fielding pictures the changes already taking place:

. . . each village managed its own affairs, untroubled by squire or priest, very little troubled by the state. That within their little means they did it well, no one can doubt. They taxed themselves without friction, they built their own monastery schools by voluntary effort, they maintained a very high, a very simple, code of morals, entirely of their own initiative.

All this has passed, or is passing away. . . . The people are now part of the British Empire, subjects of the Queen. . . . And the local government is passing away, too. It cannot exist with a strong government such as ours. For good or for evil, in a few years it, too, will be gone.[16]

The old community ways, he points out, were breaking down, and crime was increasing.

Yet, as in many parts of the world, the simple community ways of people close to the soil refuse to die. In the villages

·of Burma fine human relations still exist, and we read in the *Encyclopedia Britannica* that Burmese children are the happiest in the world! The penetration of the Indians with their caste system, and of the English with their factory system, have not yet completely destroyed the old pattern.

A somewhat similar process took place when Japan invaded and annexed Korea, except that Korean life had moved further from the primitive village stage, and that the cynical Japanese disregard for life, property, and human dignity in Korea made the English administration of Burma seem benevolent in comparison. An account of the conditions in Korea at the time the Japanese took possession of the country, and of the treatment which the natives received, may be read in Younghill Kang's *Grass Roof*. The English tradition of freedom and respect for established rights and customs has been conspicuously lacking in the Japanese administration of Korea.

In the absorption of village community cultures by strong empires there has been great variation in method. Perhaps the highest level was reached in ancient Peru, where the old community structure was preserved and the conquered people were given equal place in the new order. The lowest order of practice is illustrated by the ravages of Genghis Khan and his successors who left waste and destruction behind them.

The toughness of the small community, and its ability to withstand disintegrating influences, has enabled some of its best qualities to survive, perhaps to a day when methods other than force shall guide the development of human society. Then they may again come into their own, and make their contribution.

There seems to be little doubt that the village community

is the oldest of human institutions, that it has played a dominant part in the total of human history, and that, considering the world as a whole, it continues to be a major factor in human affairs. The progressive disappearance of the village community in America constitutes a serious departure from the general course of human history. In the interest of social and cultural continuity it is important that we try to understand the significance of that change.

CHAPTER V

THE PLACE OF THE COMMUNITY
IN HUMAN CULTURE

THE roots of human culture are not its fine arts, its technology, its political institutions. These are the flower and fruit. The roots of culture are the underlying drives, motives, incentives, manners, habits, and purposes. If these are socially sound and vitally alive in a good social soil, then the flowers and fruit will appear. If these underlying elements are unrefined, weak, and undisciplined, then the fine arts, the technology, and the complex organization of society cannot long endure.

Young human life is avid for example and instruction which it can accept and imitate. It takes to itself whatever is available in the culture of its environment, and makes that its own. It becomes fundamentally and intimately like the culture in which it grows. The characteristics of the existing culture are acquired during the very early years, and produce a set of personality which seldom is fundamentally altered. Probably the ages up to ten years are more compellingly formative than all the rest of life taken together. It is during those years that the individual's tastes, standards, and appreciations are largely determined.

The crowning inheritance of humanity is its basic culture of community habits, traits, and attitudes. Yet there is evidence that some of the finest of human cultures have almost disappeared. The preservation and dissemination of the best of these is a fundamental human need.

When we come to observe the exact processes by which the transfer of culture takes place, we see that it is chiefly through intimate personal contacts. It is the same process as that by which children acquire spoken language and inflection. It is a process of contagion, of imitation of others. First of all there is the family, and next there is the community surrounding the family. The permanent set of personality is determined in early life chiefly through those two relationships, always influenced, of course, by inborn native quality. Supplementary influences include church, school, government, etc., and more recently radio and movies, alike powerful in their characteristics of intimacy and penetration.

Influences appearing later in life overlie and modify fundamental sets of character, but seldom change the main traits of personality. Occasionally profound change does take place in later years, but only by great personal effort, and in a relatively small number of cases.

For the most promising development of great personalities the family must have the support of the nearby environment. Very generally the home is too small a part of the child's total environment to be conclusive. If playmates and neighbors tend to nullify the influence of parents, serious stresses and conflicts may be set up in the growing personalities. A great home needs to be supplemented by a great community, so that the cultural inheritance which a child receives at home is in harmony with that which comes to him from the community. When a young person from such a home is married, the peculiar character of that home is to some extent lost unless the mate also has inherited it.

As a rule great leadership occurs when exceptional intelligence and vigor project onto a larger scene of action the drives and purposes that were learned in the intimate associations of early years. It follows that society and government in their larger units will not be moved by any more refined motives, and will have no higher objectives, than do the families and the communities from which their leadership arises. The community is the mother of society. As the community is, so will society be.

The home and the community are not only the places of origin, but also the principal preservers, of the most intimate and sensitive values of our cultural inheritance, those elusive traits of good will, considerateness, courage, patience, and fellowship, which are the best and finest fruits of the long process of social evolution. Those finest and most distinctive traits originate where but a few persons are immediately involved, and where fine qualities can be sheltered and nourished during their infancy. In the family and the community the sympathy and understanding of a few will protect such traits from destruction until they are matured and tempered so that they can make their way in the larger and less hospitable world. Human cultures, like human beings, have periods of infancy during which they cannot survive without such shelter and nurture. The higher the animal or the higher the culture, the more surely is this true.

It follows that the family and its community environment are imperatively necessary for the creation and preservation of the finest cultural values. Yet, what have we in America done with the community? We have taken for granted intimate human culture, without realizing its need for an abiding place. As individual families have come to this country from Europe, torn loose from their cultural roots, we might by conscious design have worked with them to assemble and transplant the best elements of the cultural traditions, creating new communities with a synthesis of culture beyond anything the past has known. As a matter of fact, we have tended to keep these newcomers isolated from the best and most intimate elements of American life. We have prevented the preservation and extension of cultural traits which takes place through contagion and imitation. The elements of the new-world culture which have been most visible and accessible to immigrants have been those one meets on the street, in business, in the movies. Similarly, the finer traits which the immigrants brought with them tend to be dropped as part of their old-world habits.

For several reasons the small community has been the basic source of the underlying culture of a people. In the first place, the family by itself is not a large enough group to be an adequate cultural unit. Children overflow the immediate family environment, and are much affected by the neighborhood or community environment. Exceptionally good or exceptionally poor family environment goes far to set the character of children, but the larger environment tends strongly to improve the poorest and to debase the best, and to reduce all to an approximation to uniformity. Just as the human body supplies an almost ideal environment for each of its cells such as no individual one-celled animal could provide for itself, so the community may create a favorable milieu for the development of each of its members.

A second reason is stated as follows in the *Systematic Source Book in Rural Sociology*:

Like water which flows naturally from a higher to a lower level, population generally flows naturally from rural to urban centers and from agriculture to industries and other urban occupations. Rural communities have been the centers of production of a surplus of human beings, and the urban communities the centers of their consumption. This . . . trait . . . practically speaking, has been permanent in the history of mankind.[17]

In this one-way movement of population from the small community to the large urban center or to its suburbs, the controlling basic culture of the small community carries over and provides the dominant incentives of the city. Since the small community is the controlling source of population of a country, the character of the small community becomes the character of the country.

Historically, the small community, we have seen, is the preserver of basic culture. In Greece, fine sculpture and architecture died because they were arts of the city and the aristocracy; but fine pottery and masonry lived because they were part of the life of common people in small communities. Religious liberalism was established and survived in England largely because Wyclif and his followers penetrated the small communities, where their movement became established. The culture which survives catastrophic changes generally is that of small communities.

Notwithstanding the profoundly important part which the community has taken and is taking in human history, it has been generally neglected in social planning. As a rule the small community has been robbed of its best population, economically exploited, despised, and left to shift for itself. Even public knowledge of the facts about American communities is fairly recent. Writing in 1926, Charles Luther Fry in his *American Villagers* stated:

. . . little is known about villages . . . for incorporated places having less than 2,500 inhabitants, the Census volumes furnish only a single figure—the total population . . .

The principal sources of information about villages, aside from the Census, are a small number of first-hand studies made by individual investigators.[18]

In the United States there has been much study of the isolated farm and of agriculture on the one hand, and of cities on the other; but until the last two decades the small community has been generally overlooked, and it was not recognized as the reservoir of basic human culture. During the past fifteen years the situation has greatly changed, and now there are qualified men and a very substantial literature in that field.

Because of neglect of the small community in social planning, it has tended to be stagnant and uninspiring, and to pass on its weaknesses to the city. Partly as a result of the failure of society through the ages to recognize the significance of small communities as the sources of population and as the sources and conservators of culture, the long upward climb of society is constantly impeded and interrupted. There is a constant slipping back to the cultural level of the neglected small community.

Characteristic limitations of the small village, neighborhood, or hamlet have been socially enforced conformity of thought and action, narrowness of outlook, clannishness, jealousies, tendency to gossip, and lack of recreation facilities or of direction and counsel for young people.

Such limitations tend to exist in small groups whether they are true communities or simply ununified aggregations of people. In the latter case there may be little restraint and control of social action. Where there is a true community there may be very effective discipline to prevent or to control such faults. Stefansson, in his accounts of well-integrated Eskimo communities, states that the social offense most frowned upon is "trouble making," and that social controls to prevent such faults are very effective indeed.

Just as individuals learn chiefly by imitating others, so communities on the whole, when they have endeavored to improve their designs, only rarely have undertaken original study and planning. For the most part they have imitated what was most obvious. For instance, practical management of American villages and cities by co-ordinated, business-like methods had been necessary for more than a century, but no one seemed creative enough to devise appropriate methods. Then the city-manager plan was initiated in a small city; and other communities, now having something to copy, imitated that example, until now there are hundreds of cities and villages with that type of government.

The creation of even one finely designed community, and the development there of a vital community spirit, probably would lead to that general type of social organization being imitated and reproduced many times. If skillful community leadership should grow up in such a community, it probably would be called on from many directions. It is not the size but the quality of a society which, in the long run, determines its influence. Greece and Palestine have had far greater influence on the world than have many vast empires. To work at creating a good community is not a retreat from national or world affairs, but may be the most vital way of contributing to them.

CHAPTER VI

THE RELATION OF THE COMMUNITY TO LARGER SOCIAL UNITS

THE uniting of human societies into units larger than the primitive community was necessary to the fulfillment of human destiny. Probably never again will local communities be independent of the whole of society. Lack of agreement on the manner in which such unification shall come about, and on the form it shall take, has been the cause of age-long conflict, including the present world war. Is it possible to maintain human dignity and freedom, with a large degree of local independence and cultural autonomy, and yet to achieve unity on a large scale? Except as that question is faced and a reasonably satisfactory answer is found, the place of the community or primary group in the modern world will be uncertain or insecure.

Fine community development does not call for neglect of other social relationships. Rather, when we find an excellent community we expect to find intelligent interest and participation in other social groups and organizations. Because the primary social group has been largely ignored and neglected, with resulting danger to the stability and quality of society, explicit emphasis on the small community is greatly needed; but the aim of that emphasis should be to correct a deficiency, not to monopolize all social interest. It is not the community as an isolated institution that should interest us, but the community or the primary social group as an essential and vital element in the vast, interacting network of human society.

There should be free and full acceptance of larger or of specialized relationships wherever they will increase the range and quality of life. The primary community should discover the functions it can exercise better than any other social group. It should endeavor to become excellent in those functions, while encouraging and supporting other units wherever they can be more effective.

In order to understand the place of the community in society it is necessary to understand the nature of the whole structure of which it is an essential part. Human society as a whole is blindly and haltingly feeling its way toward an ideal organization. The condition toward which it should be moving, though as yet with so much waste, conflict, and confusion, is that of regional and functional organization in which each level of society shall exercise control over subordinate levels, *but only to the extent necessary for the social welfare*. Beyond that degree of control each level of society should have complete freedom of action to work out its own destiny. At every stage of social organization all necessary control from above should be combined with all feasible freedom below. There should be absence of any arbitrary, capricious, or exploiting relationships. There can be no sharp, predetermined boundaries between social freedom and social discipline, but in such determination society must rely on the responsible good will, common sense, experience, and judgment of its members.

There are two kinds of social organization with which the community finds itself associated. One of these relates to size and extent. The community is made up of smaller social units called families. It also is part of the county, the county part of the state, the state part of the nation, and the nation part of that great family of nations (at present engaged in a family quarrel) which makes up the total of human society. These may be called general-purpose organizations.

Social organizations of another class serve special limited purposes. These are functional organizations. Education in the community may be directed by a board which has that single responsibility. Some community members may belong to the American Medical Association, which has specific and limited interests. Others may belong to the Farm Bureau or to a labor union or to a church, each with its own field of interest.

Thus the community finds itself related to general-purpose groups which differ from it in size and extent, and also to special-purpose groups which differ also in their aims. All together these organizations constitute the whole of human society. The following discussion of regionalism, especially in America, is an effort to give a picture of the structure of society toward which men are groping.

Regionalism in America*

The idea of regionalism is in part an approach to special-purpose or functional societies, and in part an approach to general administrative units. It is an idea which sometimes will tend to promote autonomous communities where local self-sufficiency is desirable. Sometimes it will lead to the giving up of some degree of local self-sufficiency because wide-range functional organization is more efficient and productive.

There is a great flux of social institutions under way.

* This discussion is taken, with changes and additions, from "Design in Public Business," by Arthur E. Morgan (Yellow Springs, Ohio, The Antioch Press, 1939), pp. 33-48.

Everywhere in America and in Europe the unified community is fading away, and special-purpose or functional-
regional associations are growing. This movement is similar
to a tendency in education during the past half-century,
when general higher education relatively declined and specialized education for specific callings greatly increased. The
result was a sudden increase in wealth-producing efficiency,
and in specialized knowledge, but no corresponding increase
in the general art of living. Educators everywhere are seeing
this mistake, and are trying to correct it.

With regard to community organization, the tendency in
America is still strongly toward functional or regional-func-
tional association, with small thought for the unifying of
community life and interest for general life purposes. That
is, all sorts of special-purpose organizations are formed, such
as school districts, chambers of commerce, country clubs,
labor unions, merchants' associations, advertising men's
clubs, and welfare societies. It is doubtful whether a civilization can endure which is supported only by functional (specialized) organization. It needs total cohesion, unity, and
integration, making it not just a collection of functions,
but a social personality. In a highly functionalized community many organizations are available to serve special
needs, but there commonly is a lack of a total view which
sees these special needs in relation to the whole, and which
keeps in view over-all aims and purposes. How to get that
integration without regimentation and loss of freedom, and
without losing the values of functional organization—that is
a major social problem. Its answer does not lie in giving up
the values of functional organization, nor in giving up the
values either of community integration or of individuality

and freedom of motion, but in achieving a vital relationship
and a sense of proportion among them all.

Americans encounter many problems which cannot well be
handled within the limits of a village, a city, a county, or
a state. Some of these are local. As an illustration, about
half the city of Texarkana is in Texas and the rest in
Arkansas. It has, therefore, a separate city government in
each state. In times past, if a crime was committed on the
Texas side of the main street, the offender needed only to
cross the street to be out of the jurisdiction of Texas law;
and he could be legally returned only through a cumbersome extradition proceeding in which the governor of one
state would request his return by the governor of the other
state. The two states finally overcame that difficulty. Several
American cities are located astride state lines.

There are more far-reaching problems in which state lines
are in the way. The Delaware River is of vital concern to
three states: New York, New Jersey, and Pennsylvania.
When an effort was made to divert large amounts of water
from the Delaware watershed to supply New York City, it
was found that the national Constitution was not designed
to meet such problems. Long and expensive litigation among
the three states ensued, and the Supreme Court finally had
to settle the issue, making constitutional history thereby.
The Colorado River is shared by six or seven states. In an
effort to work out a division of interests in its waters, and
in the power developed by Boulder Dam, a treaty or compact was made among all but one of the states, and approved by the United States Congress.

New York harbor lies in two states, yet needs a unified
administration. By compact between New York and New

Jersey, approved by the national Congress, there was created the Port of New York Authority, which not only administers the harbor, but built an interstate tunnel under the Hudson and a bridge over the Hudson.

With the advent of rapid automobile transportation, state lines do not stop criminals, though they are a handicap to enforcement of justice. In recent years there has been vast waste of oil and gas; yet when single states undertake to control this waste in the public interest it is found that restrictions in one state give unfair advantages in others. Here, again, state lines interfere with effective control.

Because of such issues, ways have been sought by which problems extending beyond political boundaries may be treated as functional or regional, by treating an affected area or region as a unit for a particular purpose, irrespective of political boundaries. About half a century ago the city of Boston and surrounding communities began the development of a vast water-supply system. This has grown until it supplies a large number of cities and towns, and goes beyond its borders for its source of supply. Following the experience of this Metropolitan Water Board of Boston and vicinity, the state legislature of New York created the New York Water Supply Commission, which goes far from the city for its water supply, and which has had a very successful history.

In flood control, ten Ohio cities and nine counties on the Miami River undertook a regional development to protect themselves from floods. The Tennessee Valley Authority, also, is an effort on a very large scale to treat a regional problem as a unit regardless of state lines. The Boulder Dam project in the Southwest, just referred to, and the control of the Columbia River in the Northwest, are other great regional undertakings.

In general, these efforts to treat regional problems from a regional point of view have been thought of as isolated cases, exceptions to the ordinary course of political government. Only slowly is there emerging the concept of regionalism as a distinct kind of social organization. Gradually it is beginning to dawn on us that in the regional treatment of regional problems we may have a key to a new social and economic order—a key that may be more significant than many so-called social revolutions. We may have here one of the essential answers to the question of why, in the midst of potential plenty, our country remains poor and insecure. From that point of view let us try to see what regionalism is.

When we speak of a sovereign power we mean a power from which there is no appeal. Ordinary political government is an ascending scale of sovereignties. In the United States the national government is the sovereign or ultimate authority over the states and their subdivisions in such matters as national defense, foreign relations, and interstate commerce. The states, in turn, are the ultimate authorities on marriage and divorce, land taxation, and many other matters. Counties, townships, cities, and villages may be ultimate authority on the width of sidewalks, the zoning of lands, the operation of street lighting, or building standards.

In matters where a government is sovereign it does not have to take account of the wishes or interests of other governments, but can ignore them. In the engineering work of the writer he repeatedly has met cases where a drainage system in one state required an outlet in another state. The other state, being sovereign in that respect, could not be compelled to allow construction across its land to a natural outlet. Some necessary developments thus have been halted for years by arbitrary state boundaries.

Now, the concept of regional government is in striking contrast to this concept of a hierarchy of sovereignties, any one of which may disregard the wishes or interests of any other of equal rank. The concept of regional planning and of regional action includes several elements. First, there is the idea of organizing government or other activity to include the entire area which should properly be dealt with as a unit for the purpose in view, regardless of political boundaries. For example, the New England Conference includes the governors of all New England states, which in several respects constitute a natural region. The Metropolitan Water District of Boston and vicinity includes all the communities which can co-operate with profit in developing a common water supply. The Catawba River power project in North and South Carolina, a private undertaking, treated the entire Catawba River in two states as a unit for a program of power development.

The second element in the concept of regionalism is that regional plans shall not arbitrarily conflict with or injure other areas or regions. Inherent in the regional idea is recognition of interdependence. Under the old idea of politically independent sovereignties, Nevada can pass divorce laws to entice to Reno the people of New York who want to evade the marriage and divorce laws of their own state. Florida can advertise the fact that it levies no state income tax, and thereby entice capital from states which do. Consideration for other regions, and for the whole of which they all are parts, is essential to the concept of regional government.

The third element in the concept of regionalism grows out

of the preceding. It is that there shall be super-regional authorities which will get a total view and bring about harmony between the plans of any one region and the plans of
other regions. The Natural Resources Board, set up by
President Roosevelt, is a suggestion of such a centralized
authority.

A fourth element of the concept of regionalism is that
regions may be functional, relating not necessarily to the
whole life of a people, but to certain limited interests. The
same area may belong to one region for one purpose, and
to other regions for other purposes. For instance, New
Haven, Connecticut, in its business relations is part of the
New York City area, in its culture is part of New England,
and in its river-control problems is part of the Connecticut
River watershed region.

Although many regional programs have been planned
and executed, regionalism as a way of deliberately organizing society is relatively new, and there is much confusion
concerning it, even among professional planners. Many planners have carried over old ideas of political government,
and think of regions largely as the old type of governmental
subdivisions, with the boundaries changed so that they will
conform to regional characteristics. They try to divide the
United States into geographical regions that are regions for
all purposes.

Such all-purpose regions do not exist in fact, though some
parts of our country are so distinct that they are true regions for a number of purposes. Examples of geographical
areas which may be true regions for many purposes are
Alaska, Puerto Rico, and to some extent the Pacific Northwest. Alaska and Puerto Rico are so far from the main body
of the United States, and have so many special problems and

characteristics, that they may be efficiently treated as administrative regions for ordinary political government. But even in such extreme cases the tie to the central government is definite. In national defense, in the postal service, in control of immigration, in money and credit, in constitutional rights and obligations, Alaska is an integral part of the nation, and not a distinct region. The fisheries and lumbering of southern Alaska have more in common with those of the states of British Columbia and Washington than with northern Alaska.

In any mature society, some phases of the common life will be administered through geographical subdivisions of government and industry for administrative convenience, with little or no regard for regional differences. Among such common functions are mail, telegraph, and telephone service; the administration of justice; the naturalizing of foreigners; and the collection of national taxes. Functional or regional planning, on the other hand, comes about because of characteristics and problems that are peculiar to an area, making desirable a unified administration of that area for a particular purpose or for a few purposes. The following are examples of such areas.

An area, including all the Gulf states and a few others, was infected with the contagious disease of cattle known as Texas fever, spread by the Texas fever cattle tick. This region was put under a federal livestock administration of its own. As the disease has been pushed farther south, the infected area has shrunk in size from 728,000 square miles to 14,500 square miles, and it probably will be eliminated altogether. When the Mediterranean fruit-fly attacked Florida citrus groves, a regional administration was set up for its control. The pest was eliminated, and that regional administration was no longer needed.

The Tennessee Valley is almost a perfect region for river control. On the other hand, it is not a natural area for power distribution, for fertilizer distribution, for soil-erosion control, or for crop regulation. Part of it is in the Appalachian Highlands region, which has very distinct problems. Part of it is in the cotton belt, with other problems.

Thus we see the difference between regional or functional government on the one hand, and local political government on the other. States and counties, and to some extent cities and villages, are arbitrarily set up as permanent political structures. They have definite and relatively inflexible boundaries. Their business is to administer the general issues of government, and each of them uses much the same methods as others of its kind. State and county boundaries, and to a less degree those of city and village, tend to be static. No American state has gone out of existence because it no longer fits the realities. The concept of sovereignty, which involves a feeling of permanence and inviolability, clings to these political subdivisions.

Regionalism must be a servant of the general good, and not its master. It is a means, not an end. It denies absolute sovereignty to any limited area or people. It departs from any concept of political sovereignty which would see the state as the ultimate value. Regional government need be no more permanent than the issue it seeks to solve. Its boundaries may change as conditions change. Regional administration may outlive governments. The writer has rehabilitated regional irrigational systems among the Pueblo Indians which had been in operation for about four centuries before the coming of Columbus, through five centuries of

Indian rule, two or three centuries of Spanish rule, and a century under our own government. On the other hand, the Mediterranean fruit-fly regional administration lasted only a few years.

The concept of dynamic regionalism tends to increase and to displace the idea of static absolute sovereignty, with its rigid "sets" in political boundaries and functions. This is a fundamental change of outlook. It means that at all times, and in all societies from the village community to nations and groups of nations, men shall face the realities of social and economic life, shall adjust their organization and their boundaries to those realities, and, most important of all, shall develop peaceful, orderly, and accepted methods for such adjustments. Part of the trouble in Europe today results from the fact that political powers which seized control of natural resources when they were vigorous and expanding peoples have tried to confine other vigorous and growing peoples in straitjackets, where they cannot grow according to their vigor.

Also, much international stress is due to the absence of a well-developed idea of functional regionalism in government; that is, it has been taken for granted that government of an area for one purpose must be government for all purposes. Because a nation needs iron or coal it feels it has a right to iron-bearing or coal-bearing areas. Then, when it has annexed those areas it feels justified in suppressing the culture of the inhabitants and in substituting its own prevailing culture. If the idea of functional regionalism should be accepted, then an area might be a part of one region in its economic relations, including tariffs and banking connections, and a part of another region in its cultural relations, and possibly even with other relationships for transportation.

The Danube River, for instance, ought to have a single regional administration for water transportation, regardless of whether it is flowing through Germany, Austria, Hungary, Rumania, Jugoslavia, or Bulgaria. But the fact that the use of the river should have a single administration is no adequate reason for submerging the several cultures of those nations under a single national control.

The concept of regions and regional administration for special purposes, that is, functional regionalism, from the smallest community to the greatest association of nations, would be a very great addition to the art of human association. An international auxiliary language, such as might develop from Esperanto, would enable nations to work together for common purposes without one trying to submerge the culture of the other. Full adoption of regionalism would largely solve the problems of international relations.

The idea of regionalism requires that the administration of any region must be made to harmonize with the interests of the surrounding regions. Otherwise we may run into provincialism, which tends to see itself as in opposition to other areas and interests, rather than in organic relationship to them. Regionalism should not wholly displace political subdivisions, but should supplement them, taking over such functions as are truly regional. To some extent political subdivisions and functional regions may largely coincide, as with Alaska, the Pacific Northwest, and New England. Thus there will always be a twilight zone between the part to be played by general administrative units and the part to be played by functional regions. Questionable cases must be decided by judgment and experience.

Regionalism can be a key to a new social and economic

order, a positive process for achieving balance and fullness of development in an area, and vital productive relationships between areas. It can be a way to avoid great competitive, wasteful, and sterile expenditures of energy and resources. It can help give diversity, fullness, and good proportion to localities, to countries, and to the world.

Regionalism can stimulate local economic self-sufficiency. As our pioneer economic period passes, and America settles down to plan for stable and adequate living, we shall need to achieve a large degree of local and regional self-sufficiency. We probably shall not ship apples in quantity from the state of Washington to rural Ohio, when Ohio can raise equally good fruit. Neither will heavy unspecialized equipment, such as cast-iron stoves, be shipped from Ohio to the state of Washington. Rather than ship unspecialized products back and forth across the country, we shall achieve a higher standard of living by being more nearly locally and regionally self-contained.

With highly developed regional self-sufficiency, a great part of our economic maladjustment could be solved. For planning the most satisfactory degree of self-sufficiency, a minimum region may be no larger than a local neighborhood or a township. A village and a surrounding area of ten or twenty square miles may be regionally self-sufficient in many respects. This area in turn might be part of a larger region of perhaps four or five hundred square miles, with many more elements of self-sufficiency. Such regions of self-sufficiency would be independent of political boundaries. A local area might be part of one larger region for one purpose, such as food supplies, and of another larger region for another purpose, such as medical and hospital service. Community integration is simplified, though provincialism may result, when the same area constitutes a unit for several purposes, such as marketing, shipping, education, recreation, and local government.

Economic development in America has been partly arbitrary and accidental. There are vast potentialities for efficient local production for local use which have not been realized. A nation-wide development of local and community regionalism might greatly enrich our national life, add variety and indigenousness to our culture and industry, greatly raise the standard of living, and furnish more interesting careers for young people. As in any pioneering, the achievement of this will be a long, difficult job, though a great contribution to American culture.

Always such regional self-sufficiency should be approached realistically and not sentimentally. It should go only so far as the economics and the social values of the situation justify. But that is much further than the public yet realizes. There is no wealth created and no over-all good served simply by shipping goods back and forth, when they can as well be produced locally, with increased variety and income for local people. Many a small community could economically supply more of its own food, services, and supplies.

But just as our country is immature in not developing local self-sufficiency where it would be socially desirable, so also is it immature in its delay in developing many possibilities for regional specialization. Such specialization often contributes to the general welfare. For instance, a small area in southern California is peculiarly suited to raising dates, and perhaps can supply the needs of the United States. That is a genuine regional advantage which should be developed, along with enough local self-sufficiency to save the region from the insecurity of too great reliance on cash crops.

In western North Carolina are perhaps the world's greatest known deposits of fine primary kaolins. That product now is being shipped away almost as raw material, while there is an abundance of cheap coal and water power in the area, and a large surplus population with scanty source of livelihood. It would be reasonable to develop a regional porcelain industry there, as well as other industries in ceramics.

Such peculiar regional advantages should be fully used. In our national development, regional self-sufficiency and regional specialization each must play its part, as determined by intelligent design, not by inertia or chance.

Regional planning is beset with difficulties both from within and from without. From without it is influenced by old political ideas of a series of provincial and competing sovereignties and tends to become contaminated with that attitude. One of the most necessary changes in our thinking is to cease to see sovereignties as absolute and fixed, and to regard them as relative, dynamic, subject to change of boundaries and powers as conditions change, and interdependent.

As a government function, regional planning may tend to be non-democratic in the political sense. The very concept of a region implies that some person or organization with a comprehensive outlook appraises a larger area and defines the boundaries and functions of its natural regions. The outside view is necessary in order to see regions as such. The alternative is competition for territory, with the shrewdest or strongest taking the best.

The electric power industry illustrates this competitive process under private management. The great private power companies did not always represent the most effective regional organization. Sometimes the areas included in power systems were the result of wars of ambition between empire builders in the power field, rather than careful determinations of natural power regions.

The boundaries and areas of Ohio school districts represent the undesirable results of similar competition in democratic government. When the Ohio School District Law was passed, it was left to each locality to include in its district such territory as could be persuaded to enter. In the scramble for the best territory there resulted some prosperous and large districts where organizers were vigorous, forehanded, and persuasive, and some small or weak districts where the citizens were not quickly aware of the competition that was under way. This violation of the principle of natural regions was similar to that resulting from the American habit of separating village administration from the administration of the surrounding area of which the village is the business and social center.

From within there may be a tendency for regionalism to drift toward totalitarianism. The overseeing power necessary to bring regional projects into right relations with each other has in itself an instrument of coercion and control, unless it is disciplined by a sense of social responsibility. Regional planning need not be undemocratic. Sometimes it is a step away from democratic methods. Sometimes it is an approach to more effective democracy. It still needs to be developed to bring about the optimum degree of participation of all concerned. To avoid a tendency toward undemocratic methods, certain general standards should be observed.

First, regional planning organizations should be impartial bodies. Clear and adequate presentation of facts is a first step toward sound public policy.

Second, regional planning should include co-operation with local planning bodies.

Third, coercive legislation or other compulsion should be used only when other means of co-ordination fail, and when the general public interest cannot otherwise be protected.

What would our social and economic order be like if the regional concept should be clearly and fully developed? In government there would continue to be administrative hierarchies for administrative convenience, co-ordinated by a central sovereignty. These would correspond somewhat to nation, states, counties, townships, villages. Their functions would include patents and copyrights, vital statistics, marriage regulations, the administration of justice, the mail, telephone and telegraph, recording of deeds and contracts, collection of taxes, and many other matters.

For many other activities there would be functional regions and sub-regions, not according to any rigid plan, but as particular needs and interests should dictate. For problems of water control, single river systems or groups of adjacent systems generally would determine regional boundaries. In forestry, there might be such regions as the Southern hardwood region, the Southern pine region, the hardwood region of New England, New York, and Pennsylvania, the Great Lakes pine and hardwood region, the Pacific Northwest fir and cedar region, the southern Pacific Coast region, with a few others in the Rocky Mountain area and elsewhere. In the Federal Reserve banking system there would be another set of regions, depending on channels of commerce. Crime prevention would probably be regionalized, with urban centers as headquarters. The country might be regionalized in one way for the coal industry, in another way for the con-

trol of certain insect pests, in another way for the development of recreation facilities. Regions of self-sufficiency might
be as large as the Pacific Northwest, while sub-regions for
limited self-sufficiency might be as small as a village and the
surrounding farms.

For the larger public regional functions, some organization, such as is suggested by the National Resources Board,
should serve as a co-ordinating and integrating force. The
functions of such a central authority would be:

First, to co-ordinate the work of a region with that of
other regions and with the national interest.

Second, to harmonize different regional functions, such as
flood control, power development and transportation, or soil
conservation and forestry, where these functions would fail
otherwise to be co-ordinated.

Third, to achieve an outlook for the whole, so that regional
planning may become part of a national or world vision.

Fourth, to guide local planning authorities concerning
methods and possibilities, and to acquaint the nation with
the significance of regional planning.

Regional planning should not be wholly a government
function. It is well for government to be modest, and not to
assume that a single organization has a monopoly of all
wisdom, experience, and judgment. Many sources of initiative and creativeness are good for a people. Government
should encourage and co-operate with industrial, professional, educational, fraternal, and philanthropic organizations, and should allow such organizations as free a hand
as possible in the development of regional interests. Regional
planning need not be a road to totalitarianism.

How large should a region be? The trend to larger units

of government and industry is world-wide. In earlier times there were hundreds of independent tribes and governments. Today there are about fifty of consequence; half a dozen of the largest include more than half the population of the earth. How long the change will require we do not know, but it seems inevitable that there shall be one world government with much local autonomy and with much regional administration of specific functions.

For instance, it seems probable that such rivers as the Rhine, the Danube, the Congo, the St. Lawrence, and the Amazon will be treated as water-control regions somewhat independently of national or other boundary lines. The transportation of Europe doubtless will be organized as a functional region. The control of tropical diseases probably will be administered on a regional basis, regardless of national boundary lines. The mining of metals which, like tin, are found in quantity in only a few restricted localities, might have similar treatment. The whaling industry is distinctly an international interest, and should have regional administration, divorced from national sovereignty. International regional administration is essential to civilization. On the other hand, regions may be as small as one village and its contributory area. In regionalism we have not a specific plan, but an attitude toward society and its problems.

Unemployment in America is not wholly a phenomenon of politics or of industrial exploitation. It is partly a phenomenon of social and industrial immaturity. Regional planning and development are a necessary condition of a permanently high standard of living. This regional development will include regional and sub-regional self-sufficiency in those things which can be supplied more economically at home than by long-distance trading; it will include, also, regional specialization where significant regional uniqueness exists. It will include co-ordinating and interrelating of regions, so that the whole public good will be dominant, and it will include the development of such new professions as those of regional planner, regional engineer, and regional administrator. Intelligent and competent regional planning is one of the most essential and productive steps for achieving a stable social and economic order on a high level of well-being, and with variety and diversity which will add greatly to range of opportunity and to interest and zest in living.

Regional planning does not necessarily imply a regional plan. Planning is essential to effective living in any field. Yet a regional plan, that is, an effort to make a single plan or pattern into which the whole regional life must fit, may be disastrous. Planning should remove conflict and inconsistency, and should bring about harmony and integration. But it should leave the way open to free creative initiative. It should guide, unify, and inspire; but it should not regiment or thwart, except where the specific long-time interests of society clearly require such action.

This discussion of regionalism is included in a study of the community in order to dispel any impression that the community can be an isolated social unit, and in order to indicate the nature of the relationships which a community can have toward other social units. Between the one extreme of dissolution or disintegration through being submerged by larger units, and the other extreme of being an isolated and provincial social unit, the community must seek its best place. In this effort it will be guided by experience, judgment, experiment, and free inquiry, by understanding of the peculiar and important contribution which the community can make in preserving and transmitting basic culture, and by a vision of what the community may be at its best.

COMMUNITY SERVICE VERSUS REGIONAL OR WORLD SERVICE

No matter how high a level society may reach, there will continue to be vast differences in natural ability, experience, and skill. Sometimes, but not always, exceptional ability should have the widest possible range of action. Sometimes even great ability can be most effective with small groups. In some cases parents who are persons of exceptional quality may have the greatest total influence by deeply impressing great character upon the children of their own family, rather than by having slight influence over a very large number of children. A great teacher may do his best work by very intimately transmitting his spirit to a few students. The founder of Christianity was able to transmit his teachings, not chiefly because he spoke to the multitude, but because he lived intimately with twelve disciples, and gave them an intense and intimate acquaintance with his spirit. In many cases a man may do his best work by concentrating his efforts in a small community, thereby bringing about a penetrating and fairly complete perpetuation of his own quality; whereas if his influence had been country-wide it might have been superficial and might quickly fade away.

Very generally, however, the larger units of society can make best use of exceptional excellence. Copernicus was wise in spreading his ideas before the whole world in a book. In his village his great concept might have died. Mendel's epoch-making discoveries in the principles of heredity were published only in a local journal, and not one of his local readers combined the insight to get the significance of his great work with the vigor to transmit it. So his discoveries lay unknown for decades. Long after his death copies of the local journal fell into the hands of two scientists far away. Because of that fortunate discovery, Mendel stands probably next to Darwin at the head of nineteenth-century biologists. Have there been other great men whose work entirely perished because their neighbors could not understand and perpetuate it?

For the transmission of deep-seated character and of a way of life, long-time, intimate, first-hand association with a few people, with the gradual spreading of that way of life from group to group, far and near, often is most effective. Widespread dissemination is often best for the transmission of intellectual concepts, especially such as can be grasped by only a few.

Yet even such a statement is insufficient, for, through the process of organization, limited changes in ways of living can be enforced for very large numbers. National bank examiners, who presumably are exceptionally able, experienced, and well-trained men, may visit large numbers of individual banks, and enforce standards of practice which relatively few individual bankers could achieve by themselves. State departments of education, directed presumably by the ablest educators in the state, prescribe or pass upon the design of school buildings, the qualifications of teachers, the quality of textbooks, and the general range of the curriculum. That centralized supervision, while it may put an enterprising school system in a straitjacket, probably has improved the general level of instruction.

A striking case of the superiority of large social units over small is in the building of public roads. Three quarters of a century ago roadmaking in the northern states was largely in the hands of local authorities. Township officials largely determined roadmaking policy, and often farmers "worked out their taxes" on the roads. Under this system America was said to have the worst roads of any civilized country. Local officials lacked standards, skill, equipment, and discipline. Their road administration was in contempt throughout the country.

Then gradually the building of roads and bridges was taken over by counties, and there was marked improvement in roadmaking, though inefficiency and graft were notorious, and there was little long-range planning. With the coming of the automobile, roadmaking was largely assumed by the states, definite standards and plans were developed, and while graft and favoritism were not unknown, roadmaking became a fairly well-developed art, with efficient administration.

Then the federal government began to contribute to the cost of state roads on condition that it determine the standards of roadmaking, and again the development of highways reached a new level of quality and efficiency. A single group of specialists, working in the Office of Public Roads in Washington, could carry on research, could make designs, and could enforce standards of planning, contracting, and construction for the entire country. In general, in the case of highways, the more centralized the administration, the better have been the results.

Yet there is a limit even to this process. Local country roads and village and city streets, which carry much the greater part of the total traffic, still are under the supervision of local governing boards. For the central government to try to administer all these minute details would result in a vast cumbersome bureaucracy and a killing of local initiative. Only by experience and judgment can the best distribution of administration be made between various degrees of centralization and localization.

The small community can be the testing laboratory and the nursery for society. There, on a small scale, men can actually live by the good will, mutual respect and confidence, helpfulness, tolerance, and neighborliness, which are the ideal of all human society. There, and almost there only, men can become indoctrinated in their early years with those qualities that are the foundation of society, and can carry those qualities with them into larger relationships.

The larger units can unify and co-ordinate efforts. They can raise the standards of backward local units. And they can keep the peace among the smaller units, as the United States keeps the peace among the states, the states among the counties, and the county and other regional governments among the local communities. Large units teach men to think large. A Swiss once remarked to an American, in discussing relatively simple construction methods in Switzerland, "It is hard for a man to think large in a small country."

Not only in public affairs are large units necessary. Modern American industry could not have originated in a small country, and is possible only because both producers and consumers are organized on a vast scale. The meeting of highly specialized wants is possible only by large-scale organization. One can buy extremely specialized scientific apparatus, books on very specialized subjects, anti-venom for rattlesnake bites, rag-paper editions of the *New York Times* for library files, and numberless other products used by very few persons in any community. They are accessible to us because our life is organized on so vast a scale.

THE RELATION OF THE COMMUNITY TO THE CITY

A city is an aggregation of persons, families, communities, firms, congregations, and other associations for varied purposes, and with no necessary unity or harmony. The people do not undertake to know each other personally, and aside from a few elemental functions, do not feel personally responsible for each other and do not feel the necessity of working together in unison for common ends. What they do in common is to provide certain economic elements, such as water supply, fire protection, policing, and sanitation; and certain limited cultural advantages, such as schools and musical entertainments. Beyond this minimum basis for living, individuals are usually left to pursue their own courses.

No such description of a city is fully accurate. The impulse to create communities is at work wherever men are, and we see frequent efforts to make the city into a community. Music may be furnished to the city as a whole. Educational facilities sometimes are extensive and varied, reaching from the nursery school to graduate professional schools, and sometimes extending to varied forms of adult education. Community Chest organizations undertake to develop in the whole city a community feeling of responsibility for varied needs. Park systems, museums, municipal golf courses, city stadiums and city auditoriums tend to serve varied needs of all the people. City hospitals and visiting nurses care for the sick of the entire city. City libraries with their branches give universal service. Newspapers have their "people's opinion" columns in which citizens may discuss issues with each other in a community spirit. Even in great cities like New York and Philadelphia personalities emerge who view the city as a community, and who come to be known as public-minded citizens. Every city in some degree comes to have elements of community spirit and community traits.

Within cities there may be smaller community units, often the carry-overs of small community traditions. The following account of a city community is a good illustration of this possibility:

In about 1927 a new development was started in one small area of Great Neck, Long Island. All the people in that area moved in about the same time. They were young married couples with one or two children. A few of them had their own cars. These families were more or less segregated from the typical bustle of city life, and it seemed quite natural that the families in this block (258th Street) should become intimately acquainted.

Permission was secured to use the private beach adjoining the Chrysler Estate, several miles away, and the families would get together, hire a taxi, and spend the day there. The men have a volunteer fire department, and have recently built a beautiful fire house which is equipped for recreational purposes as well. Families congregate there in the evening for relaxation.

The women very often do the shopping co-operatively. One shops for herself and her neighbor. The distance to the shopping center is an influencing factor. If anyone is ill, everyone will do her bit to help. One woman will cook the main meal, another the dessert, another will bake some rolls—and in this way a "pot-luck" dinner is assembled for that family.

The church is a community church. The minister is young, and has done much for all ages. A social is held once a month for the married couples. There are frequent dances for the young people. It seems that something is going on every week.

This small block is closely knit, and the community feeling, the seeds of which were planted fifteen years ago, still persists.

The concept of the city as a community has a long history. It probably will continue to live and grow, and will continue to furnish able and public-spirited men with great careers in public service. To ignore it would be to overlook an important social reality. Yet, having paid tribute to the community spirit as expressed in cities, we must recognize the city as a difficult and none too promising field for the creation of a real community. Personal acquaintance is necessarily limited. Men must deal largely with strangers. Those who govern and those who are governed cannot know each other personally. Where community spirit and activity does exist in a city it usually is restricted to a small and influential part of the population, with the general citizen taking little or no part. The major needs of life are not satisfied by the entire city planning and working together toward common ends, but rather by pursuing separate and sometimes conflicting interests, often in the spirit of getting as much as possible by giving as little as possible. Even most of the so-called community cultural activities of the city are concerns of small elements of the population. The city as a community is still an unsolved problem, though not wholly impossible of solution.

The Relation of the Community to the Nation

Our modern cities are coming to be the economic, political, and social nerve centers of a great, partly evolved super-community in which the nation itself or national organizations seek to perform those community services which in most early societies were performed by local villages. Thus our national government undertakes to feed the hungry, to care for the aged, to promote 4-H clubs for the social and economic development of rural children, to guard food supplies, and to perform numerous other community services. Nation-wide private organizations such as the Boy Scouts and the Parent-Teachers Association endeavor to perform similar services. The community impulse, seeking to find expression in every social unit from rural neighborhoods to nations and to associations of nations, with the help of modern technology is creating unprecedented forms and functions. Through psychology, economics, surveys, and statistics, the modern head of a nation or of a national organization may have much of the knowledge about average individual conditions over the country that the head of a primitive village had about his fellow villagers. The people of a great nation may know almost as much about each other's thoughts and about the general state of affairs as did ancient or medieval villagers, while the press and radio give the people of a widespread nation a feeling of intimate personal acquaintance with their leaders.

The community impulse in men strives to express itself in all stages and dimensions of human society. To some extent this effort to create vast communities can be successful; but to some extent it will arrive at success, if at all, only after long periods of painful effort, and perhaps after great social catastrophes. The reason for this pessimistic view is the absence in the larger units of conditions which made for the vitality and permanence of primitive community organization. Only by development through the fabric of society of the spirit and attitudes of community can this lack be corrected. The spirit of community is the key to enduring peace.

CHAPTER VII

THE COMMUNITY IN AMERICA

IN MOST countries existing villages are outgrowths of past communities, sometimes with a continuous existence for thousands of years. In the United States, with the exceptions of Pueblo Indian villages and a few other communities, this is not the case. In a *Gemeinschaft* or natural community most undertakings arise spontaneously out of the background and spirit of the people, and are carried through with a minimum of formal organization. Lacking deep roots and long cultural traditions, Americans have developed habits of deliberate planning and formal organization. When something is to be done, the first step an American takes is to appoint a committee or to create an organization, adopt a constitution and set of by-laws, and elect officers. That custom, growing out of the absence of folkways, has itself become an American folkway. In that process formal voting has become almost a sacred process, whereas in more spontaneous groups an informal "sense of the meeting" or sense of the community is relied on. This informal process takes account not only of the number of persons involved, but also of the weight of their judgments and personalities.

Some American villages, as in New England, Minnesota, and other parts of the central West, were transplanted from Europe as organized communities with continuing traditions. Others, like those of the Mormons, were consciously designed as cultural unities. Many American communities have been built around various social, religious, economic, or political purposes. Oneida, New York; Fairhope, Alabama; Amana, Iowa; and Gary, Indiana, are examples. In numerous cases groups of people went as communities from the east coast to new settlements farther west.

There are American communities which are continuations of old democratic community tradition. Some of the most distinctive were settled by more or less organized or integrated groups from Europe which represent unbroken traditions of democratic community life from prefeudal times, or originated in localities where those prefeudal traditions had persisted. The Mennonite communities are typical. The Waldensians, another example of this process, have already been mentioned. The Dunkards, the Amish, the Dukhobors, the Hutterites, and a few other groups also are examples. New England had to some extent this continuity of prefeudal democratic community tradition from close to the soil in Europe. The New England town meeting was an adaptation of ancient democracy, and not a new creation.

Democratic church organizations such as the Baptist, Congregationalist, Unitarian, Quaker, Mennonite, and Presbyterian, which to a considerable degree carry on the old democratic prefeudal community tradition, have been among the most important schools for training people in democratic methods. They are not complete communities; but, especially in rural areas, they have many of the characteristics of communities. For the most part these are not new creations, but are adaptations of ancient ways.

Most American villages have grown in a heterogeneous way as aggregations of dwellings, rather than as living social organisms. Over a large part of the country settlers went as individuals. Energetic men guessed at what would be strategic points and laid out towns in advance of the peopling of the country. Others built dams and grist mills or set up stores at promising locations. Groups of houses, occupied by people with no previous interest in each other, sprang up at such locations. Most American villages have an advantage over those of Europe and Asia, in that, beginning as real estate developments, they are laid out on definite plans, with reasonably adequate streets.

The United States Government divided most of the territory west of central Ohio into townships six miles square, and made these into "sections" one mile square. In general the federal law allowed a settler to choose a tract of land half a mile square—a "quarter section" of 160 acres—for a homestead. This practice automatically put farm homes on the average half a mile apart. Thus the whole character of a rural civilization was deeply influenced by an Act of Congress. The Mormons of the West, however, followed a different type of settlement, with the well-laid-out village as a center, surrounded by farm lands.

When state legislatures began to make provision for local political government, they generally set up counties, and within them townships, following the rectangular township lines of the Land Office Survey. These state laws also provided for election of township and county officials by uniform methods. Whereas in Europe and Asia local government was usually a matter of slow growth through centuries, with cities and villages far older than the nations of which they were parts, in America west of the Appalachians these subdivisions generally were created artificially by legislation. They largely lacked at the beginning what the *Source Book in Rural Sociology* calls *gestalt*: that is, the personality, character, and individuality which might be said to come by the process of emergent evolution.

Within these law-made, artificial political subdivisions the hamlets, villages, and cities grew up. Where settlements were established by organized groups a considerable degree of common life was present from the first. Otherwise some integration took place out of the common background, experience, and needs of the new settlers, and out of their innate drive to community. But the results were very different from European and Asiatic communities. In some respects the results were better; in other respects not so good. The people had fewer cultural interests in common, and therefore community life was relatively bare. On the other hand, long-standing feuds and jealousies, and what is more important, the habits of feuds and jealousies, were left behind. This was a very great social gain. The chief ways in which the American hamlet or village differed from the Asiatic or European were in heterogeneous population, in absence of traditions, and in expectation of change as a normal course of life. It is much easier to change an American than an Asiatic or a European village.

During the pioneer period American villages tended to grow into true unified communities; but with the development of technical society this community character has tended strongly to disappear, to be followed by unity around special interests, such as church, chamber of commerce, labor union, farm organization, or civic club. In many cases the modern American village has become in effect a small city, in which there is little over-all community spirit and few community undertakings except those of the relatively impersonal government. The *Source Book in Rural Sociology* points out that the American village is over-functionalized:

On the average one village has 5.6 churches, about 16 church organizations, from 6 to 8 lodges, several civic organizations, 27 social organizations, and from 8 to 10 economic associations. On the average there are 21.1 village organizations and 16.1 church organizations, or all together about 37 different organizations per village.

The differentiated groupings of the rural population are becoming similar to the differentiated organization of the city, though the urban network of differentiated groupings is even more differentiated, complex, and fanciful than that of the rural population.[19]

Both advantages and disadvantages of the city result from this change. The modern "citified" village has acquired freedom from restraint, and its citizens are less subject to public censorship. Though a variety of associations is normal and desirable, if multiplication of organization is carried to excess the unity of community life is undermined. Yet to a very considerable degree vestiges remain of the old community spirit and habits, and especially during the last decade there have been many deliberate efforts to develop community consciousness and make it effective.

Does not this condition provide opportunity for a new kind of community life, with recovery of the old unity, combined with freedom and wider range of interest? In the old community, habits, customs, and purposes were controlled by tradition, and often by inertia. In the new community the unity will result from free inquiry, the scientific spirit, education, and the process of critical synthesis, given force and vitality by a spirit of aspiration and social purpose. Such a result would be a new development in the evolution of human society.

Heretofore sophisticated culture has been urban. The flow of quality has been cityward, with very little return flow to the small community. The result has been the impoverishment of small communities—one of the chief causes of the failure of society to make greater progress. Today small communities have more of the conveniences of life than were possessed by the city of a century ago, while even dwellers on separate farms can be as closely integrated with the village as were dwellers in its outskirts a generation ago. The village now includes them, and they can acquire any tempo or mores that is achieved by the village or city of which they are now a part.

The agencies of consolidation—schools, automobiles, telephones, newspapers, radio, etc.—tend to ignore the village and to center interest on larger units. So the problem of recovering community unity is not easily mastered. In the disintegration of real communities which has taken place in America, there has been a tendency for the farm to detour the nearby village and to make its connections with large centers. It reads the metropolitan daily paper, listens to metropolitan radio with its advertisements, does its shopping in the larger centers. In part, this change is natural and desirable. In part, it has taken place because the nearby village was not a real community but only a little city, and as between cities, the metropolis is in many ways preferable.

If the small town tries to be a little city it will lose the values of the community and will make a poor comparison to the big city. If a real community develops from the village and the surrounding farm area, it will reclaim such a share of rural interest as is normal and desirable.

Small communities and rural life sometimes are assumed to have to do almost solely with agricultural life. Even some rural sociologists have had this point of view. T. Lynn Smith, president of the Rural Sociological Society, wrote in *The Sociology of Rural Life*: "Agriculture and the collecting enterprises are the basis of the rural economy; farmer and the countryman are almost synonymous terms. 'Rural non-farm,' one of the United States Census categories, is almost a contradiction in terms . . ."[20]

As a matter of fact, a very considerable proportion of the dwellers in small communities do not follow agriculture. Among other industries which are pursued chiefly in small communities are the production of minerals, including coal mining; iron, copper, lead, zinc, and other metal mining; the production of petroleum; the production of sulphur and salt, kaolin for pottery, bauxite for aluminum, and a great number of lesser minerals which enter into technical industry, such as mica, feldspar, glass sand, vermiculite, kyanite, and pigment earths such as ocher. Other industries chiefly carried on in small communities are quarrying, cement manufacture, clay and gravel production, lumbering and sawmilling, turpentine extraction, fishing (including oyster farming, shrimp and lobster fishing, etc., and the canning of these products), cotton ginning, flour milling, vegetable and fruit canning, hydro-electric power development, decentralized manufacture (especially textile and paper mills), and summer and winter resort service. Perhaps under "collecting enterprises" would be included the maintenance and servicing of railroads, highways, waterways, pipe lines, and transmission lines. In addition there are the very considerable number of people who are not in agriculture, but who directly serve the agricultural population. These would include storekeepers, filling-station operators, mail, telephone and telegraph staffs, doctors, lawyers, dentists, bankers, auto mechanics, carpenters, and a large number of other persons engaged in personal service.

When we include the large number of suburban communities, we see that small community life is by no means identical with agricultural life. Taken all together, and considering recent shifts in population, the non-farm rural population may be not far from equaling the population actually engaged in agriculture. In the treatment of small community and rural life in America, agriculture has had almost a monopoly of attention, to the neglect of the large number of small community dwellers who are not engaged in agriculture. The great diversity of non-agricultural rural life, and the relatively small part played by each class, is the chief cause of this neglect.

CHAPTER VIII

THE CREATION OF NEW COMMUNITIES

IN A period of transition and flux like that of the present, when men are groping to find footholds for significant living, opportunities are as great as they were in pioneer America for the development of communities dominated by the aim to achieve the good proportion characteristic of a well-developed human body.

Throughout the course of history the successful planned creation of new communities has occurred more often than is generally realized. The Greeks definitely planned new colonies. Sometimes they had ideal legal codes developed by specialists and had the lands laid out by professional planners. The Hebrew nation was a colonist enterprise. Eastern Europe is dotted over with cities populated by people from other regions, chiefly Germans, who came as members of organized colonies. For centuries the Teutonic Knights followed the policy of extending German-Christian civilization through colonies. Millions of people in East European cities are descendants of these colonists. In the history of India and the East Indies the planning and creation of new colonies and communities sometimes was a major element of national policy, and some of these new settlements grew into great empires.

In the South Seas, when an island became fully populated it was customary to prepare large double canoes that would hold fifty to two hundred people, with food for two or three months and with seeds and animals for beginning new settlements. These, manned by young men and women, would start out into the unknown ocean, hoping to discover new lands before their supplies were exhausted. Sometimes they were fortunate enough to come to islands in the vast expanse of waters, and then they would begin as integrated communities, with continuing customs, traditions, and arts.

The planning and founding of new communities has been a common undertaking in America, as it has been the world over. Hundreds, and perhaps thousands, of American communities have been originated deliberately as new creations. There is an impression that planned communities in America generally have failed. Such is far from the case. Of the many American communities which were deliberately created, very many in large degree realized the picture of their founders. The most influential single element in the formation of American life, that of New England, began as premeditated new communities, not as an unorganized movement of individuals. For some time in early Massachusetts, settlement was limited by law to those who lived within a mile of the community center. When that area was occupied the surplus inhabitants started other communities, which often retained the name of the original. Thus we have Newton, Newton Center, Newton Highlands, Newton Lower Falls, Newton Upper Falls, and West Newton, as reminders of the manner of early New England settlement.

The founding of Pennsylvania by the Quakers also made a deep impression on the national pattern. The Fenwick community in New Jersey, also a Quaker colony, had a similar successful career. Many semi-idealistic communities, such as Oneida, New York; Greeley, Colorado; Amana,

Iowa; and Fairhope, Alabama, have lived for long periods. Some, built from an economic motive, like Gary, Indiana, and Pullman, Illinois, also have continued to grow. The original Mormon colonies have multiplied and increased to a population of three quarters of a million. Much of the quality of American culture has been the outgrowth of community efforts. In many cases, whether they originated with idealistic purposes, as did Oneida, or primarily with economic motives, as did Gary, there has been lacking a mature and well-proportioned concept of the community as a fundamental element of human culture.

But also there are scattered over our country the vestiges of many communities which were built by enthusiasts or by one-track minds. Even where these have taken root and have grown and prospered economically, which is true of many cases, there has resulted a narrowness of life and a provincial outlook which must be outgrown before a community can become a significant factor in cultural evolution. The difference between those emotional or naïvely inspirational developments and a soundly designed community undertaking is somewhat like the difference between the methods of "Darius Green and his flying machine," on the one hand, and the methodical and analytical work of the Wright brothers on the other.

Many American undertakings to create new communities have been tragedies because they lacked a spirit of inclusiveness and a sense of good proportion. Brook Farm had only dreams and transcendental theories. It had no economic roots. Its members lacked patience, steadiness of purpose, and self-discipline. Fairhope had little more than single-tax and a good climate. New Harmony depended unduly on a theory of social organization. A thousand vigorous Americans have created as many villages or cities with economic production as their principal interest. That is, they built mill towns, factory towns, and mining towns. Often these were dreary aggregations of families, housed in sordid shacks, assembled with no hint or vision of human dignity. Kingsport, Tennessee, was an effort to add to the quality of living by creating an industrial community with employees continuing to live on surrounding farms. Its chief shortcoming arises from its phenomenal success, which has led to overgrowth and to the consequent partial loss of some of the qualities aimed for. Sometimes industrial men built model towns, such as Kohler, Wisconsin, but often their ideas went little further than provision for physical conveniences and architectural design, and too often the creators of these paternalistic communities were made bitter by the ensuing "ingratitude."

Each of these industrialists embarked on the most interesting adventure he knew. Had such a man possessed a more lively imagination, had his cultural inheritance included more understanding of men, more respect and good will for them, more of friendly interest and neighborliness, a wider range of cultural appreciation, he would have sought for his community a diversity of satisfactions, including greater participation on the part of the community members in directing their own lives and that of the community. He would have broken through the prevailing industrial habits and interests of the day and would have seen that, by including the whole range of human values in his concern rather than financial profits or physical convenience alone, he would have had a more interesting life along the way, and would have left behind a greater residue of human values, and for his children better character and greater prospect for social and political security.

Fundamental to all living is a philosophy of life which gives it content, direction, and a sense of worth. Without it men are only educated animals. Communities in which this quality of life purpose was strong have survived much better than others. A common way of putting it is that communities with a religious purpose and motivation have maintained their original quality much better than those which lacked such purpose.

The limitations of American communities have not been primarily that they have not fulfilled the dreams of their founders, but that those dreams were commonplace. Adequate design is not spontaneous; it must be worked for and practiced for. It is because those pictures as a rule were rudimentary and lacking in imagination that American communities have no more character.

Community making sometimes is looked upon as an escape process for people who shrink from rough-and-tumble competition, but that is an inadequate view. The determination to build a favorable social environment would seem to be more reasonable than to create a great estate for one's children while leaving them in a social setting which does not stabilize or refine their characters. The creating of new communities always has been one of the ways by which men have tried to begin again to realize their hopes for a good society, and there is no reason to believe that the process will not be used in the future. The chance for like-minded men to work together in order to realize their common aims is too alluring to be abandoned. Such a course makes possible to an unusual degree the securing of unity of purpose in community life and work, and the achievement of new values.

It may provide happier and more productive adventure than political or financial ambition.

From time to time in America opportunities or necessities occur to create new communities. The establishment of new industries, public need for reducing unemployment, or desire to create better social and economic conditions may provide the occasions. For such projects to be restricted to minimum housing and economic needs is a waste of opportunity, and as in the case of Pullman, Gary, and other industrial towns, may fail to result in best conditions for economic production. The writer has found in several cases in his work as engineer and administrator that even the special economic purposes of such communities can be better assured by looking beyond the immediate utilitarian requirements and making possible well-proportioned community life.

For persons determined to make such occasions yield their fullest possible economic and social values, they offer chances to create and develop new communities which, both in the people who compose them and in the concept of what a community might be, may provide opportunity for originating community types of widespread significance. Few contributions to our national culture would be more important than actual cases of communities in which all major human needs and interests were recognized and developed in good proporᴸtion. Few experiences would be more satisfying to the persons involved and to their children than participation in competently designed undertakings of that kind. Only rarely are people creative. Far more frequently they are ready to imitate whatever of excellence may appear. Wherever men of competence and creative intelligence are willing to pay the price in preparation and in the arduous, persistent effort which creation always involves, the designing and developing of new communities is a worth-while field of effort.

One of the first difficulties encountered in undertaking to build a new community is that such an undertaking tends to attract persons who are misfits in society, or single-track minds searching for a panacea, as well as those who deliberately and competently seek to create an environment favorable to significant living. In this we see a repetition of the incentives which brought about the settlement of our country. Comparing the temper of life in an American community with that in most small European communities, one gets the impression that America to no small extent was settled by individuals who were ill-adjusted or discontented. In most cases, each man or family emigrating from Europe to America was so dissatisfied with home conditions as to be willing to pull up by the roots and remove to an alien land. Both the strength and weakness of America lie in that fact. With some who came, discontent was largely due to personal maladjustment, while the dream of a promised land was naïve and undisciplined. With others, the discontent sprang from mature imagination and disciplined purpose.

Just at present there is a great outburst of new community building in both Great Britain and America. In the United States the central government has been doing it, though often with tragic results due to bureaucratic and autocratic fumbling and interference. Some of the private undertakings are by persons or groups who have enthusiasm, but who lack the disciplined skill and the experience to make a success of any substantial undertaking. The failure of these projects—and many others will fail—does not condemn the process any more than the failure of nineteen out of twenty merchants is a reflection on the process of storekeeping. But such failure of ill-designed and poorly managed community projects wastes valuable human and material resources, leads to discouragement and disillusionment, and brings the process into disrepute.

A deliberately planned and created community has the best prospect for all-round success if it is a neighborhood of people who have in common enough of cultural life, social purpose, and capacity for mutual understanding to be good neighbors, and who have in common such discipline of life and refinement of purpose that children growing up in that community would find the cultural influence of the family supported by that of the neighborhood. In the development of such a community, or in the regeneration of those already existing, there should be effort to provide variety in economic undertakings and in cultural interests, so that young persons of differing tastes and abilities could find opportunities for their lives. There should be wholehearted commitment to a spirit of free inquiry and of critical open-mindedness, as a recognized quality of a good community. Otherwise some form of provincialism and atrophy will appear.

In such a community there should be range and variety of cultural contacts. Even where the occasion for the creation of the community is economic, as the development of a new industry, or educational, as in the case of a "college town," no one factor, such as economic self-support, or religious uniformity, or political or social views, should dominate, but rather there should be effort to recognize and to develop in reasonable proportion all the major interests of men and women. The analogy of the highly developed systems of stimuli and controls, of checks and balances in the human body, with the aim of maintaining good relations and good proportion in structure and in function, is especially applicable to a community. It is not any single kind of excellence, but diversity and balance and good proportion of excellence, which make a good community.

CHAPTER IX

THE PROBLEM

THE preceding chapters have presented evidence that, as a continuing source of population, and as the social organization which, next to the family, has been the chief agency for perpetuating and transmitting human culture, the small community has been of vast import in human affairs. In the long run the basic culture of human society can maintain itself on no higher level than the culture of the small community.

Yet, as we have seen, the small community has been neglected, exploited, and despised, while society has paid a very high price for that neglect. In many cases even the neglected thread of community culture has been eliminated by conquest and destruction. This neglect of a basic cultural unit may be one of the primary reasons for the failure of human society to advance with greater surety.

Serious as has been this neglect, a process is under way today perhaps more fundamental and more serious than anything which has preceded. The seriousness of that process may be illustrated from the biological world. The higher plants and animals are made up of cells and tissues and organs which co-operate to the common good of the organism. Yet each cell has its own individual life and carries on its own individual functions in a little world of its own. To protect that individuality each cell is surrounded by a cell membrane which separates it from all others, and tissues and organs are similarly protected. If the cell walls or tissue walls of the human body should be dissolved, the body would quickly die.

Similarly a social organism, such as a state or a people, is composed of cells and organs—individuals, families, and communal and functional societies. Each of these in its way has its own cell or tissue wall, its own individual life. Only by maintaining its separateness and identity can its indigenous culture be kept alive and transmitted with dependableness from generation to generation.

Today, as seldom, if ever, before, society is dissolving its cell and tissue walls, and as a result is losing power to preserve and to transmit its basic culture. Old social outlooks and convictions and habits that gave men a sense of validity are fading away, because the social units through which those values were preserved and transmitted are disappearing, leaving little but immediate self-assertion to give meaning and a sense of worth to life, and leaving the way open for the development of crude expressions of group loyalty.

Where community life is dissolved and the only remaining sense of social identity is with vast societies, such as great nations, serious-minded young people who wish to be socially effective often measure their small powers against national or world movements, and develop a feeling of frustration and futility. On the other hand, where they are members of small communities they have opportunities to deal with problems within their grasp. They can be realists and can be effective within the community, and so can have a feeling of validity denied them when their primary relations are to vast social aggregations.

It is doubtful whether there can be social health until

this process of preservation and transmission of basic culture is renewed. In the great world disturbances of today, stable seed beds of fundamental culture are especially necessary.

To what extent is the integrated community possible and desirable in our present-day society of rapidly shifting populations and multitudinous contacts, influences, and associations? Few populations shift faster or have more contacts than those of colleges, yet integration of college life is possible, partly because the concept of integration exists there. The problem is to recover the essence of the integrated community, and to achieve for it a set of mores, a code and a temper of inquiry, of critical-mindedness, of intellectual freedom and intellectual interests, which, so far as possible, will leave it without inhibiting barriers. Today the conditions of life have changed so that the small community can be culturally abreast of any other. Is not this a significant fact in social evolution?

How can there be community of standards, aims, and purposes, without regimentation and dogmatism? This is one of the oldest and most universal issues of community life. Can unity without regimentation be achieved by eliminating arbitrary and capricious standards and by seeking universal and fundamental standards?

One of the standards most difficult to maintain is that of freedom of thought and inquiry. Everywhere vested interests and dogmatism strive to entrench themselves by claims to special sacredness, revelation, or other authority, demanding that men accept the orthodox position without inquiry. The small community, because of its relative isolation, often retains the results of indoctrination and propaganda of an earlier period.

One of the most disrupting influences in the American community has been the competition for loyalty of different religious groups. Each has tried to create dominant loyalty toward itself, somewhat regardless of loyalty to general community interests. Community possibilities never can be fully realized so long as any group or groups claim a monopoly of truth or wisdom. Unity of the whole community can result only to the extent that claims to unique authority are given up. We can see how Mohammedan and Hindu in India have prevented unity through the centuries by each claiming to have the one true faith and indoctrinating children so deeply that they feel it would be a sin to doubt that claim. Yet our own indoctrination may be so deep that we may be offended by the suggestion that the cases are similar.

One of the problems of village communities the world over has been that of feuds, sometimes internal and sometimes inter-community. The flux of population to and within America has largely eliminated traditional feuds. In this respect loss of tradition is fortunate. Can traditions of unity be maintained without also maintaining traditions of discord? Can the development of community codes and standards contribute to this end?

In normal primitive life men commonly had periods of stimulated living alternating with periods of quiet vegetating. The nervous and physiological reserves consumed during periods of stress were renewed during quiet periods. This was the general condition of primitive village life. Under city influences, especially under modern conditions of constant over-stimulation, there is small opportunity for renewing these reserves. There is reason to believe that periods of in-

tense urban life may consume the reserves of human energies
to such a degree as to bring about general decadence. Can
development of small community living add to its stimulus
and interest and yet give opportunity for renewing these
reserves, and might such an achievement be a major factor
in lengthening the period of vital life of a people? Can the
increased stimulation of small community life be selective,
and can a normal balance be reached between the accumulation and the consumption of physiological reserves?

It is necessary to recover or to achieve a community way
of life which will make possible the full and well-proportioned
life of its members, and which is not in fundamental conflict
with the makeup of humanity, and then to find for it a tolerable environment.

The problem of the community has commonly been viewed
in its superficial aspects. Only slowly is it being seen as
dealing with a way of life, rather than simply with economic
or social arrangements. For instance, Cecil North, writing
in 1931 in his book *The Community and Social Welfare*,
said: "The author frankly shared the opinion that organization and correlation were the prime needs in American
social work. As the study progressed, however . . . it became clear that the lack of organization is not the fundamental weakness. . . . Underlying organization is personnel
and professional technique."[21] Even here he has not reached
the foundation, for underneath personal and professional
technique there must be the slowly developed spirit of community, which will give vitality to both organization and
technique.

There are many aggregations of families in America that
are waiting for leadership to turn them from aggregations

into communities. In the course of time capacity for community participation becomes atrophied from disuse, and efforts to create community spirit may meet with initial discouragement. Persistent purpose may be necessary to recreate an appetite for integrated community life. That redevelopment of atrophied community spirit may be one of the most difficult elements of community undertakings. That is the work of community leadership.

Every addition to human culture, every development of good will, courtesy, fair play and dependableness, originated with pioneers who in their own living demonstrated those traits. Then gradually other people, seeing and admiring those traits, imitated or deliberately achieved them. By that process civilization advances. The problem is, how to find or to develop or to encourage such leadership. For the leaders, the problem is how to bring into being a picture of the full, well-proportioned community as it might be, and how to turn indifference and unconcern into critical but active interest.

CHAPTER X

AN APPROACH TO A SOLUTION OF THE PROBLEM OF THE COMMUNITY

THERE is possible a new synthesis of small-community life. While recovering the unity which tends to emerge when all the people live and work and learn and play together and develop common interests, as in the primitive communities of ancient and medieval times, this new synthesis will include also the universality, the culture, the critical-mindedness, the sophistication, of the city and of specialized functional groups. The new synthesis will take advantage of technical developments in communication, transportation, power transmission, and other fields. It will make extensive use of specialized organizations for special purposes. But also it will strive to see the community as a unified whole, not just as an aggregation of men and of special interests and organizations. Men again may live and work with and for all the members of the community, and may have the deep emotional satisfaction which comes from common experience and association.

The wider and more numerous contacts of the present day need not destroy community traditions, but may make possible the conscious creation of greater traditions. The community can be a reservoir for the preservation and transmission of basic culture on a higher level than at any time in the past.

A clear concept of the community as a fundamental element in human affairs—as a way of life and an attitude toward life—cannot be counted on to spring up spontaneously. The idea of self-conscious, critical design for the small community, with a spirit of universality instead of provincialism, and with a conscious striving for a sense of proportion, will develop slowly, and must be transmitted by the contagion of both word and example. In the long history of numberless communities that concept seldom has emerged. When it has appeared, the results have been important in world history. Such results have been seen in the founding of Greek colonies, in the origin of the Hebrew state, and in the settlement of New England, Pennsylvania, and southern New Jersey, not to mention similarly significant undertakings in ancient East Indian civilizations.

The small community should use and recognize special or functional organizations, such as scientific and business associations, as well as its total-way-of-life or community organization. It should welcome and encourage pioneers who advance to new positions for which the community as a whole is not yet ready. There should be recognition and respect for individuality. There should be deliberate planning for active but orderly step-by-step transition from things as they are to community relations as they might be.

From the old organic community and from the modern outlook this new synthesis can borrow the elements of its purpose and program. In so doing the aim will be to seek unity, fellowship, and a sense of good proportion, so that the community shall be united in the aim of making possible for each of its members a full and varied development of his life according to the needs of the community as a whole and the needs of his own individual genius. The following are some elements of such an objective:

1. The development of neighborliness, with mutual good will, helpfulness, tolerance, and personal acquaintance.

2. A budget of community interests, consisting of matters on which the community has substantial unity, so that it can act effectively; development of the broadest possible base of unified social purpose; a policy of common efforts to common ends.

3. Suitable and effective relationships with larger units, such as region, state, and nation; common, united representation in outside relationships and issues which affect the community as a whole.

4. A policy of free, open-minded, critical inquiry, with the habit of striving for unity through sincere, patient, tolerant inquiry, rather than through compulsion or arbitrary authority.

5. The largest possible agreement on ethical principles, with conscious development of common ethical standards; no interference with pioneer standards or sincere and tolerable divergences of individuals.

6. Common community programs of education, cultural and social life, recreation, health, and other major community interests, with inclusion of the entire community population in those programs to the full extent of individual capacity and interest.

7. Recognition of community interest in land and improvements, both public and private, through programs of zoning, etc.

8. The development of co-operative community effort

or group co-operative effort for supplying basic economic needs where the general welfare can be advanced thereby; community consideration of such possibilities as community-owned and operated utilities, co-operatives, credit unions, etc.

9. The habit of regularly meeting together as a community without division into social and economic classes, for the discussion of general and specific community problems, and for general community recreation and acquaintance; the attitude of working together as a community of people who have cast their lot together and who will stand or fall together in working out common problems.

10. Respect for individuality and for individual tastes and interests—the maintenance of a wholesome balance between community life in which the entire community acts together, and individual or smaller group life where diversity of individuality is recognized and respected.

The beginning point for community development is person-to-person relationships. Every person can learn the fundamentals of community life by learning to live in harmony and good will with the persons next to him. Almost every problem of the community, state, and nation, is met with on a small scale in our relations with people closest to us. This is not a rhetorical expression, but a statement of specific fact. Unless we can be successful in those relationships we have not yet mastered the art of building a community. We need not wait for great programs. Each person in his day-to-day relationships can be mastering the art of community.

Regardless of the form of government and of society, most of our contacts from week to week and from year to year are these first-hand personal relations with people close to us. If these relations are fine, then the greater part of our lives is fine, and that fineness will constantly infect the community and all social units beyond the community.

Part Two

COMMUNITY ORGANIZATION

CHAPTER XI

COMMUNITY DESIGN

Community organization is . . . merely an improvement or perfecting of the relationships which make a community. The very idea of community carries with it the correlative concept of organization. The community is itself a form of organization.[22]

—Sanderson and Polson

1. General Comments

THE aim of community design and development should be to understand the actual nature and potentialities of men and to make possible their fuller realization. Community design should be in accord with what men really are, not in accord with theoretical abstractions about them.

For instance, in planning for community development it sometimes has been assumed, as in the case of the French social reformers Cabet and Fourier, that since association is good, the more association the better, and that the closer the personal relations in all respects, the happier will be the result. Contrary to this favorite theory of community planners, it seems that individuals thrive best with a considerable degree of spacing. Too great proximity and too close association violate deep-seated cravings for freedom of motion and for privacy. Various community undertakings have suffered or have failed through failure to realize this need. Several of Fourier's "phalansteries," not greatly different in appearance from pre-elevator apartment houses, were built in the mid-nineteenth century. Most of them failed, partly because they violated this common human craving for reasonable separateness and individuality. One of them, at Guise, France, made a remarkable success financially, but after half a century died out because the pattern of life lacked range and depth and was too confined. Economic success alone was not enough.

Where physical proximity is compulsory men tend to set up emotional partitions. Among the northernmost Eskimos, who of necessity live in close communities and are highly communal, there is great respect for privacy and for individuality. Except where they have been influenced by outsiders, they generally live in separate houses, though combined houses might be easier to build and to maintain, and would be safer. Among them it is bad form to pry into others' private affairs or to use strong pressure to persuade others to a course of action.

Among polar explorers, and other men who are compelled to live in small groups in great intimacy, the strains of too intimate personal relations often become a major difficulty. In Paris apartments it is bad form to know anyone in the same apartment house. Prisoners chained together often come to hate each other.

Too great physical proximity sometimes has been a disadvantage of small community life. Today, as never before, because of the automobile, the telephone, and electric power transmission, liberal spacing and correspondingly favorable environment for individuality can be combined with acquaintance and community. This matter of the best spacing of people in communities is discussed as an illustration of the many respects in which a knowledge of men as they actually are is essential to sound community planning.

The Relation of Community Size to Community Activity.
How large should a community be? Only large enough to
supply necessary services and to serve useful and productive
purposes. If there are enough food stores or gasoline filling-
stations in a community, then for others to be added, simply
because they can divide the business and thereby support
additional families, is a social waste—a form of parasitism.
In general, no one should join a community and tax it for
his support unless he has some service to render which will
result in its being a more desirable community. A community
should be like an excellent automobile, which has all the parts
it needs, but no more than it needs. If a large number of
spare parts are available, to add extra wheels, bumpers, car-
buretors, etc., would only cumber the automobile and make
it less useful. Such parts should be used to make another
automobile.

No one should join a community unless the service he can
render will add to the completeness or to the quality of that
community. A professional writer may live in a small community where few if any of his writings are sold. He may
serve the community by bringing in cash income which will
help to balance money sent out of the community for goods.
He may add to the intellectual life and make the community
a more interesting place. He may serve in community organizations.

The adding of a new industry which supplies employment
and income may be a gain, whereas the multiplying of community services already well supplied may be a useless tax
on the community. In most communities there is an over-
supply of some kinds of services, such as stores, and at the
same time an undersupply of some other necessary service,
such as good recreation for children, or suitable hospital
service. It should be the aim of community design that vital

needs and values be supplied, and that waste, duplication, and parasitism be eliminated.

In the best interests of a social organization it is important that the number of persons included shall be properly related to the purposes of the association. In general, the more intimate the relationships, the fewer are the numbers that may satisfactorily belong to it. For the most intimate social groups, from a dozen to thirty would seem to be the limit. Sometimes even smaller numbers may be more satisfactory. But such very small intimate groups are not what we usually think of when we speak of a community.

A community should be large enough to support a feeling of belonging; it should be small enough so that the members quite generally can know each other personally, and especially so that persons in different callings or of different degrees of authority or status can be fairly intimately acquainted. It should be large enough to supply diversity of ability and interest, as in business, education, art, the professions, etc., and large enough to provide a variety of careers for young people. It should be large enough to provide reasonable choice of intimate friends and acquaintances. It should be small enough to make possible a sharing of burdens, and to encourage a feeling of all-round community.

For a fairly complete and effective community of people who are working out a way of life together with the necessary acquaintance, understanding, and good will, the membership may be from a few dozen to a few thousand. If the numbers are too large, either community relationships will be restricted and more formal, or the community will break down into aggregates made up of several partial communities, often along economic or other class lines, and the total unity of the community will be partially lost. Nevertheless, tech-

niques and methods for developing some characteristics of
community in larger populations can be developed.

If we are engaged in creating new communities, or are
deciding how large a community we should settle in, then
comments on desirable community-size are much to the point.
However, in general we find ourselves living in certain communities whether or not they are the size we like best. Our
business then may be not to decide what size community we
should like, but rather, what elements of community spirit
and design are feasible in our own community.

Towns and neighborhoods of different size will have the
characteristics of a community in different degrees and in
different ways. In community study and planning it is desirable to come to a conclusion concerning the extent to
which the population group in question may become a true
community, and what kind of community interests and activities would be practicable and appropriate.

Consider first a small neighborhood of only a dozen families. To what extent can it become a real community? Many
of the programs discussed in books and articles on community organization are impossible for such a small group.
Yet there are other ways in which its size is ideal for community organization. If the members of this neighborhood
should make a habit of spending one or two evenings a
month together, the time to be divided between recreation
and study or planning, they would find the group to be as
large as is feasible for general discussion in which everyone
takes part. For mutual neighborly help in trouble a neighborhood of that size may develop finer relations than a larger
group.

A dozen families may make one of the finest communities,
or one of the worst. If jealousies, quarrels, and personal

antagonisms are eliminated, and if tolerance and good will control, then young people growing up in such an environment may look back to it as the most valuable formative influence in their lives.

If such a neighborhood consciously undertakes to make a community of itself it should make a point of finding out the ways in which it can be a real community, and the ways in which it cannot. It will not try to be a poor imitation of a large community. It probably will not try to promote paid music courses and lecture courses. It probably will not try to secure the services of professional recreation leaders. It will not try to create a community council in the manner described in a later chapter. It may well have a study program for all its members; they may meet occasionally to hear and discuss exceptional radio programs. A fairly definite program of picnics and other recreation may be worked out in such a community.

What is undertaken will depend on the abilities and interests of the different members. If one should be musical he or she might guide occasional neighborhood sings. If some member should be skillful at woodwork, his shop might be a place for an evening a week of handicraft work for both children and parents. Various pieces of equipment might be purchased by the community for co-operative use, which would otherwise be too expensive for any one family. Such equipment might include a small canning outfit, a large tractor for the heavier farm work, or a community refrigerator.

The combined effort of the group probably would bring agricultural experts, a representative of the state department of health, representatives of the state co-operative organization, and others, to address neighborhood meetings.

Unless the members already belong to larger co-operatives they could profitably buy fertilizer, seed, stock feed, cans, sugar, and other goods together, often at great saving. The local merchant generally will co-operate in such buying. There are many opportunities for buying supplies at wholesale from the original producers—figs and dates from California, pecans from Mississippi, unpolished rice from Louisiana, at half or two thirds the retail price. Textile mills sell "mill ends" of cloth at similar reductions from the retail price. By bringing the community needs together very considerable savings can be made. If a small neighborhood will explore for ways to do things for which it is just about the right size, it will discover many opportunities for community undertakings, and the process of working together will make the spirit of community grow strong.

On the other hand, consider a small city of ten or twenty thousand population. Many persons would consider such a city to have exceeded the limits of size for a true community. Yet, if it will face the facts and do what it reasonably can to create a community spirit, without trying to imitate either a community of one or two thousand people or a city of a hundred thousand, it may develop many of the characteristics of a true community. It probably will need a community council. Where class differences actually exist, as is true in most cities of such size, there may well be an effort to have every element of the population become directly acquainted with every other through "cross-section clubs," the members to be selected from the entire population in proportion to their relative numbers, by scientific sampling, after the manner of the Gallup polls.

Since many of the available discussions of community planning in health, recreation, music, education, and other fields deal largely with urban conditions, it is not in place to discuss such possibilities here. The point we are making is that there can be no standard pattern of community design. Each potential community should undertake to discover in what ways it can become a real community, and should pursue those ways. It should realize that in many respects the relations of its members will naturally be with larger or smaller groups.

Conditions Affecting Community Design. Various local groups more limited than the community are normal and wholesome, and should be recognized and encouraged. Among such are local intellectual and cultural associations, such as science clubs, musical organizations or recreation associations with special interests; ethical, religious, and reform groups of persons who are pioneering beyond general community standards; and commercial, agricultural, professional or other groups with specialized economic interests—all of these groups perhaps as local sections of widespread organizations. Members of such groups should see themselves also as members of the community as a whole. Their special interests should not be kept to themselves alone, but should be made to serve the entire community as well. It is wise for members of a community to limit the number of special-interest groups to which they belong, so that a substantial part of their time and interest shall be available for the general community. Otherwise the community as such will become anemic and atrophied. A vigorous, wholesome community can exist only at the price of conscious determination for its achievement. In many communities local groups become so numerous and distracting that they tend to submerge a consciousness of community, and become factors in community disintegration.

The community feeling which originates and develops in the intimate community tends to spread beyond it and to give some of the characteristics of community to larger groups, such as city, state, and nation. It is a social fact of great importance, which ordinarily has been overlooked, that the spirit of community in large groups generally is the outgrowth of the development of that spirit in small groups.

Within a real community there will be an absence of arbitrary exclusiveness. The formation of small social groups within a community may be desirable for the sake of intimate association or because of particularly exacting cultural, intellectual, ethical or esthetic standards. But there is danger that such groups may divide the community into cliques, classes, and factions. Conscious effort should be made to insure that such small groups shall harmonize with and contribute to the common life of the larger group. It should be contrary to the standards of a community for any social or economic class to insulate itself and build up exclusive communities within the community. A smaller cultural group should be an element of leadership *in* the community, not an escape from it.

There should be readiness in such limited associations to share their fields of interest with anyone who is interested and qualified. That sharing should not be left wholly to chance. Persons or small groups with special interests should endeavor to contribute their interests to the community as a whole whenever that is feasible. For this purpose they will use various community functions, such as music programs, meetings for discussion, lecture programs, community picnics, and other social events, as well as more serious community undertakings. They will explore the community for young people capable of sharing their interests.

The community will be broadened and enriched, or made superficial and debased, by outside influences. Newspapers, magazines, radio programs, parent-teacher associations, colleges and universities, are but a few of such undertakings. Their selection and use can be influenced to a large degree by the development of strong community purpose and standards. Also, the community must learn to maintain its own existence and individuality while continuing relations with civic and educational organizations for common undertakings and for the exchange of data and experience. It should be a loyal part of the nation without losing its character as a community. The local community will never again be an isolated area, and there should be no effort to make it such.

A community will thrive best if there is unity of plan and action on matters concerning which there is substantial identity of need and purpose. Individual or smaller group action may be retained for interests that are not general, or on which there is no general unity of opinion. In the new community there will be conscious effort to discover what activities and interests can well be the concern of the whole community and what activities can best be left to individuals or small groups. Still other activities will be the concern of the state or nation, or of great private industries. There will be no effort to force all life into the community mold, but there will be constant effort to discover what phases of life can best find expression through the community.

Complexity of the Community. One of the aims of this general discussion is to indicate the complexity of the community issue. In that respect the community is like the family. The interests and issues which arise in the family are too varied and complex to be foreseen or accurately described or to be worked out by any single definite plan. A family which should work wholly by a plan would be a deadly affair. Yet a family needs to plan. Will there be enough money to send the children to college, or to buy a new auto or to pay for the house? Which is more important, or how much should be spent for each? Family planning is necessary, not only in financial matters, but in many other respects; but a family "plan," by which all the activities of the family would be controlled, is neither necessary nor desirable. While a "community plan" to govern all the activity of the community would be most undesirable, community planning—a constant effort to eliminate waste, increase economic and social values, discover community possibilities, and work out designs for their realization—is both good and necessary.

No one could reduce to rules all the spirit and attitudes which go to make up a well-bred family. The members of such a family do not live chiefly by rule, but by motives and intelligence and training in what is appropriate to the occasion. So a good member of a good community will not live chiefly by rule, but by motives of good will and mutual confidence, and by a sense of security and of belonging, learning to act as an intelligent person of good will would act in the circumstances. Some definite rules are possible and necessary, such as obeying traffic signals, but community life as a whole is too complex for anything less than community good breeding.

One is not going to learn community planning as an engineer learns to design a bridge, but rather as a member of an orchestra learns the spirit of co-operating with the whole, whatever may be the music. Community planning will not be good or bad, it will be better or worse. It always might be worse, and always might be better. In the process of making it better everyone can help, though some will help more than others, as a good conductor of an orchestra may help more than a first violin, and a first violin may help more than the drum. Yet all are necessary. The man who plays the drum does not feel irresponsible and does not play carelessly because he is not the conductor or first violinist. He does his part as well as he can. Without that attitude there cannot be a good orchestra or a good community or a good nation.

The picture of the community as a classless society in which all association rests on loyalty, on community interest, and on qualification, and not on vested privileges and possessions, is a very radical picture. In most large towns and cities it will be smiled at or frowned at as chimerical. Yet it is approximately the actual condition in numberless small villages and neighborhoods. The reality of a classless society must be won by actual experience. It was easily approached in Russia because it was already the status of the greater part of the people. The revolution simply broke a very thin and very rotten shell of caste. The situation is very different in America. No violence will achieve that goal.

To bring about cases of such communities may be easiest with small groups where there are no inflexible economic or social barriers. Yet such small communities often are provincial, lacking cultural breadth and depth. Is it easier to take advantage of the actual democracy of very small rural communities and to try to develop cultural quality, or to try to develop a democratic spirit in larger communities with a greater cultural development? Wherever we work we shall find disadvantages, but also in almost every place we shall find encouragement and hope. The small community is about the only place in America where democracy is actually a way of life, and many of those who wish to promote that way of life may find their best chance there.

2. THE AIMS OF COMMUNITY PLANNING

In planning for the welfare of the community it is necessary to keep a sense of proportion and perspective. Many community projects have been marred or destroyed because those who planned them gave attention to only a few of the elements that constitute a good community, and overlooked others. Industrial towns like Pullman in Illinois, Gary in Indiana, and Kohler in Wisconsin are cases where chief attention was given to industrial production and housing. In Brook Farm, Fairhope, and New Harmony some idealistic concept had the right of way, while practical considerations were overlooked. Most American small communities suffer from lack of an all-round idea of community life.

Various students of the community have outlined what they believe to be the chief issues with which community planning should be concerned. Sanderson and Polson of Cornell University, in their book *Rural Community Organization*, present substantially the following aims:

1. To lead the people of the community to become conscious of the existence of their community as such and of the significance of the community as a basic unit of civilization, and to encourage them to feel that they are members of it.

2. To satisfy unmet needs, whether economic, cultural, or physical.

3. To incline the people of the community to plan and to act together for common ends, and for development of common acquaintance and interests, so that

there will be "all-round participation in the thinking, the feeling, and the activities of the group."

4. To develop a community spirit and common community standards, and to maintain them in a spirit of loyalty.

5. To get the groups within the community to increase effectiveness by avoiding duplication, interference, and waste in programs and undertakings, and by pooling their efforts where that is desirable.

6. To prevent the entrance of undesirable influences and conditions.

7. To co-operate with other communities, with public and private organizations, and with the larger units of region, state, and nation.

8. To develop ways of mutual understanding and agreement, that is, of consensus of opinion.

9. To develop leadership within the community.*

Most of these, it is evident, are general, long-time aims which cannot be fully realized by any quick campaign or program, but only by patient conviction, determination, and loyalty of community leaders and of others who will not be discouraged. When we get down to actual work in order to realize these aims we come to more definite undertakings. A community development program should not aim to take over the work of local government or of other agencies, but to understand and to support and co-operate with those agencies. Such a program should offer constructive suggestions or criticisms where that is necessary, supplying elements of planning not otherwise supplied. Its aim should be to do or

---

* These aims are summarized from pp. 77-83 of Chapter V, "What Is Community Organization? Its Aims and Objectives," *Rural Community Organization,* by Sanderson and Polson.

promote what is not being done but what can be done for the improvement of community life.

The following may serve as suggestions for some of the practical things a community, or the people in it, can do to create a strong, wholesome community life:

1. Increase the range of community interests. A thorough and careful study of community needs and possibilities by a small but deeply interested group or organization, with the help of what experienced men in the field have written concerning community surveys, is a good beginning of community development. This cannot well be turned over to paid experts from outside. A community may profit by outside advice on how to undertake such a study. Its members may need the help of specialists on technical problems after they have educated themselves on community affairs in general and on their own community in particular. But the job of learning one's community cannot be delegated to outsiders.

2. Interest the people of the community in the significance of communities in general, and in their own community in particular. The local newspaper may subscribe to a community column, telling stories of interesting and successful community undertakings in this and other countries, and discussing the philosophy and possibilities of community life. Then the people of the community who are undertaking to help in the development of community life should supplement such a column by articles on the history, accomplishments, needs, and possibilities of their own community.

3. Perhaps organize a community council. After the development of general interest in community life, that may be the most important single step in the program.

4. Continue active support of the community council, as

that will be necessary to give it life and strength and standing.

5. Include efforts for town and country co-operation, so that they will constitute one community. For every person who lives in an American town of less than ten thousand there are on the average two living in the surrounding country. To some extent the rural families have neighborhood community life of their own, and that should be encouraged. Yet often the people in the surrounding country have no community center except the town. They trade there, go to shows there, meet their neighbors on the streets, often send their children to school there, and frequently belong to churches in the town. Notwithstanding these many relationships, the people of the surrounding area often are not considered to be part of the community. They should come to be an indivisible part. In time, many communities should be so reorganized that the town and the surrounding country shall have a single local government. The possibility of enlarging the town boundaries to include the surrounding rural areas should be studied.

6. Study and co-operate with the local government, to the end that local tax resources shall be budgeted, and efficient and useful government shall be developed. Officials need support in their efforts to provide good local government.

7. Consider the possibilities of planning streets, sidewalks, parks, building subdivisions, transportation facilities, zoning real estate, eliminating smoke, smells, and other industrial handicaps, planting shade trees, preserving natural beauty spots, removing roadside dumps and unsightly billboards, correcting dangerous road and street crossings, plan-

ning attractive signs on the business streets. All such activities come under the head of town planning.

8. Become familiar with problems of public safety, crime prevention, and the elimination of carelessness and destructiveness, so as to encourage and support public and private efforts to those ends.

9. Give attention to problems of public health—water supply, milk supply, sewage disposal, the keeping of animals in the town, and the prevention and control of communicable diseases.

10. Study the economic life and welfare of the community and work to make the community a well-balanced economic unit, with reasonable economic opportunity for everyone and wholesome economic relations with other or larger units.

11. Plan and develop community recreation as a vital part of community life.

12. Study the educational program of the community, which needs help, encouragement, guidance, and co-operation, not only in the public schools, but in adult education. Schools in which the public is not deeply interested cannot maintain very high quality. The home economics or homemaking program of the public school should be broadened to include all young people in a period of training for better home life and management.

13. Take into account the interests of young people. Provisions should be developed for treating youthful delinquents in such a way as to develop character and self-respect. A program of vocational guidance should help young people to appropriate callings. Interesting and useful ways of spending spare time should be developed and maintained. Through high school the time and interests of young people are highly

organized. Then they are suddenly dropped and left to shift for themselves. Transition programs should be provided.

14. Study the general cultural interests of the community and see that they are encouraged, planned, and promoted. These include a library, music, handicrafts, dramatics, a possible village institute containing museum, library, and community center, and various other undertakings.

15. Give consideration to common community undertakings, such as the development of a community calendar of meetings, with effort to arrange meetings to result in the least possible conflict. The co-ordination of relief and charity work, the support of a community chest, and other common community activities require study.

16. Give attention to that part of the population which is left out of community activities. Even in an over-organized community it generally will be found that a considerable number of people have little part in community affairs. This may be true of tenant farmers and their wives, of elderly people, of foreigners, and of low-income people. A good community will be concerned with making life interesting and wholesome for such people, as well as for others.

Of course, not all these activities will be undertaken in any community at any one time. In almost every community some of these activities never would be needed. It is the business of a community to discover which issues are of greatest importance, and to give greatest attention to them, not forgetting lesser issues that are vital to some of its members. Care should be taken not to undertake too many projects at one time.

The first step toward a better community is a study of its needs, interests, and possibilities. The next chapter is devoted to that subject.

CHAPTER XII

A STUDY OF THE COMMUNITY

THERE may be some needs in the community so clear and so pressing that there is no doubt of the necessity for supplying them. Perhaps the milk supply is unsafe, or there may be some disreputable business undertaking in the town which should not be tolerated. Common sense may urge the correcting of such situations without any prolonged study of general community needs. Nevertheless, as a rule it is good policy to spend some time in learning about communities in general and about one's own community before starting out on any general program of improvement. Without such a background, good perspective will be lacking.

The development of the community is not a short-time undertaking such as might be brought about by one year's program of a Rotary Club or a League of Women Voters. A year's intensive study by such an organization may be a good way to discover what the problem is and to develop ways of working with it. Community development, however, is a never-ending job. It should have some of the time and attention of all the people. It should be the chief interest, aside from home and making a living, of a few people who will qualify themselves to be leaders and the hardest and most consistent and persistent workers in that field. Without such leadership of a few people who will take the trouble to study and to understand the subject, and then to work at it, community development will be unbalanced and interrupted.

How to Begin the Study of a Community. Because sociologists are inclined to take the attitude of experts and to make studies, in many books and bulletins on community planning we find the advice to be: "First get an expert and have him make a study." Not only is such a course expensive, but it is of doubtful wisdom. It tends to make a community feel that what it needs is to have something done to it, rather than to work at its own problems. Unless some understanding of community issues exists in the community before the expert comes, he will take most of his knowledge away with him, and the community will be little better off. If expert guidance is secured at the beginning of a community study, its aim should be to help the people of the community study their own problem.

Community planning must be lived with and worked with by those who greatly care. Some one or more people must make it their chief avocational interest. When they have become well grounded in a general understanding of community life and community problems they may well call in technical help, as in case of public health problems, or in financial management. An informal serious study by members of the community may be much more productive than a dramatic and expensive "survey." At best the expert can be an indispensable guide to local people who are deeply concerned. At worst he can be an expensive nuisance.

Generally the best way to begin the study of a community is for a relatively small group of members of the community to make it a major social interest. In a Nevada town of about two thousand the Women's Twentieth Century Club undertook that service; and in the years which have followed, that organization has been recognized as the leader and the best source of information and judgment in community affairs. In case no organization is inclined to take up the project, perhaps some one person who is deeply interested can find a few others sufficiently interested to unite with him in such a study.

In such a group, one-track minds and men with social panaceas should be absent. Also, it may be fatal to such an undertaking if those engaged in a study have axes to grind. A community should beware of studies dominated by utility representatives or others who are concerned to commit the community to their programs, or by representatives of certain religious organizations which hold that they alone have authoritative truth, or by representatives of political parties bent primarily on making converts. Such persons often are "available" and "ready to serve." Everyone engaged in such a study should be a sincere learner, not a person of fixed ideas determined to impose those ideas on others.

Suppose that some organization in the community, or some informal group of five or six, should undertake to begin the study of the home community. How should they begin? This book, or Colcord's *Your Community*, may be followed as a guide. A general idea of the nature, history, and significance of the small community will supply a background and a basis for judgment which knowledge of one's own community alone will not. A knowledge of communities of other times and places, and of the origins and background of present-day customs and problems, is essential to an understanding of our own times and our own community. However, an historical study of communities and a study of one's own community in some cases may well go along together.

Alternate meetings or parts of each meeting of the study group might be given to such general and historical study as is covered in the first chapters of this book, alternating with the study of one's own community, such as is outlined in this and succeeding chapters.

A Working Library. For an effective study of the community a small working library is highly desirable—almost imperative. Several able men have spent their lives in an effort to understand small communities and their history and problems; and not to take advantage of the life-work of such men will result in a waste of time and effort.

For a very few dollars a small nucleus of a library can be secured. For an expenditure of fifty dollars a very helpful collection of books on general community planning can be purchased. A few hundred dollars will make possible a very fine library on community development, covering general community planning and also such subjects as local government, community economics, sanitation, parks, streets and public buildings, community health and hygiene, delinquency, education, music, recreation, other cultural interests, relations with other communities, and various other fields.

For a group beginning the study of their community three books are recommended as the beginning of a library. *Your Community*, by Joanna C. Colcord, should be owned and studied by each member of the group. It is an excellent guide to practical community planning, but provides almost no historical background. Two other books will supply that larger view. *The Rural Community*, by E. Dwight Sanderson of Cornell University, is an excellent treatment of the history, the nature, and the significance of small communities, with discussions of their future possibilities. *Rural Com-*

munity Organization, by Sanderson and Polson, is perhaps the best book on that subject. Another excellent book is *A Study of Rural Society*, by Kolb and Brunner.

A remarkable collection of information and literature on rural society is contained in the three volumes of *A Systematic Source Book in Rural Sociology*, by Sorokin, Galpin, and Zimmerman. Still another good book, made up largely of descriptions of individual communities, is *The Changing Community*, by Zimmerman. *Elements of Rural Sociology*, by Sims, is almost a condensed encyclopedia of data in that field, though the index is inadequate.

With this little nucleus of a library, or even with the first four books mentioned, which cost all together about twelve dollars, a group of people in a small community will be equipped to approach its study intelligently. Other books are mentioned in the suggested readings for this chapter. As the study proceeds, books will be helpful which deal with special fields.

The Objects of a Preliminary Study of the Community. This preliminary study of the community should have two principal aims:

First, the members of the study-group should become generally informed on their subject, so that they may continue to be a source of judgment and information. They should not get lost in detail. The careful study of detailed projects should be the work of individuals or of special committees, to continue through the years.

Second, they should become acquainted with those persons in the community who could be added to their group, and with those who, after a study of general principles and methods, might prepare to assume leadership in particular phases of community life. Someone might be willing and able to prepare himself for a study of community music, to learn what other communities have done, and perhaps to develop leadership in community music. Others might be found who would be interested in vocational guidance, in local government, in community economics, in recreation, and in community health. Their detailed work might follow a general survey.

One of the principal undertakings of the preliminary study-group might well be to become acquainted with the membership of every active public-interest organization in the community, and to find one or more persons in each organization who would be most effective as members of a community council such as is discussed in a succeeding chapter. Having found such persons, effort should be made to interest them one by one in the general undertaking, and to get them to spend time in preparing for greater usefulness in the community. Such persons might read this book, and one or two of the principal writings on the subject, and should be asked to attend meetings of the study group.

The next step might well be the formation of a community council. This phase of community development is so important that a chapter is devoted to it.

CHAPTER XIII

THE COMMUNITY COUNCIL

THE community council may well be one of the most important inventions of American democracy, perhaps not even second to city-manager government. The movement seems to have had several independent origins. During the first World War such organizations were proposed as a defense measure; and it is said that thousands were organized, but nearly all of them disappeared after the war. From 1912 to 1919 community councils were promoted by the Massachusetts Agricultural College, under the leadership of Dr. E. L. Morgan. The first publication on the subject, *Mobilizing the Rural Community*, by Dr. Morgan, issued in September, 1918, outlined methods and policies strikingly similar to the latest pronouncements by proponents of co-ordinating councils. However, his program looked more to long-time planning and concerned rural communities chiefly, whereas the co-ordinating council has been a movement of large city and suburban communities. Dr. Morgan also called for a greater degree of direct community participation than the co-ordinating council requires. With his retirement from Massachusetts, and with the after-war relaxation, the movement largely stopped; but his bulletin spread the idea.

In the fall of 1919 Dr. Virgil E. Dickson, Director of the Bureau of Research and Guidance of the Public Schools of Berkeley, California, and August Vollmer, Chief of Police of Berkeley, began to have lunch together to co-ordinate their work. Then, after some years, with four other department heads, they organized to form the "Berkeley Coordinating Council." In 1929 the California Commission for the Study of Problem Children recommended the spread of the Berkeley idea, and by 1933 there were about fifty co-ordinating councils in the state. In 1935 an organization of the ninety co-ordinating councils of California was formed, as the "California Coordinating Councils." In March, 1938, "Coordinating Councils, Inc.," was created, and has since been the active head of a movement for the organization of such councils. Its headquarters is 145 West Twelfth Street, Los Angeles. The organization is ready to be of service to communities everywhere.

In 1929 the village of Alexandria, Ohio, organized a community council which has had a continuous and successful career. At the present time there are twenty-five or thirty community councils in Ohio, and the number is increasing.

In 1929, also, community councils were organized in Clarence and Clarence Center, New York, both of which have continued to the present. These have been responsible for a large number of activities, such as summer band concerts and a bandstand, playground equipment, Old Home Day celebrations, mosquito prevention, sidewalk construction, community buildings in the school park, clean-up days, new street signs, an essay contest, a volley ball league, horseshoe pitching courts, a reorganized fire department, and tree planting on highways.

At Norris, Tennessee, under the Tennessee Valley Authority, a community council, organized in 1936, for some years constituted the sole governing body of that community of 1500 people. In 1934 "Neighborhood Coordinating Councils" were formed in Cincinnati. They have increased until eight are now active. Doubtless numerous other similar organizations have originated in past years quite independently of each other. The American Legion, after a brief study, reported six hundred co-ordinating councils in the United States. While this figure is frequently quoted, it includes a large number of organizations that are not community councils, and there may be a much smaller number in effective operation.

A community council may be made up of one representative of each live, active, public-interest organization in the community. That is, the Chamber of Commerce would appoint one member, as would the Parent-Teachers Association, the League of Women Voters, the Garden Club, the Rotary Club, the Trades and Labor Council, each church, the Farm Bureau or Grange, and so on through the list of community organizations. These representatives would constitute a council to plan the fuller development of the community, to study its needs and shortcomings, and to co-operate with governmental bodies and with the member organizations, for the improvement of the community.

A great value of the community council lies in the fact that it represents every public-spirited interest and organization in the community. It cuts across all party lines and class lines and gives representation to the entire community. When constituted as indicated above, it is exceptionally resistant to political or other manipulation.

Great credit is due to the unselfish efforts of those in California who are chiefly responsible for this movement. As is natural, it has not arrived suddenly at perfection. In planning the organization of community councils difficulties may be avoided by observing early shortcomings which are in process of being eliminated.

One weakness is the tendency in some cases for public officials and public employees to dominate the councils. In the original Coordinating Council, of Berkeley, California, and in several others in that region, the entire representation was made up of public officials or public employees. A local government should have a co-ordinating committee, with representatives from each department or agency, to prevent overlapping of effort or failure to cover the ground, and to develop understanding, unity, and economy in local government. Yet such a committee of public officers and employees does not take the place of a community council made up largely of non-governmental representatives.

Public officers or employees should not dominate the community council. It would be well for each major official department or agency concerned with local government to designate one person to meet with the community council when desired, and to be a connecting link between the community council and the government department or agency, but not more than perhaps one fourth of the community council members should be public officials or employees.

The value of working with public officials is well expressed by Kenneth S. Beam in "Coordinating Councils in California":

It has been the experience of coordinating councils in California, with some exceptions, that the public officials are ready to participate in the council program and that they welcome the opportunity to cooperate with the private agencies and civic organizations. The very assumption that this cooperation will be forthcoming often produces cooperation, when any other attitude would have failed. In those instances in which the council feels that some public service

THE COMMUNITY COUNCIL 149

needs improvement, they have found that they can usually serve such improvement by working with the official concerned and offering cooperation, rather than by criticism or opposition.

It frequently happens that the improvement in service or additional service sought by the coordinating council has long been the objective of the official in charge, but that he has been unable to secure the improvement because of lack of funds or lack of approval of other officials. The weight of opinion registered by the coordinating council in many cases has provided the support that the officials have needed to secure the service that they have long desired.[23]

In addition to members representing public-interest organizations, the community council may itself select a few "co-opted members," that is, persons chosen for membership because of special personal ability to render service. These may be full members with voting powers, or associate members with opportunity to discuss, but not to vote. For instance, a physician in the community may be greatly interested in public health, and yet he may not be chosen to represent any civic organization. Such a person might well be chosen as a co-opted member.

The co-ordinating council movement has lacked a clearly defined basis for selecting members. As the community council becomes a more and more important element in our national life, this shortcoming may have serious results. What kind of organization is qualified to have representation in the council? Suppose the largest church in town has a Men's Club, a Ladies' Aid Society, a Sunday School, and a Boys' Club: can each claim a representative? Suppose the Trades and Labor Council is made up of half a dozen craft unions, should each union have a representative? Unless clear policies are developed, such issues may make trouble.

The following general principles or standards are suggested for membership in community councils:

1. Government officials or employees shall constitute not more than about a quarter of the members. Where some public official not on the council has special knowledge or skill which would be of particular service to the council, as for example the public health officer or the teacher of school music, such person, if co-opted by the community council, may be an associate member without a vote. If any general class of people in the community should be found to be without representation, such as the farmers adjoining the community center, or some foreign population group, the community council may appoint representatives of such groups. The total number of co-opted members shall be not more than a third of the whole membership.

2. Only civic-purpose organizations are eligible to appoint representatives. This classification does not include amusement organizations, such as country clubs, golf clubs, or bridge clubs, though it may include such an organization as a sportsmen's club whose interest is largely that of game preservation. The criterion is that the organization shall be committed to the public service. Purely commercial organizations like advertising men's associations or coal dealers' associations are not eligible to choose representatives. Cultural societies concerned only with the interests of their own members, such as dramatic clubs and private music clubs, are not eligible. Labor organizations constitute a marginal case. They are organized to promote the economic benefit of their own members, but unless they have a place on the council their members may have little representation.

3. Political or propaganda organizations, such as the Democratic or Republican Committees or the Communist Party organization, or the Single Tax Club, are not eligible.

4. No organization will be eligible to appoint a repre-

sentative if the organization has been created chiefly for that purpose, or if it has been in active existence for less than three years, or if its membership is less than one per cent of the population of the community, or if it is a secret organization.

5. The term of membership shall be for one year. A member who has served for three consecutive one-year terms shall be ineligible for re-election until one year has elapsed. This provision will tend to prevent entrenched membership of inactive members, and will create openings for new members of promise. It will lessen the accumulation of "deadwood" on a council.

6. The secretary need not be a member of the council.

7. In case an organization has subsidiary or component organizations, only the central organization shall be represented. A loose association of officers, such as a town ministers' association, does not constitute a central organization, and is not qualified to appoint a representative to the council.

8. There shall be no restriction of membership on the basis of race, sex, creed, or national origin.

9. Any civic organization meeting the above conditions for membership may appoint a member to the community council. In case of disagreement on eligibility of an organization, the vote of the majority of the council shall be conclusive.

10. In addition to members, a community council may well provide for "committee associates," that is, persons who would be chosen by the council as members of its committees because of their marked ability and interest in some field. For instance, if the community council has a standing committee on housing, it might add to that committee a few members of the community who are best qualified in that

field. Such a policy, if consistently observed, would make the community council committees representative of the best community talent. Committee associates would be members in full standing of their respective committees, but appointment as committee associates would not make them members of the community council.

Community Council Publicity. Another frequent shortcoming of co-ordinating councils has been a policy of avoiding publicity. Many communities know little of the work of their co-ordinating councils, the near secrecy being justified by the councils on the ground that since much of the work is for delinquents or for persons or families in trouble, publicity would be humiliating to those being dealt with. With a larger view of the place of the community council, publicity becomes imperative. The public has a right to know what is being done by such an important organization. Publicity can help to clarify issues, and can make the public aware of the significance of the small community in the life of the nation. It need not make public specific cases where personal or family embarrassment would result from publicity. By a wise handling of publicity the idea of community integration and unity can be developed little by little, and a feeling of pride in and loyalty to the community can grow. (This shortcoming also is now recognized and is being overcome by the co-ordinating council movement.)

The Field of the Community Council. Still another shortcoming of the co-ordinating council movement is that in its origin and in much of its development it has been concerned chiefly with juvenile delinquency and with underprivileged boys and girls. Important as is this field of work, the scope of the community council should be much greater—nothing less, in fact, than the development of every phase of community life in good proportion to every other. Leaders of the co-ordinating council movement are coming to recognize this need. Juvenile delinquency is largely the result of unbalanced community development. While not forgetting that it is an important community responsibility, the chief consideration should be to create such a community that juvenile delinquency will seldom originate there.

While the co-ordinating council movement has been of great value, it has needed a clearer definition of purpose and method, and a broader vision of its possibilities, in order to make the very great contribution to American life which is inherent in the idea. The steady growth of the concept is illustrated in the excellent bulletin of Coordinating Councils, Inc., "A Guide to Community Coordination." This should be in the hands of every person concerned with such activities.

It may seem to the reader that the terms "community council" and "co-ordinating council" are used indiscriminately in this discussion, but such is not the case. The term "co-ordinating council" is used with reference to the movement which developed first in California, and which is served by Coordinating Councils, Inc., of Los Angeles. This movement was initiated, and generally has been led, by heads of departments in local governments who got together to compare notes, to harmonize and unify their efforts, and to prevent duplications and omissions in their work. In the view of the early organizers, the value of their "co-ordinating council" was to enable them as department heads to do better the work of their several governmental departments or agencies. In this development the state government, and the federal government through W.P.A. workers, have shared expense and have been helpful. In the literature of that movement repeatedly one meets the statement that the co-ordinating council is not to undertake projects on its own account, but is only to co-ordinate the work of other agencies. The co-ordinating council movement to a considerable degree is outgrowing that attitude and is recognizing the need for undertakings by the council itself.

In contrast, the community council, while undertaking to co-ordinate the work of existing public and private agencies, does not hesitate to assume projects of its own. Typical examples are the community council of Alexandria, Ohio, and those of Clarence and Clarence Center, New York. All of them have long periods of successful work second only to that of the Berkeley, California, council. The Alexandria council originated a public library for the community, and in connection with the library provided a social room for farm women. It developed a public playground. It worked out a community calendar of meetings. It directed three community pageants at intervals of five years. It plans an annual Hallowe'en party. It promotes the community musical program through an existing agency—the public school system. The New York councils mentioned had an even wider range of activity. At Yellow Springs, Ohio, the "Youth Council" both informally co-ordinates the work of other agencies and initiates projects of its own.

The co-ordinating council had its origin and much of its development in large cities, or in suburban areas which had facilities largely financed by cities. In such cases there were well-developed public departments and agencies to co-ordinate, including health officials, the juvenile court, probation officers, and recreation officers. The movement has the color of a large city or suburban area. Its literature constantly emphasizes the need for paid professional workers, which means that it is to some degree impersonal, like large city government.

On the other hand, the Alexandria community council is in   village of 500 people, with 1500 in the farm population wh ch is included in the community and shares in the pro-gr m. In such a community there are relatively few public or private agencies to co-ordinate. There is no juvenile co rt, no recreation department. Short of the entire county the e is no governmental or other organization except the co munity council, which coincides with the entire com-mu ity of village and farm area. There is little money for pa'd workers, so the people must rely upon old-time neigh-bo liness to serve their own needs. In creating the Alex-an ria community playground by filling a gully and remov-in an eyesore, the actual labor as well as the planning was the unpaid volunteer work of the villagers and farmers.

n producing each of the three pageants every member of the Alexandria community in village and country who was old enough to participate had some part, and no one had mo e than one responsibility. The chairman of the council is   farmer living outside the village. Thus the community co ncil, as represented by Alexandria, is a movement to over-co e the separateness of denominations, school board, village co ncil, farm organizations, and business men's clubs, and to   reate in reality a community of friends and neighbors wh get acquainted with each other by co-operating in com-mu ity undertakings. This element of becoming a real co munity is no less important than that of preventing du lication and omission in the work of the several depart-me ts, agencies, and organizations. The very fact that the whole community works together on a given project creates a bond of neighborliness.

There is room for both types of community organization, and for various grades between, but the small community will lose something very valuable if it sees its council as chiefly a means of preventing omissions and duplications in the work of its various agencies and organizations. Its chief work is to recreate the community of friends and neighbors, and to bring it to a well-proportioned development.

There is a growing tendency for small communities to have available the same kind of paid social services as large cities have. These are furnished by county, state, and national governments.

The Work of the Community Council. First of all, it should be the business of the community council and of its members to understand the history, principles, and problems of communities in general; to know their own community thoroughly; and to appraise its needs and possibilities. With that background of knowledge it should be the business of the council to know how the public work of the community is being carried on, to point out weaknesses and ways of correcting them, to support able efforts and to recognize good work. It should aim constantly to promote the co-ordination of the work of various organizations and agencies, so that waste time, effort, and expense may be eliminated, and a higher degree of efficiency may be achieved.*

* Co-ordination and integration may not mean consolidation or elimination of organizations of similar purpose. Small units often are desirable because they allow more intimate relations. Several small churches, if they are not too small and weak, may serve their members better than one or two large ones in which intimate acquaintance would be lost. Different churches and other organizations appeal to different temperaments. Such small organizations with similar aims should not be looked upon as necessarily com-

he community council should not do the work which oth r organizations in the community are willing to do and capable of doing. Where no organization exists in the community which is willing and able to perform some necessary service, then the community council should not hesitate to perform that service if it is able to do so. Such cases usually will be limited to general community projects, such as the development of a calendar for community meetings, or the establishment of a public library. When any practical need of the community is not being taken care of, the community council or one of its committees should bring the need to the attention of the appropriate government department or other agency, and follow up the matter until suitable results are achieved.

The community council should keep the public informed of the state of community affairs, including facts, needs, and possibilities. It should seldom if ever try to enforce its opinions by legal or other drastic action.

The Organization of the Community Council. The initial members of the community council may well be proposed to the various organizations by the initial study-group heretofore discussed, for appointment as members of the council. Before making such recommendations to the several organizations, the study-group would, of course, discuss the various possibilities with the best informed and most responsible

---

peting with each other, any more than squads or divisions which make up a regiment, or the artillery, cavalry, and infantry of an army, are competing. They may have friendly and helpful relations with each other. It may be better for a community to have several Ladies' Aid societies, and several luncheon clubs, rather than to have a single large organization of each kind. There can be too many or too few organizations in a community, or too many of one kind and too few, or none at all, of another kind. There needs to be a sense of fitness and a sense of proportion in establishing and maintaining organizations.

members of the community. Perhaps a committee of such men and women might be appointed informally to draw up a list of proposed names. After the initial organization of the community council, reappointments would be made by the several organizations as they should see fit. Member organizations may become thoughtless or careless in appointing members to the community council. In each case before an appointment is made the council might well write to each organization, drawing attention to the importance of the appointment, or it might have a conference with the officials. When subsequent appointments are in order, in case certain members of organizations are especially qualified to give good service, the council might suggest that their names be placed in nomination among others. Care should be taken that the community council does not become a self-perpetuating oligarchy. That has happened in a few cases.

When the community council is organized it may be divided into several committees. One or more of these may be concerned with the general theory and philosophy of community organization. Any group will do better work if it is familiar with the history and background of its problems. It would make the community council a more useful group if perhaps the first third of every regular meeting were spent in a study of the history and philosophy and problems of communities in general. One or more committees might be responsible for that part of the program. If no better plan should emerge, at each meeting a chapter might be read from one of the best books on the subject, or a description might be read or given of significant and successful work elsewhere. It is important that the council keep a broad and long-range view, and that it shall not be completely buried in the details of current undertakings.

Other committees will be concerned with various specific subjects, and special committees may be appointed for limited periods to deal with temporary or special issues as they appear.

To a considerable degree the work of most co-ordinating councils has been the outcome of concern for juvenile delinquency and for the needs of underprivileged boys and girls. The community council should have a wider range of interests. It should be concerned with the efficiency of the local government, with the economic possibilities of the community, with cultural opportunities and possibilities—in fact, with the whole range of community life. This need for increased range of interest is being recognized more and more by the co-ordinating council movement.

It is sometimes unwise to have committees on all phases of community life at one time. A committee should not be organized just for the sake of having a committee, but only if there is some definite need for it. However, when some member or members have a definite interest on which they wish to work, a committee may well be provided for that purpose. For instance, one or a few persons may feel very strongly that boys and girls finishing high school should have help to prepare for definite callings. In that case they may be made a continuing committee for that purpose.

Attention might well be limited at first to a few major issues, except as individual members are willing to be continuously responsible for definite interests. In addition to the day-by-day work of meeting the current needs of the community, it might be well for the community council to give its major attention for six months or a year at a time to some single issue. The major issue for one year might be a study of the economic life and possibilities of the community.

Such a concentration of attention would not prevent any other committee from going ahead with its work.

The initial study-group, if it should not be absorbed into the community council, could well continue its work, for the organization of a community council will not suddenly result in community consciousness, even among council members. Unless their interest is maintained, some of the members may be willing to let the council die. Someone must continue to work hard and patiently against repeated discouragement in order to put flesh and blood and life on the dry bones of organization. It might be that for years the fate of the whole movement might rest on the persistent work of one person or of a small group, some of whom probably would be members of the community council. If the council as a whole seems listless, perhaps some committee chairman is alive, and with the help of the initial study-group, might make his own small part of the program such a success as to give life to the whole council. Often it is by such a course of taking any legitimate opportunity which presents itself, that success finally is achieved.

From the literature of the co-ordinating council movement the following suggestions are culled. Their value is largely due to the fact that they are the product of actual work with co-ordinating councils, and they should not be taken as applicable in all cases. Most of them were assembled by Kenneth S. Beam, Executive Secretary of Coordinating Councils, Inc.

Suggestions for new councils:

"In starting a Council one should concentrate on a few interested individuals rather than try to form an organization with a large number of people." [During the early days of a council, and until community interest is well established, one thoroughly interested person might represent two or more organizations, but the aim should be to interest others to become representatives, each of a single organization.]

"Start with a small group, then increase by inviting representatives from other organizations in the community, until all are represented."

"Sell the idea to three people who will devote their time and efforts, and the job is begun."

"Take plenty of time to secure good representation from each member organization."

"Get young people on the committees."

"Secure the broad, inclusive participation of all possible interests and agencies."

"Work very closely with the law enforcement bodies."

"Include in the membership the people's groups, so that the Council is not superimposed on a community."

"Secure an active and discriminating membership chairman."

Suggestions for the program:

"Study the community, find actual needs; then select one need and meet it."

"Find a vital basic need, and concentrate all efforts to fill that need."

"Start work immediately on some problem, however small, which can show tangible results."

"Begin with a small group attacking a definite project, one that can be completed within a reasonable time, so that interest can be maintained."

"Go slow. Analyze needs, but do not expect to accomplish everything at once."

"Do not attack too many problems."

"Limit the scope of the project to that which can be well done. Expand as resources and understanding permit."

Surveys:

"The Council's first activity should be to study the neighborhood from the social viewpoint."

"Have a thorough survey to find facts before starting."

"Definite understanding of community problems must precede program building."

Leadership:

"The one person who represents the Council in the eyes of the community is the chairman. If he is a person in whom the community has confidence, and is one whose interests go far beyond his own organization, the Council has a good chance of succeeding. Ordinarily he should be a person who has already demonstrated his ability by having served as the leader of other organizations in the community."

"No one person can possibly have experience or training in all the fields touched upon by the average Coordinating Council."

"He should not be known as an extremist in any field, political, religious, or professional. He should not be a fanatic, a radical, or a reactionary, and not one who is inclined to ride one hobby to death."

"He should be one who does not try to capitalize on his organization contacts for personal gain, or to make use of the organization for political advancement."

"He should be able to detect and emphasize points of agreement and to minimize points of difference until common ground is discovered."

[Some of these suggestions seem to emphasize tactfulness rather than courage and conviction. A real leader will do more than tactfully prevent friction. He will have conviction and creative ideas, and will not shun unpopularity when that is necessary.]

"Never allow politics to enter."

"Select a chairman who will lead from the community point of view, not from a church or a P.T.A. point of view."

"Be cautious lest you have publicity seekers."

"If they don't want a lot of hard work without pay or credit, or if they are not able to give a lot of free time, don't organize."

"It would be an advantage to start out with a paid director." [In most small communities this is not feasible. Sometimes a woman who does her own housework would be able to give a good deal of time if she should receive the actual cost of hiring help which would free her own time.]

"Provide a secretary with sufficient funds to keep activities before membership and public."

Keeping the public informed:

"Acquainting the public is important, getting its confidence and co-operation."

"The press, the governmental and private agencies must be with you; the community must have confidence in you."

Council meetings—programs and policies:

"Be sure to have thorough preparation of interesting programs for every announced meeting."

"Have informative programs related to problems in the community."

"Establish committees only as there is felt need for them, and definite projects for them to work on."

"No important information should be concealed, whether it indicates success or failure of the plans adopted." [This of course does not refer to matters where publicity would be unwise, as in cases of personal or family difficulties where help or guidance is needed.]

"Every representative should have some responsible part in the organization."

"Avoid taking authority and responsibility for initiating and carrying on activities in the name of the Council." [This applies where there are organizations in the community to whom the work and credit can properly be assigned. Sometimes the Council will initiate its own projects, where no other organization will undertake them.]

"There is no pattern for a Council to follow, no fixed program to be carried out in all communities. No two towns and cities are alike, and no two should expect to have exactly the same program." [This statement by Kenneth S. Beam expresses his experimental, democratic, non-regimented attitude in co-ordinating council promotion. That attitude should be jealously preserved. Naturally some methods and policies will be found to be so generally sound that they will become widespread.]

"One of the axioms to be followed religiously by Co-ordinating Councils is that of requiring full information regarding a given need, condition, or problem before a program of action is mapped out."

"Satisfactory results will come only after hard work and dogged persistence over a long period of time."

"City and county organizations contemplating the sponsorship of a number of Coordinating Councils should recogñize the importance of providing qualified and experienced persons on full time to direct the work of the Councils. One such person can serve a number of Councils."

"Reports from 57 Coordinating Councils indicated that the average annual budget of a council was $42. The funds were secured in various ways." [For an effective community council a much larger budget is desirable.]

"Coordinating Council work should be related to all vital aspects of the community. Only by being so related can it maintain its balance."

Other Forms of Community Organization. Sanderson and Polson, in their very useful and interesting book *Rural Community Organization,* give descriptions of various types of community organizations. This book reflects such clear insight and such a wealth of experience that it should be read by all persons planning community councils. Their final comment on community organization is pertinent:

. . . it is questionable whether there is sufficient experience in this field of endeavor to warrant the advocacy of any stereotyped procedure in setting up a community council. The presumption is that circumstances will differ materially in each community and that the important thing is in the beginning to get the various organizations to working together in joint community projects, rather than to spend too much time in trying to work out the best type of organization or to give much attention to long-time planning. The need for long-time planning may better evolve out of the situation, when it will be felt as a real need and will have better support. When this stage has been reached, or as a means for determining the essential facts upon which to base certain projects . . . surveys of community conditions will usually be found desirable.[24]

Especially for small communities where there are not several local organizations to be represented, a simpler form of organization than that described for the community council may be desirable. In such cases thought should be given to find the method of selecting members of a community council who will most fully represent the whole community and who will be most efficient and useful. Direct, general participation of the community under the best leadership should be the aim.

When a community organization has been developed, its members will find that most of its work has to do with specific community interests. While taking account of these one by one, it will endeavor to keep them in good proportion, with the aim of bringing about a well-balanced all-round community. Insofar as it is feasible and leadership is available, the work of the organization probably will be distributed among committees, each with a special field of interest. Most small communities contain people of varied interests and abilities who, if they should learn to use those abilities in the community interest, could make it a good place to live. The general community organization should aim to encourage, support, and unify such efforts.

Best results for the community often may be secured if the organization as a whole gives its major attention for a time to a single subject. For instance, the chief interest for a season might be the removal of community health hazards. Yet even then the several committees should continue. A community is very fortunate when it has several persons willing to prepare themselves in their several fields and to do the persistent and painstaking work on which the results of community efforts finally depend. One person may make it his or her life contribution to the community to develop community music, taking the trouble to become familiar with the best methods and most successful undertakings in that field. Another may study thoroughly the local government expenditures and help the community to understand them and to plan them.

The needs of the community have to do with such matters as local government, public safety, relations with county, state, and national governments, economics, co-operation of town and country, co-operation with other communities, town planning and housing, health, provisions for handicapped persons, education, delinquency, the welfare of young people, recreation, cultural activities, community ethical standards, and religion; and often with special problems, such as migrants. Any one of these subjects covers so large a field that no more than a few suggestions can be given concerning it, with a few references for study, and perhaps a few examples. Part Three of this book deals with these special fields.

CHAPTER XIV

COMMUNITY LEADERSHIP

MOST writings on community organization assume that funds and professional workers are available to supply paid health officers, paid recreation managers, paid music program directors, etc. In small communities this very often is not the case. Sometimes county, state, or national funds may be provided for specific purposes, and this supply of assistance has steadily increased during recent years. However, it still remains true to a large degree that the well-proportioned development of the small community must come about by the voluntary, unpaid work of members of the community.

Especially for the leaders, such voluntary work must be more than occasional short undertakings. Some community members must become at least amateur experts and specialists in their fields. One may become expert in leading meetings and guiding discussions. Such a person will not depend on common sense alone. He will find out what the ablest men and women have thought and written about the subject of leadership. He will read such books as *The Art of Leadership*, by Ordway Tead, Sanderson's *Leadership for Rural Life*, Follett's *The New State* or her *Creative Experience*, and Walser's *The Art of Conference*. Also, such a person will take occasion to attend meetings directed by skilled leaders, and will carefully observe their methods.

Competent, prepared leadership is necessary for good community development. Slavson, in the book *Creative Group Education*, remarked, "Common observation indicates that a group of average type, without any leadership or with inadequate leadership, degenerates into a destructive or petty-tyrannical group, with the stronger members as the tyrants." In many communities long experience of living together, and the carry-over of wise leadership from the past, have resulted in mutual respect and good manners which prevent this petty tyranny, or conflicts between would-be petty tyrants. In some communities good leadership in the family and good community leadership have made such an impression that the work of the community gets done with very little evidence of personal dominance.

If a few people in a community will qualify themselves to be chairmen of meetings and leaders in community affairs they can raise leadership and habits of co-operation in their community to new levels. A vast amount of time can be saved at meetings; there can be greater order, promptness, efficiency, and good will in getting things done. As young people learn the methods of such leaders, the community in the course of years may come to have a reputation for producing business leaders and executives. In a relatively small business in a certain American city the founder and owner of the business trained his assistants so thoroughly in the art of administration and management that as the years passed his company supplied more chief executives to large American corporations than did probably any great American corporation during the same period. Any small community in which a few persons will thoroughly master the art of democratic leadership may be making a very great contribution to that community and to the country.

Leadership in a community does not require striking personality or prominent position. In the labor union movement some of the most effective leaders are mechanics or office clerks or other people in everyday positions. Any reasonably intelligent person can take any little committee chairmanship as his experimental laboratory. He can read up on methods of leadership, correcting his own faults, observing good leaders when he has opportunity. By keeping at his little committee job until he has done it thoroughly and well he can make himself into a more efficient leader than most people who now handle small community affairs.

In various special fields individuals may become specialists, experts, and qualified leaders. Joseph K. Hart, in his *Community Organization*, wrote, ". . . every human being needs some real experience of leadership. This is not only necessary; it is becoming definitely possible."[25]

Sanderson comments as follows in his *Leadership for Rural Life*:

> Not infrequently persons of ordinary ability, who lack self-confidence, and who have no experience as leaders, when they are encouraged to assume positions of leadership and are given some concrete help or training for it, develop into excellent leaders for specific groups . . . they become excellent leaders because of their devotion to a cause in which they were sufficiently interested to try to learn how they might help in its advancement.
>
> On the other hand, there are many persons of undoubted ability who seem to have all the qualifications for leadership, but who are unwilling to assume its responsibilities, or who are so self-centered that groups will not trust them as leaders.[26]

Very often a community is greatly harmed by an itch for leadership which results in competition and hard feeling, and which may undermine the effectiveness of community action. It is not a craving for recognition, position, authority or dominance that is helpful, but a live interest in some work which needs to be done, a willingness to take the trouble to understand the problem, and willingness to assume the responsibility and the hard work of getting it done.

By the time one has thoroughly qualified himself to get a small piece of work done well, the way generally will open for more important work. In a small community a young woman who had prepared herself to lead a community music program found the local program firmly in the hands of an older person with less useful qualifications. She gathered some young people of high school age who were receiving little attention in the community, and within a year or two had made them the center of young people's activity, in addition to creating a well-trained musical group. When opportunity finally came for her to take over the community music program she hesitated to assume a responsibility which would interfere with work that had come to be both useful and pleasant.

Ordway Tead in *The Art of Leadership* remarked very truly:

The opportunity to lead fairly shouts aloud for its chance in *every* organization and institution which brings the citizens of a democratic community together. For in every area of action people are seeking to fulfill themselves. They want deeply to rise above a nominal or legal equality to an assertion of their own intrinsic superiorities of capacity and achievement. But to do this they have to be led. They have to be brought into effective group relationships which are certainly not spontaneous, but the creation of those in the vanguard.[27]

Democracy is one of the hardest lessons humanity has to learn. It must begin in the home. Husband and wife must be partners, each one the leader in some matters and the follower in others. Children should share in responsibilities to the full extent that they are able; otherwise they will never be truly democratic, but will be either dictators or people seeking someone to manage them. In the same way, community responsibility must be widely distributed and widely shared if community democracy is to be a reality. Unless there is democracy in the community there will be little in the nation.

The habits of feudalism and autocracy, which were so deeply imbedded in the old world, were not escaped in the settlement of America. The new world could not have lived comfortably without those old habits, because the new habits of democracy had not yet fully developed. The transition to democracy, which is a very difficult process, can best take place in the small community where it already has roots from the distant, prefeudal past. Hart pictures the difficulty of this transition:

Democracy needs a completely new organization of the technique of administration, which will be consistent with the factors and the aims which a democratic community seeks to achieve. Democracy requires leadership. Autocratic bossing of the job is not real leadership. It may be "executive ability" but if so it is an ability to "execute" the aspirations of democracy, to suppress them, and discourage and destroy them, rather than to lead them. All too long democracy has had to fight against these unsympathetic attitudes of the typical administrator. One phase of the work of the deliberate community council should be the more complete analysis of the kind of leadership and administration which the democratic community must have.[28]

The democratically-minded leader in the community will find that he cannot always wait for results until he has educated his people in the spirit of democratic responsibility. He will find many of them inert, uninterested, concerned with their own affairs. Men who are competent in their own fields see the fundamental social economy of giving a leader full authority in a field where he is competent. Too much deliberation and participation may wreck a program as surely as too little.

No universal rules can be made for the democratic management of community affairs. Sometimes a program of necessary work may be delayed or killed by waiting too long on democratic participation. Sometimes it is necessary for the community leader to "take the bit in his teeth," and get the job done in a somewhat autocratic manner. Sometimes the seemingly quick results of such methods do not last or are ineffective, because the people have not had enough part in the undertaking to become interested, because they have not been educated to carry it on, because they resent the autocratic methods used, or because the leader in his haste to get results has failed to understand the problem as some of the people did who seemed to be obstructing his program. In choosing his methods the leader must be guided by his common sense, by the best counsel available, by a willingness to learn and to change his opinion, and by persistence and firmness against discouragement or blind opposition. He should be on his guard constantly against a desire to be conspicuous, to dominate, to gain recognition and power. His aim should be to learn what his community needs and how he can be most helpful in meeting those needs. He will go as far as possible toward making himself unnecessary or unimportant by helping his associates to develop the capacity to carry on without him. This will free his time and attention for pioneering, if he has it in him.

CHAPTER XV

COMMUNITY FOLLOWERSHIP

THERE can be no leaders unless there are followers. Good followership requires intelligence and preparation as surely as does good leadership. Many a time a good leader finds his careful efforts of no avail because no one has taken the trouble to prepare to be an intelligent follower. In a well-balanced community at least as much thought and effort and interest will be spent in being good followers as in being good leaders.

An efficient and well-selected board of directors of a large corporation commonly is made up of men who are good followers as well as good leaders. Each member of such a board is a successful man of affairs who does not feel a suppressed urge to gain a place for himself. He already has that place, and feels secure in it. His aim is not to create an impression of his own importance, but to help get the business done in the best possible manner and with the least possible waste of time.

Very often at a board meeting some member of the board is much better qualified than others on the subject under discussion. The other members turn to this man, and he becomes the natural and informal leader for the time being. It is the business of the others to follow him, to understand what he says, to approve his position except where they see some apparent weakness or possibility of improvement. In such cases they make suggestions or ask questions, not for the purpose of seizing leadership, but to help clarify the issue and to help get it wisely disposed of under the leadership of the man best qualified.

A large corporation often employs a general manager, who presides at most board meetings. The manager may have a smaller income than any member of the board. On the whole he may be a less able and experienced person than the members of his board. Yet for the purpose at hand they have chosen him to be a leader. He not only acts as manager, but often defines general policies. The directors pay him to free them from the necessity for leadership in the affairs of that organization. They want him to succeed as leader, and they endeavor to make themselves his efficient followers. In such a situation, if some member of the board tries to impress the other members with his importance, and undertakes to act as leader for that purpose, he becomes a conspicuous nuisance and tends to get left off such boards.

On the other hand, the board members are not "yes men." They are ultimately responsible for the success of the undertaking, and are keenly on the watch for any weakness in the program, or for any opportunity to improve it. They do not hesitate to criticize when criticism is necessary, but in order to criticize effectively they must first understand. That is, they must first be good followers—they must have followed the leader until they know what he plans to do. Sometimes a single board member who thinks he sees a serious fault in the program will stubbornly present his position almost alone. If he is a man known for good judgment the other members will hesitate to decide until his doubts are removed. In many good boards of directors a formal vote seldom is taken. Definite action of such boards nearly always follows general unanimity of opinion, quite generally acceptance of the opinion of the man or men best qualified to judge the question.

The good leader in such a situation fully discloses his plans and purposes. His aim is not to be sustained, but to find the right course; and any disclosure of error or weakness in his plans, or of any possibility of improvement, is welcomed by him. The aim of the entire board and of the manager is not to have a program emerge with the honor of its origin attached to some person, but rather to get the best possible results.

A long experience with a great variety of public and private boards and organizations leads to the conviction that the most able, experienced, and successful men make the best followers. A man who must be responsible for large undertakings has a great sense of relief when he finds that those he must lead are men of intelligence, responsibility, and judgment—men who know how to be good followers.

Every community needs people who are not concerned with leadership, who perhaps have no large plans of their own to promote, but who can tell the difference between a good and a bad plan, and who have trained themselves to be good followers in case they thoroughly believe in the project to which they give their help.

In many communities there are such persons. Mr. A. knows the status of every building and meeting place in town. He has no ax to grind, and can be depended on to find a meeting place or a location for an undertaking. Mrs. B. knows who would be interested in any worthwhile project, and will be responsible for sending notices and making announcements in the newspapers. Miss C. is a good secretary, and will keep clear and adequate records. Mrs. D. or Mr. E. will

be responsible for telephoning or writing or visiting everyone who should take part in an undertaking, and will see
that no necessary person is overlooked. Mr. F. can be counted
on to look after the janitor work, to see that meeting places
are clean, the furniture in place, and the heating satisfactory; he is a good mechanic, and will take care of any mechanical needs or arrangements. Young Mr. G. is ready to be
general flunky and assistant to the leader, running errands,
doing chores, picking up loose ends—doing anything that
will make the leader's efforts more effective. All these special
services are in addition to participation in making plans and
programs.

For persons who are free from an itch for conspicuous-
ness, or who can overcome that weakness, there often is as
much pleasure and usefulness in being a good follower as in
being a good leader. One need not be a blind follower. He
can limit his work to undertakings which he sincerely ap-
proves. A community which has competent, intelligent, dependable and experienced followers is very fortunate.

When a leader plans for a talk and a discussion it is of
enormous help to him to have followers who are interested
and prepared. The ideal attitude for a follower is to try to
understand the leader and the subject he is discussing, to
secure information on it in advance, to see the difficulties
and weaknesses in the leader's position as well as its strong
points, to ask intelligent questions, to throw light on the
subject from the follower's experience and observation.
Unless at the end of a discussion the leader has found it
necessary to correct or enlarge or better define his views,
the discussion has not been greatly successful. Great followership requires interest and preparation as much as does
great leadership.

Many a potential leader with a clear and sound purpose, especially if somewhat in advance of his time, has failed because no one took the trouble and interest to understand his purpose and to work for it. Good followers in a community will not let the finest community. projects die because the leader does not quickly have popular support. By being discriminating, receptive, imaginative, and efficient, followership can be as helpful and as influential as leadership in community affairs.

At their best, democratic leadership and democratic followership become indistinguishable as they blend together in the endlessly varied interplay of co-operation. In many of his relationships every person is a follower of someone else. In some respects every normal person can be a leader, if he will pay the price of preparation. In all cases the best relationship is one of interdependence, fully recognized and accepted.

Today the lives of most persons seem to be crowded. How then can time be found for community participation? The problem is that of appraisal of relative values and the budgeting of time. The old-time farmer or merchant, even when very busy, budgeted his time so as to have his Sundays free from business. The hen with one chicken is as busy as the manager of a great industry. Much personal and social activity is essentially trivial. To eliminate less important activities and to make way for the more important is of the essence of management. A realization of the importance of the community, and capacity for the management of one's time, will result in finding places in one's budget for community interests.

Part Three

SPECIFIC COMMUNITY INTERESTS

CHAPTER XVI

GOVERNMENT AND PUBLIC RELATIONS

THERE are extreme variations in the quality of small-community government in the United States. Some are examples of all that community government ought to be, while others would qualify as examples of all that it should not be. What is the cause of such differences?

The writer recently visited two communities in the same state, each settled at the same time by "common" people who came largely without means. In one of these communities the government was so excellently administered as to be a suitable example for the country. In the other case the community and the government were politically-minded and boss-ridden, and the people expected to get most local benefits through political influence.

In each case the present residents are descendants of the original settlers. For the greater part the difference seemed to be due to different personal and social traditions. In one case the town was settled largely by people who came by two stages from rural New England. The first move, which was to Kansas, was made as part of the free-soil movement by men of courage and moral conviction, who had the tradition of the New England town meeting and were used to handling their affairs with thrift and social responsibility. The other town was settled by men and women of English descent who came from another direction, who as a matter of habit looked to the political boss, to favoritism and to political influence.

One of the chief problems of any community is the creation of a wholesome political tradition. Young people look about them, half-consciously wondering what kind of world it is into which they are born. If they see favoritism and political manipulation, with the best people of the community timidly unwilling to expose themselves by vigorous political activity, the young people of the community will have learned their lesson. Their school textbooks may discuss civic righteousness, but they will know that is only make-believe. The realities are before their eyes. They will be convinced that they live in a world of arbitrariness, favoritism, and special interests, and that they must be like the world they are in. On the other hand, whenever young people see integrity and a businesslike attitude in business management, they are likely to decide that the world they live in is like that, and they will act accordingly.

Thus the local management of community affairs is the greatest of all schools of government and of life. The university may teach how to do it more skillfully, but what is to be done will have been learned long before university years.

Selfishness nearly always is organized in the community. Unless unselfishness and public interest also can be organized they can have little chance. The community council, representing all the civic organizations of the community, and cutting across all partisan lines, can provide such organization. Very generally it will find public officials ready to act in accord with the public interest if they can but be assured of dependable backing. Even where they are reluctant to act for the general good, the influence of a well-organized community may turn the balance.

Several committees of the community council can advise

the council on various phases of public government. There may well be a committee on public finance, on community recreation, on public health, on education, and on general community administration, with special committees as the need may occur.

Public Finance in Small Communities. The public economics of the small community has been studied to a considerable degree, and yet we know all too little about public expenditures for small towns and villages. The problem is more difficult because much of the control of public expenditures lies with the county, the state, and the national government. Yet, the difference between good and bad public finances for small communities is so great as sometimes to make the difference as to whether or not they are favorable places to live and to do business. A great service can be rendered to any community by a qualified citizen or by a group of citizens who will make it their business to understand public expenditures in the community, who will help to the adoption of well-planned community budgets, and who will help to bring order and simplicity into community public expenditures. There are public service organizations which can supply counsel in this process.

Where the question arises of choice of suitable public officials, another method may be necessary. An Illinois town of four thousand has very greatly improved the quality of its public officials by means of a "community caucus." Each civic organization in the community appoints a representative, and the "caucus" meets as soon as the candidates for town offices are known, carefully appraises these candidates, and reports to the community. Where there are marked

differences of quality the caucus makes definite recommendations. Since the "community caucus" is recognized as non-
political and interested only in the welfare of the community,
its recommendations are nearly always followed by a majority of the voters. As a result this town has exceptionally
good government.

It can be taken almost as an axiom that without the education in democracy which good local government provides,
good regional, state, and national government is impossible;
whereas, if good local government becomes general, that
quality soon will project itself into national affairs.

Rural Municipalities. Rural and small-community government has made relatively little headway in the United States.
Most small communities are made up of residents of a central
village or town, and also of a surrounding tributary area,
generally extending beyond the town limits for from two to
five miles. This surrounding area often is very important to
the town because of its trade.

The people of this surrounding area not only trade in the
town and do their banking there, but they go to church and
send their children to school there, they get much of their
recreation in the town, and use it for a shipping point. They
have no fire protection or police protection except that furnished by the town. They need the town, and the town needs
them. Yet generally there are political boundaries between
the village and this area. Often there are conflicts and feuds
between the two. The surrounding region is commonly
denied a voice in determining the conditions under which it
must do business and under which its young people must
grow up.

This division between the town and its environs is an unfortunate accident in American life and should be done away with. There are various methods of accomplishing this. Quite commonly the village limits can be legally extended to include these areas, if the people are agreed. Laws should be passed providing for the creation of rural municipalities. If communities become aware of that need, occasions may arise when their wishes can be translated into law. A committee on legislation may be useful in bringing about such changes.

Community-Manager Government. One of the most important developments of American democracy has been the city-manager or town-manager government. A community which is endeavoring to put its house in order may well study the possibilities of this form of public administration.

CHAPTER XVII

COMMUNITY ECONOMICS

E VERY person and every community has an economic basis. We must have air to breathe, water to drink, food to eat, clothes to wear, housing to protect us from the weather, roads and vehicles for travel and for transporting necessities. Since these are what economics deals with, an economic basis for living is absolutely essential, and to talk of being superior to economic considerations is nonsense.

Yet, every person desires to be free from economic stress and compulsion, to be in a position to act as he wishes and according to his convictions, without being limited or driven by economic need. There are two ways by which this freedom can be achieved: first, by supplying economic needs so that a full, normal, and wholesome economic life is possible; and second, by self-restraint, by limiting wants, by simplicity of living, so that the filling of economic needs will not be an undue burden and distraction. In many communities every increase of income is followed by increased elaboration and ostentation of expenditures, with the result that increase of income does not bring increase of freedom, but makes life more hectic and wearing. When misfortune or a period of depression comes, such a community and its members find themselves in great distress.

Both ways for achieving freedom from extreme economic stress are necessary. Neither can bring good results without the other. A good community will strive to secure a fair economic income and wholesome economic conditions, while at the same time it will strive to maintain simple and unpretentious standards of living, and will undertake to accumulate reserves for times of stress. It will be considered bad taste for its members to try to show superiority to neighbors by spending more money. A community of good breeding and of a variety of interests will find the spending of money to take a relatively smaller part in its satisfactions. In a community of good breeding people will not be ashamed to do any work which adds to the quality and convenience of living. A well-bred man will not ask his neighbor to do for him what he would consider to be beneath himself to do for his neighbor. A good community is made up of neighbors in that sense.

Community Self-Support. Many communities could profit greatly by an increased degree of self-support. It may be feasible for a community to raise and to preserve more of its own food. It may be getting its craft services—plumbing, electrical work, carpentry, etc.—from nearby larger towns, while young men of the community who would make good plumbers, electricians, and carpenters, and young women who could be skillful at feeding people, or who would be good dress designers, milliners, etc., are compelled to go to the city because there is no work for them in the home community. In the fairly well-balanced community of Yellow Springs, Ohio, with a population of 1600 or 1800, it was found that about 60 men and women were making a living by serving the community in these various crafts, each directing his own work instead of working for a "boss"; and that if well-trained men and women should be available, there would be room for several more.

A productive undertaking for many a small community would be to discover what kind of craft services could be used in the community, and what young men and women are competent to learn those crafts; and then to help them to thorough training. If there is room for a carpenter, and if there is a young man who has capacity and interest to become a good carpenter, then it may be possible to find some exceptionally good carpenter in the region who would let the young man work as his assistant while learning the craft. The young man could find a calling in his home community, and the community would have the satisfaction through the years of having its carpentry work well done.

It is by such practical steps as this, taken one at a time, rather than in great dramatic action, that excellent quality in a community can develop. With suitable inquiry and advice most communities can find unfilled needs for which their own young people can be trained, thus making a career at home while making a better community. By an occasional community economic survey the feasibility of a larger degree of economic self-support can be discovered, while it is possible for one or a few persons in the community to make it a habit of knowing young people who could be helped by friendly counsel, and to find ways for them to prepare to fill such openings.

One of the limitations of the American small community is its economic monotony. A mining town generally is only a mining town. In a farm village there usually is no way to make a living except by farming or by serving the needs of farmers. Somewhat the same tends to be true of small factory towns, college towns, lumbering towns, and fishing towns.

Young people growing up in such communities have little chance at life in their home communities except along the line of the town's dominant interest.

A good community will develop a variety of economic interests, so that people of varying interests and capacities can find livelihoods there. As an example, the village of Yellow Springs, Ohio, had almost no sources of income twenty years ago except farming and a small college. Through the years an effort was made to develop a greater variety of economic undertakings. Today, in addition to the farming community and the college, a number of small industries are well established. Among these are printing and publishing, an aluminum foundry for making difficult castings, an art bronze foundry, a large hybrid seed corn industry, a chicken hatchery, a chemical industry, a local power plant, a genetics research institute, and a farm seed business. None of these, except the college, employs a hundred and fifty persons, yet nearly every person in the community, and many from the surrounding farms, have found employment, and there is considerable range of choice in fields of work. Some of these industries serve the surrounding country. Others are such as might have been undertaken almost anywhere in the United States. In this development the permanent population has been only slightly increased. The hope has been, not to have a bigger community, but economically a better community. Not every small community can arrive at such a diversified economic life, but with careful planning it frequently is possible to secure considerable variety.

In many communities there are too many competing stores, filling-stations, and poor eating places, while there may be a lack of other undertakings which would make for better living. There may be no suitable provisions for caring for mechanical equipment such as furnaces, refrigerators, radios, lawn mowers, and the many mechanical conveniences used in the home. There may be no organized recreational opportunities of good quality. There may be no local sanitarium or hospital.

One of the first principles of community economic design is good proportion—not too much of anything, and no lack of what is essential. This good proportion will not be achieved by drifting. It requires very little imagination to start another filling-station or food store or pool hall. To bring a community into good economic balance requires planning, search for persons who are competent to undertake the necessary enterprises, thorough training of such persons, and intelligent community support for them and for their undertakings.

Pioneers in developing well-proportioned communities will not have an easy task, for the small community has been neglected and exploited. Many make-believe industrial promoters have robbed small communities by selling stock and by starting unsound industries. Few if any educational institutions are prepared to train young people for competent direction of community undertakings. If some educational institution should qualify itself, with competent leadership, to train young people to administer small community economic enterprises, it might do a very useful work.

The following are some kinds of economic services which commonly are lacking in small communities:

An accounting and bookkeeping service, to help individuals and firms with income tax, social security reports, and the many other taxes and reports required by government. Charges for such services should be on the community level, and not on the level of a public accountant dealing with large affairs.

A service for maintaining all kinds of mechanical equipment.

A recreation place where, at moderate expense to their families, boys and girls can find varied recreation, intelligently guided and administered by persons who are trained for their work, and who have an interest in young people beyond getting their money.

A small establishment for collecting and processing surplus food products such as vegetables, fruit, and meat, primarily for later use in the community, but sometimes for sale outside.

A small community clinic and hospital.

A community nursery school, perhaps in a private home.

A community clearinghouse, for the exchange of services and produce. A word about this possibility may be interesting:

A Community Clearinghouse. In many rural communities there are competent persons who have not found effective use for their time and energy. An interesting career for such a person would be the development of a community clearinghouse. In most small American communities one of the principal shortcomings is the lack of money as a medium of exchange. Even within the community there are many services which the members could render one another which are not rendered because of lack of money to pay for them.

A well-managed community clearinghouse may overcome much of this handicap, and enable the community to serve itself much better. Under such a clearinghouse system, members of the community can secure goods or services from each other without money. The person supplying the goods or services can be credited on the clearinghouse books with their agreed value, while the person receiving the services or goods can be debited on the clearinghouse books. The management would deduct a percentage of credit from each transaction to pay for administration. Such a project can be started on a small scale with very little expense.

With this system in operation the community members

can serve each other to the limit of their time and resources, largely unhampered by lack of money. Good management is necessary, and a considerable period of time and experience may be required before confidence and habits develop which will make such a clearinghouse generally effective. Detailed methods for such a system have been worked out.

As a phase of a community clearinghouse, a service might be developed for renting or lending equipment which is used only occasionally. In one town a man made it his business to gather up much of such equipment, baby carriages, wheeled chairs, crutches, sick-room appliances, etc., which were made available to any person who wanted them. He found that many people were glad to empty their attics of such equipment and to give it more frequent use.

Buy at Home. In a good community the "buy at home" policy will not be carried to excess. The aim will be not to buy at home as much as *possible,* but to be self-supporting to the greatest degree that is *beneficial.* For instance, it may be unnecessarily expensive and wasteful in a region which raises livestock, to ship livestock to a distant market, and then to ship meat products back again. A local packing and freezing plant may add a new industry to the community and save much of the cost of shipping and of commercial overhead. Such a local packing house can succeed only if reasonably well equipped and well managed. Otherwise the waste incurred may be greater than the profits of large-scale packing plus transportation. A larger degree of buying at home may be desirable with canned goods and other food products, or with recreation facilities. The economic monotony of most American small communities is due only

partly to economy of large-scale operation. Partly it is due
to bad economic habits or to lack of economic education.

An Economic Survey. As a basis for understanding the
economic possibilities and needs of the community an economic survey is desirable. The following account of such a
survey of a village of about 2000 people, made in the course
of a few weeks with almost no cash outlay, indicates how
such an undertaking may be begun. This particular survey,
made under prewar conditions, had a special and limited
purpose, that of finding out how the people of a village
actually made their living, but it illustrates a method.

A list was built up of the names and addresses of all
persons in the village of income-earning age and condition,
or whose support was not provided for. The local telephone
book was used to begin the list. Then the lists of persons who
paid for water, electricity, or gas were examined, and other
names added. Then the voters' lists were similarly examined.
Most employers supplied lists of their employees. Then several persons who were acquainted with various elements of
the community looked over the resulting list, and added a
few names that had been missed.

An effort was made to learn how each one of these persons
earned a living. The lists of employees were self-explanatory.
The local banker gave information concerning several, as
did the grocer, the man who reads water and light meters,
the ministers, and others. The few remaining names required
special inquiry. All these names were then classified according to classes of occupation, and according to whether the
occupation was continuous or intermittent.

While this list was being prepared a visit was made to
every business and professional establishment in the village.

The information gathered included the nature of the business, the date established, the number of full-time and part-time employees with their names and whether they were white or colored; the number who lived in the village and the number who came into the village from outside; the area served by the business, the source of its materials, what competition it had from inside and outside the village, and what the prospects were for the business. During these visits each proprietor was asked what opportunities and needs, in his opinion, existed in the village for new businesses or new services. Various other individuals were asked what they considered to be the chief economic needs and opportunities of the village.

When this information was classified it threw considerable light on economic conditions in the community. The survey showed the need of a small industry which would employ young colored people. Otherwise it appeared that nearly all labor was employed, and that if another industry of any size should be added to the community it would have to bring its labor from outside. There was room for a number of additional carpenters and other craftsmen.

Various additional undertakings seemed possible if they should be thoroughly well managed, including a small bakery, a small laundry, and a local dairy. It was observed that relatively few businessmen had suggestions as to new enterprises. The survey would have been more valuable if it had disclosed what additional or different services could be supplied by residents of the village. Also, for a true community survey, the surrounding farm district which deals with the village should have been included.

Another type of economic survey would be to determine what foods and other goods are very generally sold in the community, and then to find out to what degree the community might profitably fill its own needs in this respect. Still another type of survey might be a study of local raw materials, with inquiry as to the possibility of processing them for local use or for general sale. No definite form can be prescribed for a community economic survey. The problem of finding the economic needs of the community and discovering or developing ways to meet them must be faced by each community in its own way.

CHAPTER XVIII

CO-OPERATIVES AS AN EXPRESSION OF COMMUNITY

THE finest relationships are those which arise spontaneously and informally out of the spirit of good will, mutual regard, and common interest and purpose which are the characteristics of a community. However, the very spirit of community leads men to want to extend their co-operation beyond the limits of spontaneous and informal action. Therefore they seek ways to co-operate on a larger scale and in more complex ways. Out of this desire to extend the range of community spirit and action has grown the co-operative movement.

In the first chapter reference is made to the distinction between the indigenous, spontaneous human relationships, which Sir Henry Maine calls *status* and which Ferdinand Tönnies calls *Gemeinschaft,* and on the other hand the more formal and deliberate organization of society which Maine calls *contract* and which Tönnies terms *Gesellschaft.* As Tönnies indicates, formal organization must grow out of and rest upon the informal and spontaneous impulse, or it will be sterile.

This distinction always should be kept in mind in considering the place of co-operatives in community life. The very nature of community is that of mutual interest, co-operation, and sharing. In every true community this tendency shows itself in many ways. A farmer going to town will take his neighbor's eggs to market, to save duplication of travel, and will purchase his neighbor's supplies along with his own. Neighbors get together in making purchases which one could not afford alone. In pioneer days log-rolling parties for clearing land gave a name to the politicians' habit of exchanging favors. Barn-raisings, husking-bees, neighborly exchange of help in threshing, and quilting parties, all were expressions of informal co-operation. They were expressions of community.

As life grew more complex it became necessary to use fore-thought and deliberate design and planning in order for the spirit of neighborly co-operativeness to be effective. Out of this need grew the co-operative movement. It was a change from *status* to *contract*, from *Gemeinschaft* to *Gesellschaft*, from spontaneous, informal co-operation to deliberate design and planning. A true co-operative movement, therefore, consists in doing in a formal, deliberate manner, with the help of organized business methods, those things which people desire to do together as friends and neighbors, but which are too large and complex to be done without formal organization. Yet it remains true that if the formal organization is to be sound and vital it must be the expression of an actual and vital community spirit. Otherwise the forms of co-operatives will simply contribute to the managerial revolution, in which those who actually and technically administer a business become its real owners and masters.

The English co-operative movement, through lack of adequate community spirit, has largely reached this condition. There is relatively little sense of solidarity and of community among its members. The average member owns a share but has little part in directing the destinies of the movement, except by deciding whether or not it is to his economic advantage to buy of the co-operative or from private merchants. The managerial revolution has captured the English co-operative movement much as it has the well-managed American Telegraph and Telephone Company, whose shareholders in theory own the company, though in fact the company is controlled by a very competent self-perpetuating management. In the Scandinavian states the element of community has been stronger, and has given greater vitality to the co-operative movement, especially in Denmark.

Co-operatives have been exceptionally effective in a small religious group, the Mennonites. Among them co-operatives have emerged by a natural, evolutionary process from the informal sharing and co-operation that is an expression of the strong sense of community and brotherhood which has characterized the Mennonite society for four centuries. With them, formal co-operatives spring almost spontaneously into being when the scale of action becomes too extensive for informal neighboring and mutual help. They are neighborliness and friendliness incorporated, as in case of Mennonite co-operatives organized to administer the estates of orphans and widows.

Recently a young friend of the writer came to tell him about the results of a year's work distributed among several consumer co-operatives. He had planned to spend his life in the co-operative movement, and began his co-operative experience with enthusiasm, feeling that he was learning the technique of a new social order. At the end of a year he was greatly disillusioned. He found people not co-operative in spirit; they joined co-operatives and retained their membership almost solely because they thought they might buy more cheaply that way. This man found little underlying loyalty to co-operatives among their members. He had been working in co-operatives whose organizers had looked upon them as of necessity leading to a co-operative society. Effort had been made to create the *form* of community where the *spirit* of community was very weak. Some of the larger co-operatives are beginning to find boss rule or demagoguery creeping in.

In contrast to the Mennonite type of co-operative are those organized by the Rural Electrification Administration of the national government. These "co-operatives" are required to conform to the original Rochdale pattern of "one man, one vote." Yet sometimes the process of organization is most impersonal and bureaucratic. On request from someone in the locality a strange organizer appears and arranges for a petition or application to be prepared, signed by persons wanting electric power, who pay a membership fee of five or ten dollars. Thereafter an impersonal government sends men who lay out and construct the system. In some cases, at least, no meetings are held, there is no consultation with the "members" as such concerning routes or standards of constructions, and no reports of progress are made to members. When work is interrupted for long periods due to defense requirements, the "members" learn of it only by hearsay, or by inquiring at the R.E.A. office. A privately owned railroad building a much desired line through a locality could be little more impersonal.

Electric power is so vital to modern life that there is a strong impulse to co-operate on the part of those to be supplied. Yet the same was true of railroad building. The expectation that on completion these systems can be turned over to a real co-operative in many cases is an optimistic dream. The prospect is that very many of them will be thrown into receiverships and operated by the government, or will become phases of political machine organization, or perhaps will be taken over and operated by private power companies, if the latter continue to exist as such. In the latter case they will have been captured by the managerial revolution. Doubtless in some cases there will be enough community spirit already in existence to bring about the development of real co-operatives, though in most cases the application of the term to this development is a fiction.

It is not inevitable that co-operatives which are "organized from the top" must fail. If the manager is a person of great and intelligent devotion to the co-operative movement, and if he carries through a well-planned educational program, such community spirit as already exists may be developed, informed, and organized until it becomes a living force. In the words of Emil Sekerak of the Ohio Farm Bureau:

> In the economic field there is a great deal of frustration among people who want to do something to make economic institutions responsive to community needs. They feel impotent to accomplish anything. However, if by dint of hard work on the part of a few good organizers, followed by good management and leadership, the co-operative demonstrates a mode for meeting economic needs of the community, while paying attention to social and moral values, the co-op then becomes a "creator" of community spirit—not merely an outgrowth of it. A co-op, with an educational and recreational program, can be a means for creating good will, mutual confidence and common interest. It may arise out of a minimum of spontaneous community spirit and go on to create a lot of it.*

The Ohio Farm Bureau, in the development of its co-operative program, seemed to be reaching a dead end. The old standbys among the organizers had become weary of campaigning for members. Then there emerged the policy of developing local "Advisory Councils." A dozen persons

* From a letter to the author.

in a locality unite to form such a council. Once each month these persons and their families spend an evening together, studying, playing, and visiting. They begin to have the characteristics of a little community. They come to like each other, are interested in each other, and begin to have common aims, common standards, mutual affection and regard, and a spirit of co-operation. Representatives of the individual councils meet in district conventions, and representatives of these, in turn, meet at the state headquarters. Thus the spirit of community extends to the larger organization and tends to pervade the whole. The thousand or more of these advisory councils have given new life to the Ohio Farm Bureau.

Real co-operatives must grow out of the spirit of community, though that spirit may be brought to life by good leadership. They generally will be soundest if they emerge gradually from informal co-operative neighboring in the community. Often they do well to begin, not in the setting up of a formal co-operative organization, but in this actual practice of informal co-operation. The *Gesellschaft* co-operative will not thrive until the co-operative *Gemeinschaft* is already strong and vigorous enough to infuse it with life. Otherwise its success will depend on the same conditions that determine the quality of the managerial control of any corporation. The co-operative movement rests on the spirit of community, and cannot thrive without it.

Given a spirit of community there are many forms of co-operatives which can add to the quality of the common life. The man who dreads to leave his estate, and the welfare of his family, in the hands of an impersonal trust company, may welcome the chance to place his affairs in a co-operative trust company made up of his neighbors. Burial co-operatives may take much of the pagan ostentation out of funerals, and reduce the cost by half. Co-operative fire, life, automobile, and accident insurance are making great headway. Co-operative food stores are the most familiar undertakings in the field. Co-operative medical service and hospitalization are becoming frequent. Other co-operative undertakings that thrive in America are bookstores, laundry and cleaning services, accounting services, woodlot management and logging, the purchasing of seed, fertilizers, farm equipment, gasoline and oil, and many other supplies. A vast amount of fruits, nuts, and vegetables are cared for, harvested, packed, and sold co-operatively, especially in California and Florida. In Minnesota, the processing and marketing of dairy products has had very extensive development. In some such cases, however, the managerial revolution is well advanced, and those who control some co-operatives are little more responsive to the members than is a modern corporation to its stockholders.

If a community desires to meet some of its wants through co-operatives it would do well to take note of needs that are least adequately met by private initiative, and begin where the need and the prospect for success are greatest. Co-operation is not the way of violence or coercion. If, for instance, a storekeeper in a small community has been doing an honest, competent job of serving his community, and has not exploited his customers, and if he has in this way built a degree of security for himself and his family, the spirit of community will not favor wrecking his business by starting a competing co-operative. There are various alternatives. The co-operative spirit can express itself by entering some field where service is poor ; or the local storekeeper may turn over his business to the community and continue to act as its manager; or some agreement may be reached whereby the co-operative and the storekeeper would carry different lines. A true community will so order its co-operative undertakings as not to cause unnecessary loss to competent, sincere members of the community.

Organizations like the Cooperative League of the U.S.A., 167 West Twelfth Street, New York City; the Group Health Cooperative, 1790 Broadway, New York City; or the Ohio Farm Bureau, Columbus, can supply information concerning the organization of co-operatives. The Rochdale Institute, 167 West Twelfth Street, New York City, founded by the Cooperative League, undertakes to train people for co-operative work.

CHAPTER XIX

COMMUNITY HEALTH

THE writer has had occasion to employ many men on work which required them to take their families to new locations, often to small communities. From this actual experience it has been found that when an intelligent family is considering such a move, the prospect for good health conditions is one of its most serious concerns. Is there a good water supply? Is there good drainage? Is the milk supply safe? Is good medical care available? Is there a good hospital? Is the schoolhouse well lighted, heated, and ventilated?

Such questions as these a well-managed community will ask about itself. By intelligent planning and consistent effort it often is possible within a few years to change a small community, as regards health conditions, from one which people are anxious to leave, into a community to which people desire to come. Because the matter is so important, a great many public agencies, organizations, and institutions have prepared to give help to communities which desire to improve health conditions.

In a study of community health it is necessary to limit attention to matters which are common to the general community, and which can be dealt with best by organized community effort, or by other public action. Individual problems, or technical medical problems, should not be included, or the issues will get entirely out of hand. Among community problems appropriate for united action would be protection of water supply, enforcement of quarantine, school lighting, and the question of whether children of low-income families should be provided with dental, oculist, and other health services at public expense. Among questions which would be outside the proper limits of a study of community health would be the best way for physicians to treat particular diseases, or the cause and cure of cancer. There are no clear boundaries between community health problems to be met by community action, and technical medical problems which are the business of the physician or other specialist, or matters of private judgment. For instance, the question of how best to provide well-balanced school lunches is partly a question for specialists and partly a matter of practical community thrift and planning. The solution of such mixed questions requires mutual respect, co-operation, and tolerance.

In so complex a field as public health, specialized counsel and help are needed, both in the development of a general program, and in particular issues under consideration. No adequate discussion of particular problems is possible within the limits of this outline.

Suppose a community council, perhaps working through a Parent-Teachers Association or a Rotary Club, should wish to undertake a year's program on the subject of community health—how could it proceed? It might plan its year's work, with the development of a continuing committee made up of persons most interested and effective to follow up unsettled issues through a period of years. As a guide the community organization might secure a number of copies of *Your Community*, by Colcord. Chapters 8, 9, and 10 of this book provide an excellent outline for the study of community health. Another excellent book, *Community Health Organization*, by Hiscock, is a well-thought-out program for a public health service for a city of 100,000. The methods it proposes are not in general applicable to small communities, yet an intelligent club or committee, with that book for suggestions, could become aware of needs in its own community and could devise ways to meet them.

Public Health Administration, by Smillie, has a chapter on rural health administration (Chapter XXX), which is an excellent brief treatment of the subject, especially in connection with the general treatment of health in the earlier chapters.

The first book mentioned, *Your Community*, could be taken as a textbook for a program of study and work in community health. The twelve subjects into which the discussion is divided would provide a twelve-months study and activity program, under such headings as "The Community as a Health Environment," "Indices of Community Health," "Health Services for Special Groups," "Aids in Planning the Community's Health Program," and "Informing the Public about Health."

In many states there are county health officers who will consult and co-operate with communities in removing the most serious health hazards. Each state has a Department of Public Health with a staff of experts. As a rule these persons can be called on for talks or advice on such problems as water supply, milk supply, quarantine of contagious diseases, or more complete sewage disposal. In most states the state university has a department, or at least individuals, who are specialists on public health problems. These are to be found in the Department of Rural Sociology, or in a Bureau of Community Planning, or in the Agricultural College, or in the Extension Service. A few letters usually will locate the help needed.

The United States government serves community health through many agencies. Chief of these is the United States Public Health Service, with its many activities and publications. Under the Social Security Law, the Children's Bureau of the Department of Labor makes studies and issues publications, and also makes grants for maternal and children's health services. The United States Office of Education also is concerned with children's health. The Department of Agriculture issues literature on public health, such as its bulletin on "Hospitals for Rural Communities." The Farm Security Administration, in association with state medical associations, has developed a far-flung program of rural medical care, especially for Farm Security Administration borrowers. This program of fixed-sum payments for medical care has been organized in more than five hundred counties, and on more than a hundred and fifty homestead projects.

Numerous nation-wide organizations are concerned with community health, among them the American Public Health Association, the American Red Cross, the American Social Hygiene Association, the American Automobile Association, the National Conference on Street and Highway Safety, the National Safety Council, and the Metropolitan and other life insurance companies.

Several large foundations have made studies of community health, or have helped to finance community health projects, and have published books and bulletins on the subject. Among these organizations are the Russell Sage Foundation, the Rockefeller Foundation, the Commonwealth Fund, the Rosenwald Fund, the Duke Endowment, and the Bureau of Co-operative Medicine.

A group working on community health generally can get needed information—or at least learn where to get it—from one of four sources: its own state department of health, the United States Public Health Service, the American Public Health Association, or one of the foundations.

Most discussions of community health have in mind a citified, commercialized America, from which old-fashioned neighborliness has for the most part disappeared. The advantages of modern medicine in the administration of public health are very great, and should never be lost. Yet in small communities there is opportunity for revival of the old-time neighborly qualities.

A mother, worn out almost to the breaking point with family illness or other trouble, might get a new lease on life by a week or two of visit and complete rest in a neighbor's home. One of the most socially useful persons we know is a woman who is observant of her neighbors and sometimes says to one of them, "Come home with me and spend a few days in bed." Or sometimes she takes a baby home for a few days, and gives the mother a rest. Such practices could be encouraged and made a community habit.

A community might well have a storage place for things used occasionally in sickness, such as a wheeled chair, bedpans, crutches, a sheepskin with the wool on it for bedridden persons, and a sick-bed table. The old-time custom of neighborly nursing back and forth should not disappear. Without questioning the superiority of trained nurses, it must be recognized that friendly neighborly help is better than the lack of any such help because the cost is prohibitive or the nurse not available. The modern community should take full advantage of modern science, technology, and organization for community health, but it will make its resources go much further and will add a priceless human quality, if it preserves and develops the friendly helpfulness of pioneer days.

CHAPTER XX

COMMUNITY SOCIAL SERVICES

THE social service agencies of the country constitute a vast and far-flung institution, with scores of thousands of workers, with millions of case records, and with a highly specialized technique and a voluminous literature—all supported by taxes and contributions. This vast outpouring of effort, together with that of crime prevention agencies, provide some indication of the extent to which things have gone wrong with human life and society.

To some degree this failure is due to shortcomings of biological inheritance, and can be overcome only by eugenic means. A combination of education, legislation, and a sense of social responsibility are needed to meet that issue.

To a very considerable degree those meeting with acute difficulty are suffering from cultural deficiency—from bad bringing-up. Such traits as slovenliness, laziness, wastefulness, intemperance, and instability very often are due, not to inbred shortcomings, but to living with families and associates who also have those shortcomings in their backgrounds. There are various approaches to this problem. The almost universal craving to be self-respecting and respected is a powerful help. Through school and recreation and through living in a helpful, friendly, self-respecting community, children are spurred to surmounting such shortcomings and to becoming normal citizens, especially if someone will believe in them.

Still another cause of social failure is economic exploitation and social exclusion. During the process of general correction of the shortcomings of the social order, victims of exploitation need to be given a lift by society to enable them to overcome such handicaps.

Lastly, there are victims of accidental circumstance, such as the death of the breadwinner, or extreme economic depression. The principle of "bear ye one another's burdens," of general social insurance, gives such persons a clear right to the assistance of society.

If these various causes of personal difficulties should be segregated, so that each person in difficulty would represent a single cause, then the handling of welfare, relief, and delinquency would be greatly simplified. However, the various causes of difficulty are inextricably mixed in innumerable combinations. A personal difficulty may result in large part from a single cause, but more often it is the result of a combination of several causes, each present to a limited degree.

In large cities there are specialized, experienced workers to deal with many phases of trouble. In a small community, unless it is a suburb, there is no such abundance of professional skill, though the occurrence of county-wide health service is increasing. Often all social services in small communities are administered by persons of no special training or qualifications, and sometimes by politicians or political appointees who have neither qualifications nor interest in their work. Even in some fine old self-respecting communities one will find these services crudely and wretchedly handled.

Little by little, national, state, and county organizations are supplying more adequate professional supervision for small community social services. Yet, these are sometimes perfunctory. A single intelligent, faithful person, or a small committee of a community council, may give intelligent direction and human quality to relief, delinquency, and other welfare problems. Such persons may become valuable leaders by working steadily through the years, keeping in touch with present-day literature and practice in the field, and co-operating with established agencies. In fact, in a community where that kind of intelligent interest is available, a common-sense human treatment can be given to individual difficulties with better results than in large cities where professional workers are compelled by circumstances to work partly by impersonal rule and routine. Such local individual direction may add greatly to the value of national, state, and county services.

This brief discussion of relief and delinquency is placed near the end of the book because, if major attention is given to creating opportunities and incentives for normal living, the residue of failures to be treated directly will be far less. A study of cases of personal trouble in a community of about two thousand disclosed a few families who seemed to be mentally deficient, and who were chronic troubles to the community. A larger number of families suffered from cultural deficiencies, that is, from bad bringing-up. The bulk of failure and delinquency seemed to be due to lack of training for vocations, to lack of economic opportunity, to lack of opportunity for social interests and outlets, and in some cases to sheer accident of circumstance. Lack of economic training and opportunity ranked as the chief cause of immediate difficulty. Back of that lies inadequate character-building, and a social order which tends often to the breakdown of character and of economic security. The kind of community development pictured in this book would relieve the larger part of these difficulties, and would ameliorate many of the others.

In a good family, if one of the children has a period of waywardness, recklessness, or rebellion, the family rallies to his support. At home there is both discipline and encouragement, sustained and directed by affection. In case of some breach of the peace, or of injury to neighbors' property, or of stealing, there is effort in the family to treat the matter as evidence of human frailty or of immaturity. The family seeks the aid of friendly associations, education, medical care, appeal to personal aspiration or to family pride. There is effort to avoid any arrest or legal action which would have a court record. Usually such effort is successful.

Modern treatment of delinquency is of that kind. Just as parents say to themselves, "What have we done to bring about this condition?," so those dealing with juvenile delinquency ask what conditions society has created or permitted that may have caused the delinquency. Effort is made to correct those conditions and to educate and encourage the delinquent in living a normal life. Studies of the results of this kind of treatment in specific cases show that it has a very considerable degree of effectiveness, which would be still greater if the environment of those in trouble could be more completely controlled.

A small community may present the best or the worst conditions for dealing with juvenile delinquency. Where there is no community organization and little community spirit, and where specialized welfare service is not available, the small town may be about the worst place for the development of juvenile delinquents and other social failures. On the other hand, if the spirit of a small community is that of a family, with an attitude of mutual responsibility and mutual help-fulness, and if even a very few friendly-spirited people qual-ify themselves in the best present methods for working with delinquency and removing its causes, the small community may be more successful than any other in helping those who have failed to maintain its standards.

In a certain small midwestern community a family with a poor background was "down and out." It had lost caste and lost its pride. The oldest boy, about seventeen, had become a clever thief, and was teaching his art to his younger brothers and sisters. Without creating a court record against him, this boy was sent to a "clinic" for six months. There he was re-educated in a friendly spirit. When he returned home he worked on his brothers and sisters, and undid the habits he had taught them. With the help of the community he got a steady job. He is now supporting himself and his mother and brothers and sisters. He knows he has at least one friend in the community to whom he can go in trouble. That situa-tion was worked out by members of the community, not by professionally trained social workers. But those few com-munity members had made themselves acquainted with mod-ern methods for dealing with juvenile delinquency, and made use of the specialized professional services of a public clinic.

Of the hundreds of community councils in America, most of them, especially those which are the outgrowth of the California movement, are concerned chiefly with delinquency and with efforts to correct the immediate conditions which lead to delinquency. A disreputable drugstore is eliminated. A newsdealer is persuaded to discontinue selling salacious literature. Wholesome recreation is provided to make road-houses less popular or "necessary." School lunches are provided, and pupils unable to pay for them are given tickets by the school principal, which are used as any other tickets without any evidence of charity. Decent clothing is assured, similarly without discrimination. Boys or girls in particular trouble may be put under the care of temporary guardians or "friends," who take personal interest in helping them to overcome their difficulties. The respectable citizen who calls this "pampering" does not hesitate to use such methods with his own children. Community co-ordinating councils may have overemphasized this part of community life, but they have helped to show the way in the treatment of delinquency.

The care of local relief and welfare problems today is partly national, partly state, partly county, and partly local. In a small community those dealing with welfare and relief can be in touch with the actual situations. It is their business to unify all the efforts being made, to prevent neglect and favoritism, to correct oversights, and in general to fill in any gaps and make up deficiencies in the treatment of individual cases.

Members of a community can turn welfare work into mutual helpfulness, and relief into neighborly, friendly sharing of burdens. That spirit very often pervaded the ancient community. Without it relief may be bitter, and welfare work may develop resentment, or a relaxation of personal responsibility, or even a scheming to get everything possible from society. The quality of nonprofessional, neighborly friendship, informed and guided by professional knowledge, will give good results in community relief and welfare work. The best results will come from a union of interested community members and skilled professional workers.

CHAPTER XXI

SMALL COMMUNITY RECREATION

MOST discussions of recreation are from the point of view of urbanized communities, in which many facilities, considerable equipment, and paid supervisors are available. Yet probably a third of the people of America are beyond the reach of such opportunities. What can they do about recreation in their small communities? Perhaps the best answer to that question is to indicate the natural place of recreation in society and the spirit and attitudes which will make recreation most fully realize its possibilities, and then to suggest numerous possibilities.

Some small communities have natural settings favorable to recreation, which others lack. Some have financial resources which others do not have. Good recreational leadership is fairly abundant in some communities, and almost wholly lacking in others. No one small community can develop more than a small part of the many possible ways of recreation, but nearly every small community can find some within its reach.

The Place of Recreation in Human Life and Society. After every heartbeat the heart has a short period of rest and relaxation before the next beat. By this rhythmical process of work and rest the normal heart is able to keep going for threescore years and ten. For a very short time under stress it can beat faster and omit the periods of rest, but if that speeding up lasts very long, death results.

That rhythm of alternating work and rest, of effort and relaxation, is characteristic of all normal life. To ignore it is perilous. A civilization which speeds up its living pace and omits relaxation may seem to make great headway, but it will quickly burn out. Even for the relatively short period during a war a speeding-up process which would omit provision for rest and relaxation may be poor economy.

Recreation is just as necessary as work. Provision for recreation is not a minor incident of good community life, but a vital element in social well-being. Human society as a whole the world over has recognized play as a primary need. Most accounts of primitive peoples deal at length with feasts, dances, and other social recreation, and indicate that such occasions are given as much dignity and importance as any part of the community life.

So important is recreation to normal living that as a rule if a people is required to choose between freedom and recreation, it will give up freedom and choose recreation. Worldly-wise tyrants are aware of this. They may rob the people of their rights, but only at their peril do they interfere with the people's play. During the period of the English Restoration, in the conflict between the autocratic Royalists and the democratic Puritans, one of the most effective means used by the royalty to undermine the influence of the Puritan regime and of democracy was a nation-wide program of sports, such as Cromwell's Puritan regime had ignored or frowned upon. Democracy should be no less wise than tyranny in recognizing the need for play.

Like the other arts of life which make up human culture, the art of play is not suddenly acquired. The folk games which provide a satisfactory outlet for primitive communities have been many centuries in development. Watching the folk dances of Pueblo Indians one may see a perfection of precision and skill far beyond anything ever seen in an American theater. That skill has been developed in each small village for probably eight hundred years. No one generation creates very much. It inherits from the past.

An interesting illustration of the slowness with which games originate came to the writer's attention. He observed many years ago that Negro children on cotton plantations did not seem to play at games in the way of some northern white children, and supposed that they were different by nature. Some time later he discussed the matter with the Director of Race Relations of South Africa and was told that in their native African villages Negro children play at their ancient folk games, as do children in their native communities the world over. The reason for the difference in America is evident. Each Negro slave brought to America was torn out of his or her native environment as an adult, and was put to work for long hours with no regard for old-time traditions. As children were born and grew up in America there was almost a complete break from the old folkways. Young children could not learn from older children, for the older children knew nothing of those old African games, and two centuries in the new world had not been time enough to create anew the folkways of play.

Another incident illustrates the fact that the play impulse was not lacking in these children. A good many years ago some colored teachers from Hampton Institute spent a year going to Negro schools through the back country, teaching English folk games to the children. Years later, when those children had grown up and left the school, the same schools were visited again. It was found that the same folk games were still being played. The entire school population had changed, but the tradition had been kept alive as the younger pupils learned by playing with the older ones. It was not the spirit of play, but the knowledge of how to play, that had been lacking.

Quality in Recreation. In every field of human activity there is a vast difference between clumsiness, vulgarity, and crudeness on the one hand, and skill, refinement, and beauty on the other. Genius, experience, skill, and leadership are necessary to turn the former into the latter. This is fully the case with recreation. What is more tragically pathetic than the effort of people to play when they do not know how?

> A holiday of miserable men
> Is sadder than the burial day of kings.

An old-time village Fourth of July celebration, or the annual county fair, were illustrations of people wanting to play and not knowing how.

As a boy the writer had seen folk dancing only as a clumsy, boisterous activity, in which there was no sense of beauty of motion and little refinement of skill, and in which the greatest fun was in jerking one's partner off her feet. From that experience he supposed that folk dancing was essentially clumsy and loutish. Then when he saw these same dances under the direction of a master, their skill, charm, and beauty were a revelation.

The transition from the one manner of action to the other, whether in recreation or in any other field, is the process of civilization. The field of recreation offers unlimited possibility for creative genius, knowledge, skill, and leadership in making play into a great art. A people is not civilized until it is creative, skillful, and versatile in its play. With the greater leisure of the machine age, recreation properly is taking an increasingly large place in community affairs, requires increasing intelligence and design, and provides increasing opportunity to add quality, variety, and interest to living.

A great people will be great in every phase of its life, and a trivial, inconsequential people will show its real character in whatever it does. Very often greatness or triviality of character is not inborn, but is the result of growing up in a great or in a trivial environment. What we are thoroughly used to becomes "second nature" to us. If young people have become used to cheap and tawdry interests, then any other kind may seem "highbrow" and uninteresting. If they have become used to fine quality, then cheapness and crudeness are distasteful and boring.

This principle holds in recreation as in any other field. The character of a people is formed in its play as surely as in its work. Leadership of skill and quality and imagination can gradually lead people to feel at home with quality, and to prefer it. Democracy in recreation should not mean holding recreation to the levels of the least developed persons, but rather the development of widespread interest in and love for excellence.

American democracy, as expressed in high school, luncheon club, and farmers' institute programs, has that lesson yet to learn. Much of the dramatics in small American high schools and rural groups is exceedingly inane and trivial. Much recreational reading is on the same level. There is a great difference between simplicity and triviality. Some great drama and some great literature is so simple that children can appreciate it. To a large degree the language of excellence must be learned, and the feeling for excellence must be acquired, through gradual acquaintance. Great leadership in recreation will first have appreciation of excellence, and then will steadily and persistently work to make people familiar with excellence, never going too far beyond their present interests and experience to keep contact.

In a certain community workshop, instruction in excellent, simple furniture design substantially affected the taste of the community, so that crude and ugly pieces tended to disappear from the shop. A good leader by skill and patience can change folk-dancing from crude loutishness to a thing of beauty and refinement. The leader of a drama group, instead of trying to find the latest popular hit, can search for the world's masterpieces which combine simplicity and greatness. In field sports, constant emphasis on fair play, sportsmanship, and considerateness can be a material influence in the development of good manners. Quality in recreation can go far toward making a great people.

Play in America. Americans have been so busy at pioneering that a large number of them have not learned how to play intelligently and effectively, as have people with deeper roots in the soil. Wherever a fundamental human need is denied or neglected, perversions, distortions, and abuses appear. The destructiveness of boys' gangs often is but an unconscious protest to society against being deprived of the arts and opportunities of normal play. Commercial interests seeking for some unfilled need to supply, may provide amusements, not with the aim of making the greatest social contribution but to make the greatest profit. The disintegration of many American communities is due in no small part to the lack of adequate provision for recreation, and of skill and refinement in play.

In pioneer American communities necessary work often was turned into play. The husking-bee, the barn-raising, the quilting party, the sewing society, were examples. With the fading of neighborly community life, with the coming of the factory, and with commercialized farming, these folkways disappeared, and the knowledge that working together could be interesting and recreational tended to fade from the public mind. One reason for the abandonment of these pioneer forms of recreation was that, lacking a tradition of excellence, they were crude and offensive to good taste and good morals.

In their place three general types of amusements have developed. There are school, community, small-group, and individual games and recreation which represent the best of the tradition of play, including tennis, basketball, hockey, golf, sand lot baseball, swimming, skating, skiing, hiking, hunting, fishing, handicrafts, community music, and many other activities. There are commercial amusements operated for profit, such as dance halls, commercial amusement parks, pool halls, and movies. And there are sports, commercial or otherwise, in which a few people participate and a large number are spectators, such as horse-racing, intercollegiate football, and professional baseball.

Under existing conditions the aim of a program of community recreation most frequently should be to increase the first type of recreation—that of noncommercial games, sports, amusements, and related occupations—which are directed chiefly by those who participate, and for their benefit, rather than for spectators. Such a program would not rule out either of the other classes of recreation, but would reduce their relative importance.

Too often the more prosperous members of the community, from which leaders are usually drawn, have the impression that because they and their associates have opportunities for games and sports, no community recreation problem exists. Yet even in a prosperous community where recreation seems to be over-organized and given too much attention, from a quarter to a half of the young people may be without any planned recreational opportunities, at least outside the regular school program. A community council or other community organization should not be satisfied with the presence of numerous recreational activities. It should endeavor to make sure that no part of the population is without reasonable opportunity for play and relaxation.

The field of recreation is so wide that a detailed discussion of recreation methods would be out of place here. Only a few major forms can be mentioned. Little or no mention will be made of forms of recreation which already are generally provided, such as bridge clubs, country clubs, baseball teams, competitive interschool athletics, and conventional school dances.

Recreation for the Community as a Whole. There should be definite efforts to have times and occasions when the community as a whole can get together for play and acquaintance. Music furnishes an excellent opportunity for such meetings. Outdoor community band concerts and community singing have been among the most successful community occasions. A union of the two—band concerts in which the people listen, and community singing in which they participate—makes an excellent combination.

Periodic community picnics and field days are desirable. Community pageants in which nearly every member of the community takes some part have had a large vogue in America. At their best, and if not overdone, they have much social value, especially as a unifying influence. As actually produced, sometimes with diluted and colorless symbolism originated by uninspired authors, the community pageant may represent prodigious effort with but relatively transient value.

Community dances and social evenings can make a great contribution to community recreation and community spirit. At Mesa, Arizona, a town of about four thousand people, is a large public recreation building, built by the Mormons, but open to the entire community. Here on one evening a week the community gathers, often to the number of a thousand or more. In an atmosphere of good order, consideration, and courtesy, young and old people dance or visit or enjoy light refreshments, or sit around the sides of the great room and watch the others. In a Maine village near the State University one finds the town hall used in a similar way, though largely by young people.

Among the most satisfactory provisions for community recreation are community parks, playgrounds, and camp grounds. Many communities have provided these, and they are in great variety. Sometimes there is simply a public park. Sometimes there is a community recreation building, as well as ball grounds, tennis courts, horseshoe courts, swimming pool, golf course, children's playgrounds, all available to the community members, perhaps on a small charge to cover maintenance.

In some communities the public school building is the social center for many purposes. However, where it is feasible a general community recreation building often is desirable. Seldom if ever should a community recreation center try to provide facilities for all kinds of recreation, but it can choose from many kinds, such as games, dancing, folk dancing, basketball, volley ball, boxing and wrestling, handicrafts, bands, glee clubs and choruses, theater clubs, and picnic meals.

Group Sports. The commonest way for people to play is in small groups, with or without audience. Most communities are so well aware of the desirability of providing tennis courts, ball fields, basketball courts, swimming pools, golf courses, horseshoe courts, etc., that little argument for them would seem to be needed. Sometimes opportunity to play can be provided without great expense. A survey by Cornell University of a rural New York area disclosed that the most popular forms of recreation for men were reading, baseball, swimming, and horseshoes—only one of which is very expensive to provide.

Educational Recreation. Recreation is more than amusement. There is a common misconception that play must be without practical value, or it is not play. That idea is in conflict with the whole of human history. In primitive life a very large part of children's play is imitation of the work of adult life. That is, it is a process of education. A girl in playing with her dolls is learning to be a skillful mother. A boy with tools is learning the skills of adult life. Scarcely any recreational device is so popular as a community workshop. Both children and adults take to it.

In a town of two thousand the community workshop proved to be about the most popular activity. Young people and their elders made boats, furniture, pewter dishes, woodenware dishes, and numerous other articles. As a rule the greatest difficulty in maintaining a community-workshop program is in finding men and women in the community who will supervise it. Activities which may be included are woodwork, metal work, weaving, printing, photography, electrical work, painting, and modeling. Since most children no longer see their parents at work, society needs to make definite provision whereby children can play at the work which adults do.

Many other forms of educational and cultural recreation are feasible. Study clubs, reading clubs, Shakespeare clubs, music clubs, poetry clubs, nature clubs, garden clubs, science clubs, and discussion clubs are among the most long-lived and most persistently attended of all recreational undertakings. Some of them have kept alive and active through generations.

Cultural Recreation. Many people enjoy recreation which has an intellectual or esthetic content. Either for the community as a whole or for smaller groups, lecture courses, music programs, drama clubs, panel discussions, art exhibits, museums of art, science, or industry, zoological and botanical collections, and other cultural undertakings, find popular approval. Even small communities may have some of these advantages if those who direct such undertakings have imagination and know their fields.

The community theater has grown to such dimensions that it is a national movement. Its prominence is due partly to its innate merit, and partly to the fact that a recreation-hungry people who have not achieved an art of play seize upon it as an outlet for their craving for activity. In some cases dramatics absorbs a disproportionate part of the leisure time and resources of school or community, and represents a psychology of escape from a real world that is not interesting.

Individual Recreation. Many public recreation programs deal with masses or groups of people, and thereby neglect an element of recreation that is of no less value. Most great men have found solitude to be a vital necessity, and the best that is in us often demands time to be alone or with one or two companions. A detailed study by Cornell University of a rural community in New York State indicated that more people chose reading than any other form of recreation. Another widespread study gave the same results. A wise program of community recreation will make provision for individual enjoyment. Today as never before this is feasible.

The community library is a primary necessity. Its shelves should not be wholly filled with the latest best sellers. There should be room for literature, science, poetry, biography, history, philosophy, and religion. It is not always the book most talked about and taken out most frequently which is most interesting. The great books of the ages often can be the most familiar friends. Many people would like great books if they were not afraid of them, and if they were willing to learn the special language which great thinkers frequently require for expressing their ideas.

A phonograph records circulating library can be a great resource to a community. It can be kept in the community library, and administered by the persons who handle books.

An art exchange also can be very interesting. Original paintings or copies, small pieces of statuary, and other beautiful things can be loaned for a few weeks at a time, as books are loaned. Often there are persons in a community who will lend some of their belongings for that purpose, while often artists will lend original paintings, with the expectation that occasionally one will be purchased by the borrower.

The toy loan library is becoming a widespread institution. In scores of communities toys outgrown by their owners are given to the library, and are loaned like library books.

The Little Wilderness. Millions of persons visit our national parks, but seldom do they do more than drive through, or perhaps stand beside a geyser or a big tree to have a photograph taken, or stop beside a waterfall for lunch. Not one in a thousand stops to relax and to make deliberate, intimate acquaintance with primeval nature.

The kind of intimate enjoyment of nature and of solitude which characterized Henry Thoreau does not come suddenly. It needs opportunity for growth. Most American small communities have been blindly insensitive to the natural beauties around them, and have tended to destroy whatever opportunities there were for saving them. A wooded river bank may have been used for a city dump. A beautiful native woodlot has been cut for the timber. In most parts of America hogs and cattle have overrun the beautiful wooded tracts and destroyed the wildflowers.

Yet in hundreds if not in thousands of cases there is opportunity for the community to get possession of wooded river banks, or rough pieces of woodland, or bits of open marshy meadows, or wooded swamps where native wildflowers are not yet destroyed or can be replaced. Few expressions of nature are more awe-inspiring than a tamarack swamp, with great trunks like gray cylindrical pillars reaching toward the sky, and the ground of the shady aisles underneath covered with tamarack needles, and here and there twinflower or golden-thread. Compared with its stately, silent beauty, a European cathedral seems artificial and commonplace. Most such places have been temporarily spoiled by cutting the timber, but time can heal such wounds, and the beauty can return.

A community does very well to acquire as it can its river banks, springy hollows, wooded hills, or marshy shorelines where the pink gerardia and the blue lobelia bloom. Even if there is no money at present to care for them, the years will be busy in restoring nature. Boys will explore these little wildernesses, and will become acquainted with squirrels and groundhogs and woodpeckers and thrushes; and some of them will develop a sensitiveness to nature which will add to the appreciation of our national parks and other great natural monuments. A few people have ability to see potential natural beauty "in the rough," through blackberry briars and tramped-over springs. On them we must largely depend for saving our resources of beauty.

Beauty Spots and Vista Points. About most villages in rolling country there are small spots of natural beauty which are of no particular economic value to their owners. Often they can be acquired and developed into nooks for picnic parties. Along the highway an acre or two may provide a picnic ground. Often there is a point from which an exceptional view may be had. A community in which there is imagination and sensitivity, and energy to acquire such bits of land and bring out and preserve their beauty for the public, may be more fortunate than a community endowed with an art gallery and a museum. A keen sense of beauty applied to the home environment may give a community quality and distinction beyond what money could buy.

A young Chicago lawyer had a keen sense of natural beauty and a craving for the out-of-doors he had left behind. On weekends he explored the environs of the city. Finding a tumbledown farm on rough land of woods and swamp he saw potential beauty in it. During weekends for a considerable time he studied its possibilities. With ax and grub-hoe he would open a vista, clear away underbrush, explore a marshy spot for an underground spring which could be made beautiful.

When the possibility of beauty in this rundown farm had been revealed he sold the farm to a golf club for a high price, and then searched out another waste place, where he repeated the process. Thus he maintained vigorous health (he is now past ninety), enjoyed the out-of-doors, gave play to his creative sense of beauty, and in the process made a fortune. Would that a thousand communities had each a nature lover who would explore his community setting to discover its natural beauty, and then, not for profit but as a community service, help his neighbors to possess the beauty he had discovered!

Hobbies. Other individual recreations are included under the general term of hobbies. Many a person finds relaxation and interest in some one of numberless special interests, among them handicrafts, printing, bee-keeping, carrier pigeons, collecting glass, corresponding with people of other nations, writing a column in the local newspaper, or raising tropical fish. The community need not conduct these, but it can make young people aware of interesting hobbies, and can encourage them. Since most of us do not have very original minds, suggestion and example are needed to help us to discover possibilities ánd to learn how to enjoy them.

A Directory of Interests. Even in a community of one or two thousand persons there may be several with the same keen personal interest, each of them unaware that anyone else has that interest. If some person, or some organization, will take the trouble year after year to develop a directory of personal interests, and make a few copies available to the public, as in the public library, persons of like interests may discover each other, and find companionship in common avocations. Such a directory can be compiled by sending a return post card to each member of the community, listing perhaps fifty subjects which can be marked 1, 2, or 3, according to their rank in the interest of the person replying. The subjects listed may range all the way from philosophy and poetry to boxing and hunting. A small space should be left on the card for a description of equipment or facilities available.

Camping, Hunting, and Fishing. Our spirits hark back to the ancient days when our ancestors lived close to the soil and depended directly on nature. Hunting and fishing and camping are in our blood. Often the camera can take the place of the gun with no loss of interest.

When well-to-do members of the community go off on their hunting and fishing and camping trips they may be unaware of any lack of such opportunities in the community, yet half or more of the population may never find it possible to satisfy these cravings. A community does well to have access to some wild country, and to make it possible for each family to have a modest share of camp life. Some-times, with the help of the State Fish and Game Commission, local streams, ponds, and lakes can be stocked, so that local boys and girls may have their opportunities without the burden of expensive fishing trips. There are thousands of spots in America where the building of a small dam would form a beautiful lake, often with wooded shores. To create such a recreation place may be the best way of providing a memorial.

Outdoor Clubs. Nature clubs, bird clubs, botany clubs, cross-country clubs, hiking clubs, bicycle clubs, science clubs, mountain-climbing clubs, geology clubs, Boy and Girl Scouts, Camp Fire Girls, Youth Hostels, outing clubs, and 4H clubs are among the possibilities for out-of-door recrea-tion, in addition to sports and games.

Work as Recreation. John Locke in *Some Thoughts Con-cerning Education* expressed an important truth:

The great men among the ancients understood very well how to reconcile manual labour with affairs of state, and thought it no lessen-ing of their dignity to make the one the recreation to the other.

Nor let it be thought that I mistake, when I call these or the like exercises of manual arts, *diversions* or *recreations*: for *recreation* is not being idle (as every one may observe) but easing the wearied part by change of business: and he that thinks *diversion* may not lie in hard and painful labour, forgets the early rising, hard riding, heat, cold and hunger of huntsmen, which is yet known to be the constant recreation of men of the greatest condition.[29]

At Alexandria, Ohio, the people of the community worked together to turn a dump into a playground. It is doubtful whether the use of the playground gives any greater enjoyment than did the making of it. Working together for community ends often is a pleasant and desirable form of recreation.

Updyke, the great printer, worked for ten hateful years at the printing trade, despising his work, and wishing he were free from it. Then he began to wonder what he would do if he were free, and he asked himself whether his own work had no possibilities of interest. The result was that he fell in love with printing, became one of the world's great printers, and by that route found an open road to the companionship of the men of intelligence and appreciation whose acquaintance he had so much desired.

A woman who had kept house for thirty years said that only recently had she discovered that the processes of the kitchen had at least as great range of possibility for emotional satisfaction as would modeling clay, painting pictures, or driving a golf ball. She has become an artist in her home, and her friends enjoy it with her. She learned that freedom may come by self-discovery and self-mastery more surely than by escape.

There are some forms of individual or family recreation which do not need public financial support so much as public encouragement. Gardening is one of these. In many small communities, especially in those far from industrial centers, money is less abundant than time. If such a community can take pride in its gardens it may become a place distinguished for its beauty and individuality. Tyler, a small town on the prairies of western Minnesota, was settled by Danish people. Although the houses were small and set on flat rectangular lots fifty feet wide, the people of the community used so much skill and imagination in planting their gardens that after thirty-five years the writer looks back to this little village as one of the most interesting he ever saw. The neighborly exchange of plants, vegetables, and flowers, and the discussion of common problems, created at least as much neighborly feeling as membership in a golf club. The Dane by tradition is a landscape artist, and turns a commonplace setting into a place of beauty. He finds recreation in doing so.

The feudal, aristocratic attitude, dating back to Aristotle and before, held that usefulness and beauty are incompatible. In the ancient democratic atmosphere of Switzerland some people know better. The writer recalls an evening at the home of a rural Swiss pastor in the Bernese Oberland. His garden was a masterpiece of design, so informal that the design was invisible. Vegetables and flowers were blended in an apparently artless unity. As he sat with his guest in the evening looking across the garden to the mountains, he remarked, "How beautiful the evening sunlight is on the beet leaves!"

How great in beauty and in recreation America might become if we could but free ourselves from the deadly pall of convention inherited from tawdry aristocracy, which leads us to feel that useful work cannot be recreation, that necessary tasks are mean, and necessary things ugly! What if Americans should treat their gardens as did the Swiss pastor! What if American women should forget fashions from Paris, Vienna, or New York, and each who had creative ability should qualify herself to design her own costumes to suit her personality and her work, whether the resulting style should follow ancient Egypt or medieval Japan or modern America! What an increase of variety and interest, yes, and recreation in a true sense, might result, though except for qualified persons the initial efforts might be far from happy.

In such a process skilled leadership would have more range of action, not less.

Recreation through Organizations within the Community. The community as such should not try to monopolize all public recreation within its borders. Members of churches, farm organizations, labor unions, and other working organizations find increased unity in playing together as well as in working together. Community recreation facilities should be made available to such organizations.

CHAPTER XXII

SOCIAL AND CULTURAL ASPECTS OF COMMUNITY LIFE

THE life of a community is not sharply divided into separate parts, such as business, education, religion, and leisure. It is a single, complex, interwoven fabric, with every part related to and affecting every other part. This total fabric is the culture of the community. Some elements of this total pattern are so clearly distinguishable or are so in need of attention that we give them separate treatment. Other elements are so interwoven that separate treatment, even for practical convenience, seems to interfere with our seeing the pattern as a whole.

This chapter is devoted to discussion of some elements of community life which for the sake of convenience are treated in relation to each other. This manner of treatment is arbitrary and only for convenience, for it is obvious that subjects treated separately in this book, as economics, recreation, and health, are no less interwoven in the total fabric of community culture.

Interest in community development should not be confined to a few chief issues, even if they include the important interests of business, education, the church, health, and recreation. A good community will give friendly welcome to every kind of activity and interest which adds to the quality of living. How to give such friendly welcome without scattering and dissipating time, energy, and resources, so that people are wearing themselves out with activities and doing everything superficially, is a problem of community leadership.

An uncrowded life, in which there is time for relaxation and refreshment, is no less necessary than range of interests. The two are not necessarily in conflict. No small part of so-called cultural activity in both large and small communities is essentially trivial, having almost no value except that it brings people together and helps time to pass. Social life for sheer relaxation is desirable to the extent that it is necessary, but to make passing the time away a chief end of leisure implies mental and spiritual bankruptcy. The elimination of triviality will go far toward providing time and resources for a wide range of interests.

The Principle of Economy of Experience. "We must avoid . . . the notion that vocations are distributed in an exclusive way, one and only one to each person. . . . Each individual has of necessity a variety of callings, in each of which he should be intelligently effective. . . . No one is just an artist and nothing else, and in so far as one approximates that condition he is so much the less developed human being; he is a kind of monstrosity."[30] Thus wrote John Dewey in his *Democracy and Education.*

We crave many kinds of satisfactions, and often these seem to demand many divergent activities. We want reasonable income, so we perform the day's work. We want companionship, so we join social organizations. We crave beauty, so we have parks and music, and buy ornaments and pictures. We need ethical principles and spiritual life, so we associate with churches or other appropriate organizations. We must have exercise, so we play golf or tennis.

If each kind of satisfaction lacks unity with the others and requires a separate undertaking, our lives will be crowded, cumbered, and confused. Too often that condition exists. The popular doctrine of "art for art's sake" may prevail—the idea that art is independent of all other values, that it has nothing to do with ethics or with usefulness. As a result, the artistic expression of the community may ignore and tend to nullify efforts to develop ethical quality in community life.

In economic life we may find the doctrine that "business is business," indicating that business should be governed by no consideration but the production of profits. Principles of honesty and fair play may be violated, a factory may be dirty, ugly, and surrounded by disorderly piles of materials, and billboard advertisements may mar the landscape and give the streets a cheap and confused appearance. The health of the community may be undermined by poor working conditions, or by the sale of unwholesome products.

Evidence of other lacks may appear in the religious life of the community. The church buildings may indicate that a sense of beauty is wanting. Various churches may compete with each other, each overstraining itself to build a larger building and get a larger part of the money of the community. In short, the church may be pursuing its own ends with little regard for other values.

The physicians of the community may have little interest beyond their particular patients. The psychiatrists may be working with persons whose lives are disturbed and disintegrated by conflicting experiences. The stomach specialist may be trying to cure ulcers that are the outcome of nervous and disordered living, and the heart and nerve specialists may be similarly engaged. The difficulties of their patients may be largely the outcome of a prevailing way of life in the community. Yet the physician may treat them as independent, individual problems, and he may himself be following the general way of life which contributed to the disturbance or disintegration of normal health.

Where such standards of separateness prevail, a person who desires a full and well-rounded life must have a multiplicity of separate interests and experiences, and the various undertakings may tend to defeat each other. Such doctrines as "art for art's sake," "business is business," and "religion is the supreme interest" are in error. Each field of interest should have relation to all the others, and each should support all the others. Also, if we can make what we want to do coincide with what we ought to do, there is great gain in the quality of living.

If the idea of unity and economy of experience should prevail, then one undertaking might supply several needs, and it would not be necessary to have so many experiences in order that life might be full and well-proportioned. Life would achieve freedom from confusion and complexity, and would have greater unity and poise, and reserves of health and power.

This principle of unity of experience is important in art as in other fields. Vital art is one of the formative influences of people's lives. We tend unconsciously to become like the art we see. The artist therefore is under obligation to be intellectually sound and ethically wholesome. That is not the same as being conventional. The artist may be an ethical pioneer, but he must distinguish between pioneering and decadence, between freedom and the expression of his own ethical immaturity and crass insensitiveness. Where the artist meets this standard, then his artistic experience is also an ethical experience. He makes one undertaking serve more than one need.

Beauty generally can be combined with economic usefulness. A home may be filled with ornaments and art objects which have no use except to supply beauty. Often a multiplicity of art objects disguises the fact that home furnishings and arrangements lack design and inherent beauty. If the furnishings necessary in the home have beauty in themselves, and if a sense of design has made the arrangement of the home a work of art, then few art objects are needed except such as by their inherent beauty provide an experience not otherwise attainable. Through such simplification there is a saving of the first cost of the "art" dispensed with, of valuable space, and of the endless work of keeping, cleaning, and caring for art objects.

Painting classes were organized in one community, and soon the walls of the homes in the community were hung with atrocious landscapes. In another community there was organized effort to make necessary things beautiful. A community handicraft shop was equipped and supplied with good simple furniture designs. This shop became a social center, and taste in furniture greatly improved as people made pieces for themselves. The garden club similarly influenced home surroundings. One woman made a study through several years of how to make a kitchen not only efficient but beautiful. She found that some manufacturers had taken the trouble to design pots and pans to be things of beauty. Several meetings of the women's club to discuss kitchen design and arrangement had the result of making several kitchens efficient and attractive places to work. Efficiency in living and a certain integration and unity of life results when beauty becomes an inherent quality of what is necessary, rather than something attached to an unlovely world.

Again, the doctrine that "business is business" tends to destroy the wholesomeness and integrity of the community. An ugly sign on a building or in front of a store may bring a merchant financial profit, but it is an offense to the esthetic sense of the whole community, and debases the public taste. For all the business men in a community to make all of their advertising and signs, and the treatment of their store fronts and places of business, conform to a well-developed sense of beauty and fitness would be a greater improvement than the founding of an art gallery. Moreover, it need cost very little, and could be an expression of the growing community taste.

A beginning could be made by bringing about the removal of the ugliest and most offensive signs or advertisements. The merchants of the town might give up trying to outdo each other in flamboyant signs, which turn a business street into an orgy of ugliness. They could unite, and through a committee, with the help of a competent designer, give their business streets a unity and beauty of design and treatment which would be a source of satisfaction to every person who should have business there. The business experience would then be also an esthetic experience, and it would not be necessary for the business man to leave ugly business surroundings and build an elaborate country place, or buy expensive pictures on the advice of a specialist, in order to have experience with beauty. Making the same experience serve both usefulness and beauty is an illustration of what we mean by the "principle of economy of experience." When such a change does take place people will look back upon the present appearance of our city and village streets as representing an age of crude, insensitive stupidity.

The doctrine that "business is business" should also give way before a sense of ethical responsibility to the community. The newsstand dealer cannot face the community with self-respect while he undermines the morals of young people by selling salacious literature. The man of property cannot call for the respect of the community while he rents his property for a use harmful to the community. Instead of trying to meet his ethical responsibility by promoting the building of a larger church, with its continuing financial burden, the merchant might go through his stock of merchandise and assure himself that he is not selling anything that is essentially harmful or useless in meeting legitimate human need. He would watch his advertising, to insure that he makes no unfounded claims and does not excite people to extravagance or wastefulness. He would train his salespeople to tell the plain truth about what they sell. In the field of government he would realize that democracy is a way of life, not just a device of government, and that it must be slowly learned. He therefore would try to educate his staff in democracy by seeking their participation in administration to a gradually increasing degree as their experience should lead them to develop interest, understanding, and responsibility. In the field of health, he would not sell injurious products, and he would try to provide wholesome working conditions for his employees.

Having in view the need of the community to care for its so-called unemployables, such a merchant might endeavor to find places where some partly disabled persons might be of such actual service as to be self-supporting, and therefore more easily self-respecting. By following this principle of "economy of experience," he would in the course of his usual work give expression to many fundamental needs and desires.

If this principle should come to be followed generally in a community the result would be an increased excellence and unity, both in the community and in the people concerned. There would be less demand for corrective and relief agencies, or for escape devices by which people flee from boredom and sordidness into an unreal world. Business experience would also be ethical experience, esthetic experience, and social experience.

We may summarize the discussion of this "principle of economy of experience" by observing that our interests in any field should not be judged simply by the standards of that field, as the standard of beauty in art, or profit in business, or religious loyalty in the church. Activity in each field should harmonize with reasonable standards in all other fields. Then an experience I have in one field can satisfy my needs in other fields, and it becomes less necessary for me to multiply experiences. Life can achieve unity and simplicity while it is gaining fullness and good proportion, and can be freed from the confusion and distraction which come from multiplicity of conflicting efforts.

While, therefore, a community will endeavor to give friendly welcome to every kind of activity and interest which will add to the quality of life, it will endeavor wherever possible to express that interest by giving quality to the usual and necessary life of the community, rather than by adding new organizations or institutions or activities which require additional effort and expense.

The principle of economy and unity of experience should run through the whole design of community life, and can be a powerful cultural influence. It will show that the life of the community is not made up of a number of unrelated undertakings and interests, but is a single, interweaving cultural fabric, in which each part adds to or subtracts from the quality of all the rest.

Achievement of that unity and economy of experience is an art which must be learned as good speech and manners are learned, or as a great orchestra is created, by long working together with the gradual development of a well understood common purpose. Each successful attempt to achieve economy of experience, however simple and however small, helps develop experience and skill for further effort.

Community Centers. The community as a whole can have a much better realization of its existence if it has some place in which, as a community, it can express its common life. Already there are some such community centers—the post office, railroad station, and school—but since each of these serves a very limited purpose it does not take the place of a general community center. Sometimes the school does, however, serve reasonably well as a focus for community life.

Because the American community has been disrupted by the self-centered organizations of churches, clubs, lodges, etc., as well as by the flux of modern life, the feeling of community is weak. As that feeling is strengthened and encouraged, it will be greatly helped by the development of a community home and meeting place. Sometimes the best that can be done is to use the school building. Sometimes a public park, where community meetings, band concerts, etc., may be held, must serve the purpose.

An ideal to work for is a community center, with an auditorium, rooms for smaller meetings, a nursery, game rooms, a place to serve meals, and outside playgrounds. If space and other conditions permit, such a community center may well be the location of most community interests. The post office may be located there, as well as the public library and the offices of city officials, who would probably be more sensitive to public opinion if they should meet the general public more frequently. Such a community center, either in one suitable building or in a group of buildings, where the common life of the community can focus, may go far toward developing a consciousness of the community as such. Even small communities, by planning through the years, may achieve this aim.

Education. The school program of most communities has suffered greatly because of this division of life into separated parts. Children often have a strong sense of the unreality of the school process. The original way by which human beings learned what their elders knew was for children to watch adults and imitate them. The more the community can have a common life, the more this fundamental learning process can be recovered. Children may continue to learn facts in schoolrooms, but they learn life itself outside. Well-organized community life supplies the best opportunity for that process, and a community center can be a help to that end. It would be desirable to have the community center adjacent to the school center, with such facilities as gymnasium, library, community theater, and perhaps even a general assembly hall, available both to the school and to the community in general. Education has become too much a world by itself, cut off from the life for which it is a preparation, and of which it should be an integral part.

Vocational Education. High school pupils may have vocational courses, often given by teachers who never had intimate contact with any other vocation than teaching. In the

average small community there is very little intelligent help
for young people trying to find their suitable places in life.
Either the school or the community council would do well to
explore the community for possible local careers for young
people. If there are young people of special bents who need
different or larger opportunities than the village can afford,
it should then be the work of the community to open the
way for such persons when their families cannot. It would
be well for the community council through the years to have
a small continuing committee on vocational guidance, a group
of persons who would make it a major interest to know the
possibilities of many callings, and to become acquainted
with every young person in the village for whom finding a
vocation is a problem. Wherever competent, professional
vocational guidance is available, full use should be made
of it.

Often the problem is not simply that of finding a suitable
vocation for a young person, but of making him aware of
the preparation and the sustained purpose necessary to
achieve competence, and of the larger opportunities and
issues of the calling. In some Mormon communities the local
businessmen make it possible for each high school senior to
work for a time in a business he thinks might interest him.
Such a chance for one or more actual working experiences
under friendly guidance should be the opportunity of every
young person who is trying to settle upon a calling.

Adult Education. It may well be maintained that only by
adult education does society progress. If each generation
teaches the younger generation only what it learned when
young, we may have an unprogressive cycle. It is by the
enlarging of our outlooks and the changing of our points

of view after we are mature that we are able to pass on to the next generation a better culture than that we acquired as children.

Adult education is necessary to make leadership effective. Some person in the community may have taken the trouble to inform himself thoroughly on some subject of great public interest, but unless there is some way for him to transmit his information, the community may be but little better off for his effort. One of the chief aims of adult education is to make it possible for people to become acquainted with facts and issues of interest or importance which someone has taken the trouble to understand. Nearly every community, even if it is made up of only a few dozen people, has within its reach men and women who are well qualified to inform their neighbors on subjects of general interest. To find out who such people are, and to make them available to people who would like to learn what they have mastered—that should be the responsibility of some group in every community.

A community council may well have a committee on programs, on the one hand keeping in touch with significant speakers or teachers or leaders who may come within reach, and on the other hand keeping in touch with local organizations needing teachers for classes or speakers for programs. Also, such a committee should see that interesting or especially well-informed persons coming to the community may be heard, when it is appropriate, by the entire community, rather than just by a small organization.

Another aim of adult education is to help people learn the ways of democracy. Good leadership will develop the habit of participation. People do not become democratic by chance, any more than they become musicians or carpenters by chance. They must learn the art of democracy, and wise leadership may teach that art in adult education.

Adult education should *educate*. As the Overstreets remark in their *Leaders for Adult Education*:

We seem to find in the land a great weariness with the way in which we have all pooled our manifold ignorances through the discussion method, congratulating ourselves all the while on our democratic tolerance. No doubt a democracy must provide places where people can talk freely whether or not they know what they are talking about. But the job of the adult educator is not primarily to provide such places. His job is to create conditions under which people can really learn . . . To create such conditions the leader himself must possess and enjoy accurate knowledge and not mere verbal facility.[31]

There is coming to be a large literature in this field, covering every phase of the subject from elimination of illiteracy to graduate work in university extension. The American Association for Adult Education has published (1941) a volume of 493 pages on *The Literature of Adult Education*. Here one finds a very large number of references to books and magazine articles, classified under hundreds of different headings, with references to scores of bibliographies concerned with special parts of the field.

In such a maze of material how can a member of a small community who wishes to be of use in the field of adult education find his way? If the prophet Isaiah, when he started out on his adult education program, had come across such a bibliography, he might have quit his prophesying, feeling that he would not be fit to teach until he had read one or two hundred of those books. In such case the world probably never would have heard from him.

A considerable amount of reading is desirable. Such books

as Sanderson's *Leadership for Rural Life*, Overstreets' *Leaders for Adult Education*, and Follett's *The New State* may give one an idea of the spirit and manner in which adult education can best be carried on. Walser's *The Art of Conference* is also helpful. Then one may as well go to work, doing his best. Sometimes there may be opportunity to see a good teacher of adults at work. Sometimes a good book on the subject may be read—there are none too many of them —but one's own experience will be his chief teacher.

Community Libraries. Seldom is a community too small to have a library. A woman in a community of a few dozen families was troubled by the aimless loafing and trouble-making of the children in the neighborhood. She got a dozen or so good children's books and invited the neighbor children to come in. Before long, on rainy days or late afternoons they would be sitting or lying in all available rooms of her house, absorbed in those books.

A well-planned investment of $100 or even of $50 in the Modern Library editions or other inexpensive books will furnish a vast amount of good and interesting reading for a community of fifty families. Some person in the community might make it a community service to catalog and loan the books.

An estimate by the American Library Association in 1936 indicated that 75 per cent of the people of America on farms and in small communities were without library facilities. Yet books more than almost anything else open up the world to inquiring minds. A person without books is almost without windows to his small world.

There is little evidence to support the common assumption that reading of itself is of value. People can be just as trivial and inconsequential, and just as decadent, in reading as in doing anything else. Worth-while reading is but a part of a total cultural process, though a vital part. Boys and girls and men and women as a rule do not "take naturally" to good reading, any more than they naturally have discipline and skill in any other field. Supplying books is only the first step.

Beginning with the actual interest and understanding of people, and gradually building substantial intellectual interests, is a great art. The existing interest may be in chickens or in clothes or in a community co-operative. Whatever that interest may be, much will have been written about it. A skillful leader can use that interest to broaden outlooks and to develop an appetite for good literature.

Whatever road may be taken to develop interest in substantial reading, the aim should be to increase range of outlook and thoroughness of understanding, not just to provide a pleasant way for passing time. Some small-town libraries are so filled with transient and trivial reading that a young person can have not much more hope of enlarging his horizon there than he could by spending as many hours about the stove in the village store. The unutterable flatness, superficiality, and monotony of leisure and recreation, and of intellectual life, in many small American communities will not be self-eliminating. Leadership is essential.

More and more small communities are not limited to their own resources for library facilities. State libraries, county libraries, "bookmobiles," and local branch libraries, are making books available to many people. Library books are delivered by auto to schools, stores, or filling stations, or are sent by mail directly to the homes. Where it is desired to secure library facilities for a community it is well to correspond with the American Library Association, in Chicago, or with the extension division of the state university, to learn what provisions are made for library service in the small communities of the state.

Where a small library does exist and one wishes to secure books in special fields of study the librarian usually can get them by interlibrary loans. Thus nearly any book in America which is necessary for serious study is available to almost any person in touch with a library.

The Arts and Sciences. In any live community, interest in the arts and sciences will find varied expression. In one community a musical leader may so arouse and develop musical interest that a reputation for being a musical community may develop. In another community a man skilled in furniture design may develop so much interest in furniture and handicraft work that the taste of the community in that respect may be revolutionized. In another case landscape design and gardening may become a fine art, with many members of the community as amateur students.

Sometimes one or a few persons with excellent training and keen interest in science may arouse such interest that young people will enjoy meeting in science clubs or going on outdoor expeditions. Sometimes more general cultural interests prevail and courses of lectures become a leading feature of community life.

There are many cases in the aggregate where small groups with special interests have maintained continuous existence for long periods. There may be singing clubs, art clubs, Browning or Shakespeare clubs, geology clubs, cross-country clubs, or simply discussion clubs. For a young man or woman to find a variety of cultural interests in the community, from which a choice of associations can be made, may have much to do with forming his or her life interests. A live organization will not become ingrown in its associations, but will continually explore the community, including the high school, for persons who can share its interests.

Sometimes such associations have a practical bent. In a small Kentucky community a group of about twenty small farmers began to study grape culture, and met one evening a week for that purpose. The Ohio Farm Bureau has found that the monthly meetings of its small advisory councils for discussion of a wide variety of subjects have been among its most significant activities.

CHAPTER XXIII

COMMUNITY ETHICS

"That which is now called the Christian religion existed among the ancients, and has never failed from the beginning of the human race, until Christ came in the flesh, whence the true religion, which was already in existence, began to be called Christian." So wrote Augustine [A.D. 427]. . . . This thought . . . belongs obviously to an evolutionary, not to a catastrophic, view of the world's history, and for this reason it took no firm root during the long period when the dominant philosophy was supernaturalistic dualism. We moderns may be glad to find that it has a recognised, though insecure, place in early Christian thought. . . . The profoundest and most original of prophets still stands on the shoulders of those who went before him.[32]

—Dean Inge

THERE is little doubt that ethical standards originated in primitive community life. People living together intimately in small groups found it necessary to be considerate of each other and of the general welfare. No matter how primitive the community, such codes always existed, and it is the fairly uniform testimony of those who have studied primitive communities that their ethical standards are quite thoroughly understood and agreed upon, and are very generally observed. While the primitive community enforced definite penalties for extreme violations of ethical usages, the most powerful enforcement was through the weight of general public disapproval of violations. The entire life of the community was ruled by these standards which everyone acknowledged, and which nearly everyone lived up to.

It seems that some of the finest ethical standards of the world today are survivals of prefeudal community life. The ethics of Christianity, except for the element of persistent forgiveness of wrongdoers and of universal brotherhood beyond the limits of tribe or nation, came directly from the Hebrew prophets, and the earliest of them were rural, small community people. The Christian teaching preserved to us just such prefeudal community ethics as Stefansson and Kropotkin found among the Eskimos.

Such ethical codes grew up gradually through generations, though sometimes leaders refined and defined them. Just as primitive people often believed that their own origin was through some divine or miraculous event, so they commonly attributed such miraculous origins to their ethical rules. Yet when we examine the nature of such codes we find them to be more or less practical standards of conduct which enable people to live together successfully. Sometimes such standards are capricious or without present value, as for instance the English rule which until recently prohibited a man from marrying his deceased wife's sister.

Ethical standards originate in efforts to define relationships for successful community living. As the community always has a real and deep stake in the individual personal health and well-being of its members, personal ethics is really a part of social ethics. The idea that there are ethical principles which concern only the individual is a delusion.

Sometimes peoples have succeeded in producing good patterns of conduct, and sometimes they have not. The Seminole Indians, apparently observing that bad results followed the marriage of close relatives, developed the standard that relatives should not marry, even if several degrees removed. In a small tribe the result was that marriage was so greatly restricted that sometimes a woman of sixty might marry a boy of sixteen, those being the only possibilities within the remnants of the tribe. Among certain New Guinea tribes similar efforts to prevent inbreeding, or to eliminate feuds by requiring intermarriage, have similarly led to grotesque results.

The customs of both primitive and civilized men have been cumbered with rules, prohibitions, and taboos which represent mistakes men have made in their effort to regulate behavior for the social good, or which—as in the doctrine of the divine status of kings or prelates—may represent the efforts of favored persons or classes to entrench their prestige by indoctrination. As in all other useful and necessary human undertakings, the development of ethical codes has been imperfect. Just as no automobile is perfectly designed, but is justified because to a considerable degree it serves its purpose, so the justification of an ethical code is not that it is perfect, but that it is useful and necessary. It is the business of intelligence critically to examine and to develop ethical standards, and to discover how best to make them serve the needs of men. Such critical examination is very, very far from indifference.

Often the ethical habits of primitive people were of a very high order. Those described by Stefansson as prevailing among the most remote Eskimos compare favorably with the best standards of civilized people, as exemplified, for instance, in the Christian code recorded in the Sermon on the Mount. The period of feudal conquest, in which community life and standards to a considerable degree were subjugated, tended to debase community ethics, and to displace them with a reliance on power, strategy, and dissimulation, just as might occur today if the Nazi or other regime relying on force and deceit were to be generally successful.

Throughout all human history one of the strongest influences toward social unity has been common ethical understanding and practice, and this has been especially true in community life. The result of such common ethics tends to be mutual respect and regard, mutual helpfulness, and a lack of internal strife and stress. Where such common standards are lacking there is inevitable conflict and alienation.

By and large people do not originate their own ethical standards. They take over the standards they see about them. They will not as a rule feel that standards have controlling value or authority unless the prevailing current of thought and feeling holds those standards to be important. Thus, the standards actually recognized in a community will largely determine what will be the standards of young people growing up in that community.

The greater the range of agreement on ethical principles, the more will a real community exist. In a dictatorship, either political or ecclesiastical, ethical uniformity may be enforced by compulsion. In most American communities that kind of unity is, fortunately, out of the question. The agreements men reach on standards of conduct must be freely arrived at, and supported by the consensus of public opinion.

The fact that ethical usage must be freely considered and appraised does not mean that one person's ethical judgment is as good as another's. In the field of science there is free inquiry, and prevailing scientific beliefs are freely arrived at. Yet no one presumes that in science one person's opinion is as good as another's. In scarcely any other field does thorough preparation and qualified authority weigh so heavily. But scientific recognition must not rest on any mystical authority. It must be based on open inquiry and on full disclosure of processes and results, so that any other qualified person by free critical inquiry can test and check the results obtained.

In the field of ethics, illiteracy, lack of disciplined competence, lack of critical, discriminating observation, and reliance on current popular impressions, are no more admirable than in the field of science. Leadership in ethics is just as necessary and just as valuable as in science. The feeling so general at present that ethical standards are a personal matter, and that one person's judgment in that field is as worthy of respect as another's, is an expression of ignorance.

One of the reasons why ethical standards have come into disrepute is that very commonly they have rested, not on the results of open critical inquiry, but on supernatural or mystical authority—a kind of authority which is not subject to critical inquiry, but must be accepted on faith, synonymous, in the minds of many people, with credulity. When such authoritarian systems of ethics compete with each other for loyalty they do not appeal to a process of critical inquiry by which they can be tested and compared. The fading of belief in divine revelation of ethical codes, unless followed by ethical principles developed by critical inquiry, will leave people with a feeling that all ethical rules are arbitrary, and that every person should be free to do as he individually sees fit.

When a community undertakes to arrive at a common basis of ethics, there will be unfortunate confusion and conflict if adherents to authoritarian systems of ethics compete with each other in trying to force the acceptance of their systems. It is partly because of such efforts to influence the adoption of authoritarian systems, and because of the resulting disrepute of ethical principles in general, that a community may hesitate to try to develop a common code of conduct. The people may feel that nothing but confusion and conflict can result from such effort.

The development of a common standard for ethical conduct in a community should be on the basis of open inquiry, with the help of competent, open-minded, critical leadership. Only those elements of conduct that have general acceptance for their sound reasonableness should be included in a community code of ethics. It is better to have substantial agreement on a simple and limited code of behavior, with a nearly universal feeling that good citizenship requires the observance of those standards, than to get superficial agreement on more elaborate standards which many people feel are impracticable or unreasonable, and which therefore do not have whole-hearted support. The widespread acceptance of the Ten Commandments provided a common body of ethical principles and for a long period was a powerful social discipline. Sometimes agreement can be had only on specific points, and not on fundamental principles.

The believer in a revealed code of ethics may be faithful himself to that code, but he should not try to force it on the community. An orthodox Mohammedan believes that the Ten Commandments constitute an authoritative code of ethics, and because they command that "Thou shalt not make unto thee any graven image, or any likeness of anything that is in the heaven above, or that is in the earth beneath, or that is in the water under the earth," he feels that sculpture and painting are sinful. He has small respect for the sophistry by which some people who profess to be bound by that code explain away this commandment. If there were Mohammedans in a community they should be free to live by that code themselves, but they should not try to force it on the community because of its supposed divine authority.

Ethical pioneers are desirable and necessary—men who have more discriminating and exacting standards than the general population. They blaze the trails and demonstrate the value of a finer management of life. Little by little the general public comes to recognize the value of finer standards, and gradually incorporates them into the accepted ethical code. Always there will be a twilight zone between what is fully accepted and what is coming to be seen as excellent, as a result of the more discriminating living of ethical pioneers. It is concerning that twilight zone that much of the community discussion of ethical standards will take place. A live community will gradually adopt more discriminating standards as the public becomes aware of them and convinced of their value. That is, it will improve in its manners and its morals.

Community ethical standards should be looked on as guides to conduct, not as inflexible rules. It is a good standard of action not to borrow a neighbor's property without asking him for it. However, if your small child were caught in a tree and you needed the neighbor's ladder, that propriety might well be dispensed with. Ethical standards will be better respected if their reasonableness is apparent.

What methods can be used effectively for bringing about general community agreement on ethical standards? In a community organization it might be well to have a committee on community standards. At first it might be well to develop only the rudiments of an ethical code, which should include what are commonly called both manners and morals. Universally accepted standards would be assumed almost without mention, such as those against murder and forgery. Emphasis could be placed on standards which, while generally recognized, are not well supported.

For instance, gossip or tale-bearing is one of the dominant evils of the small community. A recognized habit might be developed which would lead people, either separately or in groups, to protest directly against that evil wherever it appeared, and to request the talebearer to desist. If there should be active support of such a standard in the community, little offense would be taken by offenders who should be asked to desist. Considerable effort might be required to secure general acceptance and support for a standard which would lead people to refuse to make a living by any work which is a harm to the community, such as operating low-grade amusement places, or stimulating gambling for the sake of an income.

Sometimes a community ethical code can best be developed by informal education and personal influence. Sometimes, where suitable leadership is available, a definite community code may be developed, publicized in the local press, and perhaps printed in a small pocket-size pamphlet. Probably no items should be included in such a code if even as much as a quarter of the population should definitely disapprove of them.

One of the deepest cravings of men is for the respect and approval of their fellows. Unified community opinion is very powerful, especially when it is supporting standards which have been arrived at by free, critical inquiry, with the help of competent leadership, and which have been consciously and very generally accepted by the community. In the lack of such clearly defined standards, conduct is controlled largely by vague impressions of what is desirable or undesirable. The conflict between different ethical codes leads people to feel that they are free from responsibility to any, and can go their own way. In the flux of modern life the old family and neighborhood codes tend to fade until very little control of conduct is left except crude animal impulse or the fear of the law. Throughout the history of mankind the finest qualities of society have been maintained by community standards, often, but not always, supported by definite institutions such as the church, the school, the lodge, or the guild. Without fairly definite standards society will disintegrate. The small community is the best place, almost the only place, for stabilizing and transmitting the finest of those ethical standards which concern the intimate relations of its members.

Any living ethical code will express itself in action. In nearly every modern community there are discriminations, inequalities, and other stresses which prevent spiritual unity, and which tend to disrupt the community. The removal of such conflicts will be an active concern in a good community.

America suffers greatly from race discrimination. The Negro has a tragic lot which is developing a deep and lasting bitterness. The injustices which we condemn in other peoples we are practicing ourselves. Within each individual community where there are Negroes there is opportunity to work for the equality of economic opportunity and for the mutual respect and good will which are fundamental to democracy. Anti-Semitism also undermines the self-respect and dignity of many people, and brings about grave psychological stresses in those who are its victims. In many cases refugees from Europe are being treated with suspicion and discrimination which adds greatly to their already heavy burdens.

On the Pacific coast loyal American-born Japanese are

being treated in some communities with ruthless disregard for property and personality, and there are few communities in America where they can find friendly refuge. Only as such actual issues as these can be met with good will and sympathy can the spirit of community have a healthy growth.

In the states north of the Ohio River are many thousands of persons who have come from the southern mountain regions. Discrimination is leading them to develop a class consciousness of their own. As their numbers increase and they come into power in one community after another they may develop deep cleavages which decades may not remove. The older residents in these northern communities, who have been favored with a more abundant economic and cultural background, could make no better contribution to their times than to find common ground with these newcomers, and to help develop a common culture.

Such practical problems of social unity confront us on all sides. The spirit and manner in which those problems are met provide criteria for measuring ethical refinement and vitality. It is actual conduct in the handling of such issues, rather than theoretical ethical commitments, which discloses the ethical quality of a community.

CHAPTER XXIV

THE CHURCH IN THE COMMUNITY

THERE are more than 150,000 rural and small-community churches in the United States. They have an average membership of about a hundred, approximately a fifth of whom are not active, and their membership or adherents include about a third of the entire population of their communities. With improvement in transportation and with increased tendency to co-operate, the number of rural churches tends to decline, while the membership of the individual church tends to increase.

In the pioneer settlement of America the community church played an important part. To a large degree it defined the social standards of the community. For the most part, America was settled by people of small means, limited education, and vague, rough-and-ready standards, except as those standards were defined by the church. The church, almost alone among formal social organizations, had a clearly defined social and ethical code in advance of that required by law. It helped not only to maintain existing social customs, but to create better ones. It founded hundreds of colleges, and was one of the chief influences in transmitting some of the better elements of the cultural inheritance to the motley and largely uneducated mass of men and women who pressed westward.

The community church also was one of the principal

schools of democracy. Except for a few denominations that
were ruled by non-resident and anti-democratic church hierarchies, the American community church was democratic.
Often it provided much more direct, democratic participation
in policy-making and in administration than did political
government.

The community church has been a social organization,
often supplying almost the only organized opportunity in
the community for people to meet and to visit with each other.
It was one of the principal means by which young people became acquainted and found their mates. It was a recognized
agency for social service in case of want and suffering. The
democratically governed community church was a true folk
institution, and not an imposed authority. During the pioneer times when the spirit and the organization of the community were inadequately developed it supplied for its members many of the elements of community life. Its principal
value, however, was to nurture the vision and the idealism
of the community, and to keep alive that spiritual aspiration which gives the highest quality to life, but which tends
to be crowded out by the immediate pressure of economic
affairs.

Yet the community church has not been altogether an asset
in the community. The claims of the several denominations
to be unique guardians of the truth and receivers of true
revelation made it natural for each to compete with the
others for numbers and for loyalty, and tended to intoler-
ance. That tendency to competition and to isolation has been
one of the most divisive forces in American communities. It
has broken up even small communities into separate church
groups which, if they did not combat each other, yet often
did not co-operate.

A study of 140 villages in nearly all parts of America, made about 1925 by Brunner, Hughes, and Patten, under the direction of the Institute of Social and Religious Research, indicated that the home-mission policy of several denominations accentuated competition between small-community churches. More than half of the churches receiving home-mission assistance were in communities having four or more churches, whereas "unchurched" communities were generally neglected.* A continuation of that study in 1933 (Brunner and Kolb, *Rural Social Trends*), and a further study in 1937 (Brunner and Lorge, *Rural Trends in Depression Years*), indicated that this unbalance had been partly corrected. This succession of studies has shown a gradual decline in the place of the rural Protestant churches, while the Catholic churches have about held their own. Along with this general decline, however, there has appeared a distinct new vitality in a number of congregations, amounting probably to a few thousand churches in the aggregate. We find these churches and their leaders actively committed to living by Christian principles in economic, social, and personal affairs. Some of them are effectively making over their communities.

The community faces the problem of preserving and developing the values of its churches, while escaping their disadvantages. The democratically governed churches are tending to see themselves, not as the sole transmitters of revealed truth, but as associations of sincere people who are committed to a search for the truth and to an effort to achieve better ways of life for themselves and for society. Insofar as that attitude has developed they are learning to co-operate.

* See Brunner, Hughes, and Patten, *American Agricultural Villages*, Chapter VI.

Half-starved and competing churches are consolidating or are working together in harmony.

The community council greatly assists co-operation among community churches. Through community council activities the churches of a community can work together on common problems without surrendering their distinctive views. As associations of people who have set themselves to achieve more than the average level of personal and social standards, churches can be pioneer institutions in the community. By expressing their united voice through representation on a community council they can be a force for refinement of community purpose. Those elements of community policy on which the churches are united can be emphasized, and in that process of working together, mutual confidence, respect, and understanding can grow.

In many small American communities there are too many small, struggling churches, with but slight differences in actual creeds or programs, each striving to keep alive or to extend its influence, though but slightly active in affairs of the community as a whole. Yet small churches are not of necessity undesirable. If they are not too small, too weak, and too ambitious, they often may be of more value to their members than large ones. Small numbers are essential to intimate personal and neighborly relationships. A small church of fifty or a hundred active members may constitute a compact body of neighbors and associates who sustain each other's purposes and provide intimate fellowship which larger organizations miss. On the other hand, where the church tries to supply most of the community needs of its members, larger membership is necessary to effectiveness. The greater the unity of life and action in the community as a whole, the less need there is for large, impersonal churches.

The separation of church and state is relatively recent. When they were united the church saw itself as *the* center of social life, and that habit has carried over. Often the churches of a community have been in competition with each other and with the community as a whole in the effort to organize community social life, and as a result the spirit of a community as a whole has almost died. To what extent individual community churches should maintain social programs cannot be decided in the abstract. Even where there is well developed unity in the community, it is natural and wholesome that smaller groups should have still more intimate relations. But they should contribute to community integration, and not obstruct it.

If general community needs should be served by the community as a whole, and if community churches should undertake to do only those things which a small group can do better than a large one, both the community and the church would profit by the change. In the small church, if it is truly a live and active group, the members can be concerned with working out a common life purpose, encouraging and sustaining each other in their standards and convictions, and worshiping together. As for musical programs, lecture programs, and general social events, often it is well when these can represent the efforts of the entire community, with the churches co-operating. In a well developed community with vigorous and unified community life, the church might be most significant and effective by acting as a sort of social hormone, adding tone to the whole, instead of trying to be a nearly complete social organism in itself. In a small community the so-called "institutional church," with playgrounds, educational classes, music clubs, etc., often is undertaking functions which had better be performed by the community as a whole, with the help and co-operation of all local churches.

Such a view of its function would greatly simplify both the church's problems and those of the community. The church would be an association of people for inquiring into a way of life, for making that way clear to young and old, and for inspiring and strengthening each other in that way. In many cases it would need less plant and a smaller budget. Through its representation as a body on the community council, and through the activity of its members in community affairs, it could promote the unity of the community as a whole, and by example could illustrate to the community the way of life which it had set out to achieve. Its influence would be, not so much in the number of its members at the moment, as in the clearness and excellence with which it had worked out a way of life, and in the degree to which that way of life was exemplified in its members.

There may be some denominations to which such a situation would be abhorrent, especially if they are not democratically governed. Some of them may try to undermine activities of the community as a community, such as the public school. A religious institution of that kind may feel itself to be the proper supreme authority, temporarily robbed of its power. It may try to isolate its members as much as possible from general community participation, and to set up a state within a state, or a community within the community. The presence of such an influence is detrimental to efforts for community unity and to the development of democracy. The spirit of America seems to be bigger than this attitude of exclusiveness and dominance, and even these undemocratic churches are coming to give up the attitude of exclusiveness and unique authority, and are participating more and more in the general community life.

Part Four

CONCLUDING OBSERVATIONS

CHAPTER XXV

THE PIONEER IN THE COMMUNITY

SOME communities eagerly welcome new ideas in almost any field, while others are exceedingly set in their ways. Throughout the course of history small communities have been charged with provincialism, conservatism, and lack of interest in anything off the beaten track. Where there were values in danger of being lost, the small community has been a conserving influence. Where there were outmoded ways which hindered social progress, the small community often has clung to them.

Where there are no strong interests to interfere, the small community, partly because of its size, may be the best place for initiating social experiments. This has been true with reference to the co-operative movement. Community singing has had some of its most marked successes in small communities.

In a surprising number of ways, however, efforts to do things differently come into conflict with vested interests, or with set habits. The pioneer in education in a small community sometimes has a thorny path. Parents fear that a change of program may cause their children to lose conventional credits. The kind of schooling the parents have had acquires an aura of authority, and any departure from it may be frowned upon. For a teacher honestly and competently to discuss the shortcomings of democracy as it is practiced locally may bring the charge of disloyalty.

Similar difficulties may appear in church affairs. Church services may be so routine, monotonous, and uninspired as to alienate young people, yet for a minister to depart markedly from the prevailing pattern, for him to deal with present vital issues, or to change the form of church service, may lead to his dismissal.

Business and the professions encounter the same obstacles. For an intelligent and conscientious druggist to cease selling his customers useless or harmful nostrums may lose their good will. For a physician to break the fairly universal habit of make-believe and tell his patients what he actually knows and does not know about their condition, and for him to prescribe medicine only when he thinks it necessary, will almost surely bring him into disrepute, for a time at least. Years ago the writer encouraged a college physician to lay aside the conventional halo of medical omniscience, and to be candid with his student patients. The transition was a painful one, for students had come to expect an attitude of medical certitude in a doctor; but the new relationship added to the physician's self-respect, and in time led to mutual confidence. Such a change, though difficult to make, will add to the quality of life in any community.

In a score of ways the pioneer in a small community may have a hard road. Yet, as a rule, if his project is sound and within the capacity of the community, it is not impossible. Whether he succeeds or fails commonly will depend on his character, skill, and wisdom. To advise such a person to be courageous may seem to favor precipitate or ill-considered or inconsiderate action. To advise tact and patience may seem to justify timidity, cowardice, and compromise. It is not from living by rule, but by poise, judgment, character, and experience that effectiveness is achieved. A community pioneer or leader does well to give considerable time and thought to his own motives and methods, to his manners and his attitudes. If one's project is not going well, three questions may reasonably be asked: "Is the project a reasonable one to undertake under existing circumstances?" "Am I the person to undertake it?" and lastly, "In what way are my attitudes and methods at fault?"

There are a number of common-sense principles of action which, if intelligently observed, may smooth the road to pioneering in almost any community. First is the necessity for being qualified in the field in which one is pioneering. This may not mean professional preparation. Sometimes a working man or a housewife, by taking the time and trouble to become thoroughly informed, both by reading and by first-hand knowledge of the facts, may become exceptionally well qualified in the field of his or her interest. A great many unsuccessful undertakings in American communities have originated in sudden interest in some project without thorough and impartial study or consideration.

Before asking one's community to change its ways in any important respect, one should take the trouble to be thoroughly and impartially informed. One should know what has been done and written in that field, and what the results have been elsewhere. Causes of failure need to be understood, as well as causes of success. When the writer was planning adoption of the alternate-work-and-study plan for Antioch College he found various cases of failure of similar plans, with scholarly dissertations on why such a program could not succeed. Careful study indicated that in every such case the unsuccessful program had vital errors of design, and that such failures should not be considered as conclusive.

The success of the program as undertaken at Antioch demonstrated the accuracy of that appraisal.

Careful preparation does not mean that all problems must be solved in advance. A community program should be a living, growing thing. Problems will arise and take form as a project develops. If those in charge are competent in principles and methods, and are alert, they will adjust their efforts to the circumstances, just as a man running a rapids in a canoe, while he needs to be an expert canoeist and to have prepared himself as well as he can, must determine his action moment by moment to take full advantage of the actual and rapidly changing situation. Sometimes competent people never begin a project because they cannot see their way through from the beginning. Often one must rely ultimately on faith and hope, and take his chance, exploring his way step by step.

Continuous practice and accumulated experience are important. One can learn methods on very small projects. Practically all the problems to be met with on a large project may be present in a small one. Generally it is well to begin with some project so limited and simple that it is well within one's powers. To carry through a simple undertaking with thoroughness and excellence, learning along the way, very greatly increases the chance for success on a larger scale. It generally is unwise to jump from a very small to a very large project at a single step. Size alone creates its own kinds of problems. The writer has supervised the work of hundreds of contractors. One of the most frequent causes of failure of a contractor is the tendency, after success on a small job, to undertake one many times as large. If the unsuccessful contractor had made the transition from small to large by several steps rather than by one, learning the effect of size along the way, he might have succeeded.

The matter of timing undertakings is important. Sometimes a project is of such a nature that its success must be a matter of slow growth through the years. Sometimes it may even be necessary to keep an idea clearly in the public eye until a new generation has grown up that is used to it. On the other hand, it sometimes is necessary to "strike while the iron is hot." If an epidemic has occurred which is traced to a bad water supply or a bad milk supply, it may be possible to correct that condition immediately while the need is fresh in people's minds. Two or three years later interest may have cooled off. A Rotary or Kiwanis Club may be ready to take up some project and see it through. In such case prompt action may be necessary, for in a few months the interests of the club quite probably will have drifted to other matters and the project may seem like a dead issue. Timing is as important in community undertakings as in music, but, just as in music, there is no intrinsic value in slow or fast timing. It is *right* timing that is needed.

The community pioneer should carefully consider his motives. Many community projects are promoted because someone wants something to do, or craves a position of prominence. Sometimes projects are undertaken which, though desirable in themselves, are far less necessary than something else, and the community may not be able to afford both. A community pioneer might be doing better to help someone else complete an undertaking than to start one of his own. Sometimes the most successful community career consists in taking hold of necessary projects which are lagging, and in helping them to successful conclusion without seeking to take the credit. Many a person who has worked and planned intelligently and patiently through the years needs just such a lift. It is a good rule not to undertake a project of one's own if one can accomplish as much by helping a project that is already under way. A tradition of successful accomplishment is of great value to a community.

If a community pioneer or a pioneering organization has decided to undertake a project and has become qualified to direct it, then the manner in which support is assembled may have much to do with the chances for success. Often it is wise to explore the community for persons most apt to take an intelligent interest in the project, and to make them thoroughly familiar with it. Unless such persons can be persuaded and definitely interested, the project probably is mistaken or premature, or perhaps those presenting it have not mastered the problem themselves.

When a few people are one by one convinced and interested, that number may be increased by discussions at luncheon clubs and by articles in the local papers. Good books or pamphlets on the subject may be passed around from person to person. When objection is raised, it often is much worth while to discuss the issue with the principal objectors, not only to persuade them, but to get their points of view and to discover any weakness in the program. In such discussions, even if the opponent is not convinced, the range of difference may be narrowed, personal animosity may be turned to friendship, and some degree of common ground may be found. Repeated friendly contact with opposition may be important. A vigorous opponent may kill a sound project. By correcting plans to eliminate reasonable opposition, and by eliminating unreasonable opposition as far as possible by friendly discussion, the hurdles may be greatly reduced. As a rule, opponents also are human.

There are many ways in which a community project may be made successful. Sometimes an individual can carry it through by himself until the public cannot afford to go without it. He may start a library in his home, or undertake to provide vocational guidance to high school students, or he may operate a lending supply of sickroom equipment. He may organize a club of young people to study their community and its needs. Perhaps a local club or other organization will sponsor a larger undertaking. Sometimes public opinion will demand that the local government take over a new service. Perhaps the state or national government will co-operate. If a project is sound and appropriate some source of support generally can be found or developed.

Much has been written here about unity of spirit in a community. Yet sometimes a community pioneer may find that, notwithstanding good will and reasonable patience, he is opposed by some special interest or by community conservatism. The question may then arise as to which is more important: community unity, or community progress. Especially in small communities, unity often reduces to timidity and cowardice.

The school system may have dry rot because no one wants to object to the superintendent, who belongs to one of the best families. The water system may be wastefully administered, but its manager may be a good fellow, a member of prominent social clubs. A building that is a community eyesore may belong to an influential property holder. A town may go without adequate sewerage because retired farmers do not want to pay for connections.

Sometimes it is necessary for the community pioneer to take issue with conservatism or special interest and to carry on an open and active campaign for a necessary improvement. No organization may dare to support him, though individuals may compliment him privately. If such pioneering is in good spirit and without rancor it may serve a double purpose. Courageous persistence and publicity may carry a project to completion, for bad conditions seldom can stand persistent fair publicity.

But there may be a far greater gain. Children growing up in a community get their opinions and convictions from life in that community. If community policy is characterized by timidity and cowardice, if special interests and financial or other power overrules the common good, then they come to believe that is the kind of world they live in. They will expect to get ahead by favoritism, by fawning on important people, by pulling strings, by patronage—and, when they get power, by dictatorship and by favors. Everyone will be careful "not to stick his neck out." In many, many American communities that spirit rules. It is negation of democracy and invitation to dictatorship.

Let one or a few persons in a community win a battle for the public welfare against special interests, and a new feeling stirs the people. Let that happen again and again through the course of years, and young people will have new courage and self-respect. Men will dare to speak their convictions. Sycophants or "yes men" will lose caste. It is from such communities that leaders can come for a real democracy. Important as is unity of spirit in community life, that unity must represent common respect for and commitment to the general good, and the common habit of living with integrity, courage, and self-respect, or it is a unity not worth having. Such unity often must be fought for, sometimes for the time being against the general current of community opinion. Seldom does a fine community come into being unless along the way some of its citizens have been willing to endure unpopularity in the common interest.

CHAPTER XXVI

FREEDOM IN THE COMMUNITY

PRIMITIVE communities had the virtues of mutual acquaintance and understanding, mutual regard, co-operation, equality, and unity of aim; but man in the primitive community was not free. His servitude to the community spirit was as complete as the servitude of a slave to his master. So long as he was like the others in the community he had an equal share in community life. If he departed from the community way of life he became an outcast.

One of the greatest achievements of modern times has been the freeing of men from bondage to the social group. This social group might be the primitive community, the feudal society, the church with its power over both mind and body, or the empire. The strong appeal of *laissez faire*, of free independent initiative, unhampered by government and society, can scarcely be understood unless we realize the servitude to community, church, feudal society or empire, which preceded it. The enormous burst of creative energy which resulted in modern intellectual, industrial and technical civilization probably could not have occurred without that freedom.

If a large degree of freedom is to be an asset to society it cannot stand alone, but must be associated with other qualities such as social-mindedness, integrity, and self-control. Where the modern world was built upon prefeudal democracy, as to some extent was the case in Switzerland, these necessary associates of freedom were present to a large degree. Where the modern world followed feudal society, whether political or religious, with its tradition of social stratification, exploitation, and physical or mental coercion, those evil traits continued in some degree in the new *laissez faire* economy. Irresponsible individuality grew so rampant as to threaten the structure of society. The doctrine of everyone for himself has proved to be as destructive of social well-being as was the earlier servitude to social organization. Today the world over there is a swing back toward greater social control.

Totalitarian government, as in Germany and Russia, has acted on the principle that social control should be absolute. The individual is relatively nothing, and society is everything. In an industrial society, where the intimate and refining influences of small communities are rapidly disappearing, and where great, centralized, impersonal organizations are in control, this process may lose many of the values of the old community, and may retain its worst feature, that of servitude and suppression of individuality.

On the other hand, modern "free initiative," such as has prevailed in England and America, through great concentration of economic power has robbed the average man of much of his freedom, but has failed to retain a sense of mutual regard and responsibility. This form of irresponsible power is not the best defense against the evils of totalitarianism.

The problem of the community, as of all society, is to save and to enlarge the priceless values of freedom, while yet developing the qualities of mutual regard, mutual help, mutual responsibility, and common effort for common ends. That is the problem of democracy. Actual democracy cannot originate in large masses or by legislation. It is a way of life which must be learned by the intimate associations of family and community. While the community is developing a sense of mutual responsibility, and while it is working out common plans, there should be constant endeavor to save individual freedom and initiative.

Leadership in developing community interests is good. Coercion into community participation—beyond the sheer necessities of public health and safety, and the elimination of objectionable elements such as nuisances or immoral or anti-social influences—should not be used. Society has a right to insist that the contacts a man has with society shall be helpful and not harmful, but the number and intensity of such contacts should be for each man to decide for himself. In the long run society will gain by that policy.

Relatively solitary persons like Spinoza or Henry Thoreau by their very separateness may get new viewpoints of great value to society. And who knows what degree of intensity of social contacts will give life its greatest value? A man may prefer to have as his intimate associates the great minds of all times in books, or the quiet beauty of nature, rather than his neighbors. Many great men have testified to the value of such solitude. Only a crude and insensitive society will force its intimate association upon its members.

On the other hand, the man who lives much with nature or with books, if he is wise, will generally keep live contacts with his neighbors. He will find some common ground of interest, and will discover ways in which to bring to them some of the values he has found. Otherwise he may be a parasite, taking his living from society, and giving nothing in return. His community may tolerate him, but will not love him.

The community should exercise tolerance as to what constitutes anti-social attitudes, for otherwise it may be suppressing the pioneer. Society does not owe it to any man to allow him to be clearly anti-social or parasitic. It does owe him the freedom to be unsocial if he chooses.

The genius of democracy is to eliminate compulsion to uniformity, whether that compulsion be physical force or social pressure, and to develop common outlooks and aims by mutual inquiry, mutual interest, and mutual regard. That process seldom if ever takes place on a large scale. Rapid large-scale changes generally come by ignoring individual variations and by enforcing large-scale uniformities. True democracy results from intimate relations and understanding, with the emergence of common purposes. The community is the natural home of democracy, and it can be the home of tolerance and freedom.

SUGGESTED READINGS

In several cases comments on books or articles are quoted from the journal *Rural Sociology*. Brief comments also are quoted from reviews of books or periodicals in *Rural America* (now discontinued), *Free America, Recreation, The New York Times Book Review Section, The A.L.A. Bulletin, Holland's Magazine,* and the *Encyclopedia of Educational Research.* Credit is here given for these quotations, and permission to use them is gratefully acknowledged.

CHAPTER I, "THE SIGNIFICANCE OF THE SMALL COMMUNITY"

Sanderson, E. Dwight, *The Rural Community* (Boston: Ginn & Company, 1932). An authoritative discussion, with extensive bibliographical appendix and an outline for general analysis of types of rural communities. See especially Chapter XVI, "The Sociological Significance of the Rural Community."

Kolb and Brunner, *A Study of Rural Society* (Boston: Houghton Mifflin Company, 1940). One of the best general texts in the field.

Sims, Newell L., *Elements of Rural Sociology* (New York: Thomas Y. Crowell Company, 1940). A very inclusive review of the literature of rural sociology, with factual and statistical summaries of many subjects, and with briefly stated judgments on most of them. A sort of condensed encyclopedia of the field.

Chancellor and Farquhar, *Root Systems for a New Democracy* (Chicago: American Library Association, 1941). An estimate of the place of the small community in society.

Boodin, J. E., "The Unit of Civilization," *International Journal of Ethics,* Vol. XXX, No. 2 (January, 1920); included as Chapter XI in his book *The Social Mind* (New York: The Macmillan Company, 1939). One of the best statements of the place of the community in civilization.

Rural Sociology, published quarterly by the Rural Sociological Society, North Carolina State College of Agriculture, Raleigh, N. C. This journal ranks among the best professional periodicals in the field of the social sciences, and is a most valuable help to persons interested in community development.

CHAPTER II, "WHAT IS A COMMUNITY?"

Cooley, Charles H., *Social Organization* (New York: Charles Scribner's Sons, 1909). Chapter I, "Social and Individual Aspects of Mind," and Chapter III, "Primary Groups." Cooley was one of the first writers to define the "primary group" or small community, and to point out its significance.

Follett, Mary P., *The New State* (New York: Longmans, Green & Company, 1920). This book gives a clear, and to some people a new, concept of the democratic process. Follett sees community as the foundation of democratic government.

Sanderson, *The Rural Community*, Chapter I, "The Rural Community as a Sociological Group."

Zimmerman, Carle C., *The Changing Community* (New York: Harper & Brothers, 1938). "What Is a Community?" on pages 11-28, is a scholarly discussion of the question. See also Chapter IV, "Types of Communities."

Kolb and Brunner, *A Study of Rural Society* (Boston: Houghton Mifflin Company, 1940). Chapter III, "Country Neighborhoods," and Chapter V, "The Rural Community." A good general discussion of what constitutes a community in America.

Sorokin, Zimmerman, and Galpin, *A Systematic Source Book in Rural Sociology* (Minneapolis: University of Minnesota Press, 1930-32, 3 vols.). Vol. I, Chapter VI, "Differentiation of the Rural Population," pp. 305-361. This three-volume work is an admirable collection of material on rural sociology.

Sims, Newell L., *The Rural Community* (New York: Charles Scribner's Sons, 1920). One of the earlier books in the field. An excellent collection of articles on the subject.

Heberle, Rudolf, "The Sociology of Ferdinand Tönnies," *American Sociological Review*, Vol. II, No. 1 (February, 1937). Tönnies was the chief German sociologist in the field of community, and his ideas have had wide influence. He classifies communities as *Gemeinschaft* (natural or spontaneous associations), and *Gesellschaft* (consciously designed associations).

Heberle, Rudolf, "The Application of Fundamental Concepts in Rural Community Studies," *Rural Sociology*, Vol. VI, No. 3 (September, 1941). An excellent presentation of Tönnies' concept of communities as *Gemeinschaft*, in contrast to society as *Gesellschaft*.

CHAPTER III, "MAN IS A COMMUNITY ANIMAL"

Kropotkin, P., *Mutual Aid* (New York: Alfred A. Knopf, Inc., 1925). See pages 1-3, 11-15, 49-62, and Chapter III. Discusses co-operation among animals, savages, barbarians, in the medieval city, and "amongst ourselves."

Boodin, "The Unit of Civilization," *International Journal of Ethics*, Vol. XXX, No. 2 (January, 1920); included as Chapter XI in his book *The Social Mind* (New York: The Macmillan Company, 1939).

CHAPTER IV, "HISTORY OF THE COMMUNITY"

Sorokin, Zimmerman, and Galpin, *A Systematic Source Book in Rural Sociology*, Vol. I, pages 266-304, "Demangeon: Geography of Rural Habitat."

Linton, Ralph, *The Study of Man* (New York: D. Appleton-Century Company, Inc., 1936).

Stefansson, Vilhjalmur, his chapter in the book *I Believe*, Clifton Fadiman, ed. (New York: Simon and Schuster, 1939). Describes community life among the most primitive Eskimos. An interesting and important account.

Maine, Henry Sumner, *Village-Communities in the East and West* (London: John Murray, 1871). Comparisons of primitive communities in India of seventy-five years ago with ancient European villages. This book, and the author's concept of *status* and *contract*, developed in his *Ancient Law*, had an important influence on sociological thought.

Smith, Arthur H., *Village Life in China* (New York: Fleming H. Revell Company, 1900). A good account of the structure of Chinese village organization.

Liang and Tao, *Village and Town Life in China* (London: George Allen and Unwin, Ltd., 1923). A discussion of the organization and functioning of local Chinese society.

Hsiao-Tung Fei, *Peasant Life in China* (New York: E. P. Dutton & Company, Inc., 1939). "An intensive survey of the economic organization of a village in eastern China, in relation to its social structure, both of which have been undergoing a tremendous process of change through cultural contact with the Western world."

Embree, John F., *Suye Mura: A Japanese Village* (Chicago: University of Chicago Press, 1939). "The aim is 'to present an integrated social study of a peasant village in rural Japan' which in many respects is representative of most rural Japanese communities."

Yoder, Fred R., "The Japanese Rural Community," *Rural Sociology,* Vol. I, No. 4 (December, 1936). A clear and interesting description of the Japanese *mura* or village.

Tannous, Afif I., "Emigration, A Force of Social Change in an Arab Village," *Rural Sociology,* Vol. VII, No. 1 (March, 1942). Describes the social effects of emigration from an Arab village whose land could not support increased population.

Homans, George C., *English Villagers of the Thirteenth Century* (Cambridge: Harvard University Press, 1941). A rather full discussion of early English agrarian, family, manorial (community) life. An excellent, scholarly, and interesting over-all survey.

Warren, C. Henry, *England Is a Village* (New York: E. P. Dutton & Company, Inc., 1941). "Much of the village life known to Saxons and Celts of previous eras has not been obliterated by passing of centuries, the machine age, or even the war. The author sees in this survival England's chief bulwark in the current crisis. 'The best of England is a village.' "

Arensberg and Kimball, *Family and Community in Ireland* (Cambridge: Harvard University Press, 1940). Very readable for an authoritative sociological study.

CHAPTER V, "THE PLACE OF THE COMMUNITY IN HUMAN CULTURE"

Boodin, "The Unit of Civilization," *International Journal of Ethics,* Vol. XXX, No. 2 (January, 1920). Describes the primary group or small community as the fundamental social unit from which social values evolve.

Follett, *The New State* (New York: Longmans, Green & Company, 1920). Discusses philosophical basis of group organization and community organization; see especially pages 105-257.

Tönnies, Ferdinand, *Fundamental Concepts of Sociology,* Translated and Supplemented by Charles P. Loomis (New York: The American Book Company, 1940). A penetrating social and philosophical analysis of concepts in terms of natural will, rational will, community, and society.

Kropotkin, *Mutual Aid* (New York: Alfred A. Knopf, Inc., 1925). A discussion of the place of mutual aid in community life and its place in social evolution. A very suggestive book.

Stefansson, Vilhjalmur, his chapter in the book *I Believe,* Clifton Fadiman, ed. (New York: Simon & Schuster, 1939). Expresses his conviction that community life, such as he describes as existing among remote Eskimos, represents some of the highest human values.

Bryce, James, *Modern Democracies* (New York: The Macmillan Company, 1927, 2 vols.). Vol. I, Chapter XII, "Local Self-Government," Chapter XXVII, "The People and Their History" (Switzerland), and Chapter XXXII, "Concluding Reflections on Swiss Political Institutions"; and Vol. II, Chapter LXVI, "The Relation of Central to Local Government." Includes discussion of the significance of small social units.

Vogt, Paul L., "The Enlarging Rural Community," *Rural Sociology,* Vol. VII, No. 1 (March, 1942). A point of view in contrast to that presented in this book. Urges centering efforts at local action and reform on particular interest and functional groups affected, rather than on the entire geographical group or "community."

Hoffer, Charles R., "The Local Community and Social Control," *Rural Sociology,* Vol. VII, No. 1 (March, 1942). "The purpose of this paper is to examine the hypothesis that the local community has an important influence in social control notwithstanding the fact that within recent years numerous social changes suggest a different conclusion."

Mumford, Lewis, *The Culture of Cities* (New York: Harcourt, Brace & Company, 1938). An "interpretive account of the growth of cities and their present and future status" (*Encyclopedia of Educational Research*).

Chapter VI, "The Relation of the Community to Larger Social Units"

Krey, A. C., "The World at Home," *Ninth Yearbook,* National Council for the Social Studies, 1938, pages 173-181. Shows that "small-town self-sufficiency, if it ever existed, is now a thing of the past," that towns are enmeshed in a "web of life" (*Encyclopedia of Educational Research*).

Tylor, W. R., "The Process of Change from Neighborhood to Regional Organization and Its Effect on Rural Life," *Social Forces,* Vol. XVI, pages 530-542.

Kolb and Wileden, *Special Interest Groups in Rural Society, Research Bulletin 84,* University of Wisconsin Agricultural Experiment Station in co-operation with United States Department of Agriculture, Madison, 1927.

Kolb and Brunner, *A Study of Rural Society* (Boston: Houghton Mifflin Company, 1940). See pages 162-164, "Interrelationships of Rural Groups."

Hiller, E. T., "Extension of Urban Characteristics into Rural Areas," *Rural Sociology*, Vol. VI, No. 3 (September, 1941).

CHAPTER VII, "THE COMMUNITY IN AMERICA"

Brunner, Hughes, and Patten, *American Agricultural Villages* (New York: George H. Doran Company, 1927). The first of three studies of 140 villages. See Chapter II, "The Structure of the Village Community."

Brunner and Kolb, *Rural Social Trends* (New York: McGraw-Hill Book Company, Inc., 1933). Second of the three studies of American agricultural villages.

Brunner and Lorge, *Rural Trends in Depression Years* (New York: Columbia University Press, 1937). Third study in the series.

Works and Lesser, *Rural America Today: Its Schools and Community Life* (Chicago: University of Chicago Press, 1942). An excellent treatment of present-day rural conditions, and of the agencies dealing with them. Has many short descriptions of rural community projects. A good guide to the study of rural conditions, especially in education.

Smith, T. Lynn, "The Role of the Village in American Rural Society," *Rural Sociology*, Vol. VII, No. 1 (March, 1942).

Steiner, J. F., *The American Community in Action* (New York: Henry Holt & Company, 1928). A series of community case-studies.

Sims, Newell L., *The Rural Community* (New York: Charles Scribner's Sons, 1920). A good early text on rural communities. A compilation of interesting and significant articles on various phases of community life.

Jaffe, A. J., "Population Growth and Fertility Trends in the United States," *Eugenical News*, Vol. XXVI, No. 4 (December, 1941).

Zimmerman, Carle C., *The Changing Community* (New York: Harper & Brothers, 1938).

Taylor, Carl C., *Rural Sociology* (New York: Harper & Brothers, 1933). Chapter XXIV, "Rural Community Organization and Agencies," a description of the actual character and operation of present-day American communities.

Adams, Herbert B., *The Germanic Origin of New England Towns* (Baltimore: Johns Hopkins University Press, 1882). Discusses the historic background of the New England town meeting, tracing it to ancient customs in England and Europe.

Elting, Irving, *Dutch Village Communities on the Hudson River* (Johns Hopkins University Studies in Historical and Political Science, Fourth Series, Vol. I, Baltimore, 1886). Discusses the meeting of Dutch and English trends, with Huguenot influences.

Maller, J. B., *School and Community* (New York: McGraw-Hill Book Company, Inc., 1938). A "sampling of population trends in New York rural and urban communities, a work commendable for methods as well as for findings" (*Encyclopedia of Educational Research*).

Wasson and Sanderson, *Relation of Community Areas to Town Government in the State of New York*, Cornell University Agricultural Experiment Station *Bulletin 555*, Ithaca, 1933.

Mather, Townsend, and Sanderson, *A Study of Rural Community Development in Waterville, New York*, Cornell University Agricultural Experiment Station *Bulletin 608*, Ithaca, 1934. A compendium of several independent surveys of the area, with attention to agricultural, economic, religious, and educational aspects.

Hoag, Emily F., *The National Influence of a Single Farm Community*, United States Department of Agriculture *Bulletin 984*, Washington, 1921. Indicates how lines of influence may spread from a small community over the nation.

Gessner, Amy A., *Selective Factors in Migration from a New York Rural Community*, Cornell University Agricultural Experiment Station *Bulletin 736*, Ithaca, 1940. A study of records of 339 former students of Belleville Union Academy for evidences of selective factors operating in the migration of rural youth.

Cash, W. J., *The Mind of the South* (New York: Alfred A. Knopf, Inc., 1941). A decade of "thoughtful research" went into this study, which seems to indicate that the heritage of the Old South continues to pulse in the new.

Kollmorgen, Walter M., *The German-Swiss in Franklin County, Tennessee* (Washington: United States Department of Agriculture, Bureau of Agricultural Economics, 1940). The author, by means of field work, examines a cultural island community as to economic base, social structure, and cultural backgrounds.

Kolb and Polson, *Trends in Town-Country Relations*, University of Wisconsin Agricultural Experiment Station Research *Bulletin 117*, Madison, 1933. A study of twelve centers in Walworth County, Wisconsin, covering the period between 1913 and 1929 under changing service areas and changing roles of service centers.

Blumenthal, Albert, *Small-Town Stuff* (Chicago: University of Chicago Press, 1932). A picture of a small western American town of good native material from which conscious community design has been absent.

Nelson, Lowry, *A Social Survey of Escalante, Utah* (Provo, Utah: Brigham Young University, 1925). Considers historical, sociological, economic and other factors. Conclusion lists social and economic advantages and disadvantages of the agricultural community.

Dawson and Younge, *Pioneering in the Prairie Provinces* (Toronto: The Macmillan Company of Canada, Ltd., 1930). This is the eighth in a series of nine volumes dealing with the general topic "Canadian Frontiers of Settlement."

Herron, Ima Honaker, *The Small Town in American Literature* (Durham: Duke University Press, 1939). Traces the concept of the small town and rural life in American native literature.

Duffus, R. L., *That Was Alderbury* (New York: The Macmillan Company, 1941). "There is a fine balance throughout the book between the true loveliness of a small New England village and the horrors of its narrow-minded, gossipy bigotry. . . . A story that is a tribute to the New England village of the nineties."

Weston, Christine, *The Devil's Foot* (New York: Charles Scribner's Sons, 1942). The story of a Maine town, particularly of the prosperous dwellers who are still snug in their traditions and fortunes, and of their

cousins—some of whom are "flirting dangerously" with radical political philosophies—and of the townsfolk who make the place what it is.

Rawson, Marion Nicholl, *New Hampshire Borns a Town* (New York:
E. P. Dutton & Company, Inc., 1942). An intimate history of a town
for the century after its beginnings in 1753.

Lee, W. Storrs, *Stagecoach North, 1791-1841* (New York: The Macmillan
Company, 1941). A reminiscent account of great-great-grandmother's
day in Middlebury, Vermont, with emphasis on attitudes and life of
the period in a place where "self-dependence was the ideal. And then
comes the sad collapse of the small-town economy, the small-town
industry, the hard-won self-dependence. Business grew bigger, the
people grew smaller. The little town as a vital unit in the nation's
economy died."

Hamilton, Milton W., *The Country Printer in New York State, 1785-1830*
(New York: Columbia University Press, 1936). Considers the development of the American rural community, with a bibliography on the
early press and early colonial community history.

Partridge, Bellamy, *Country Lawyer* (New York: McGraw-Hill Book Company, Inc., 1939).

Hough, Henry B., *Country Editor* (New York: Doubleday, Doran & Company, Inc., 1940). A country editor with a university education views
and interprets the life of a rural community, comments on the personal character of the news in a small town, and talks about news-
gathering and publishing.

Weaver, John D., *Wind Before Rain* (New York: The Macmillan Company, 1942). "The theme of Weaver's fine novel is the conflict that
arises in a simple farming community when industry invades its territory."

Georgia Writers' Project, *Drums and Shadows* (Athens: University of
Georgia Press, 1940). Contains reports of surveys of twenty Negro
communities of Georgia, in an endeavor to describe present customs and
beliefs linked to a native African origin.

Kitch, Kenneth Haun, *Salt of the Earth* (New York: The Macmillan Company, 1941). An intimate portrait of a midwestern community based
upon material in the local weekly.

Lewis, Faye Cashatt, *Doc's Wife* (New York: The Macmillan Company,
1940). "The Lewises began the practice of medicine in a small Iowa
town, and, as far as Mrs. Lewis' story indicates, seldom wavered in
their attitude of condescending superiority toward the rural and small-
town people who supported them."

McDonald, Angus, *Old McDonald Had a Farm* (Boston: Houghton Mifflin Company, 1942). A narrative of the struggles of the author's
father as a farmer and preacher in eastern Oklahoma, "the saga of
Okies who stayed at home and made good. . . . An honest and graphic
piece of work."

Whipple, Maurine, *The Giant Joshua* (Boston: Houghton Mifflin Company, 1941). A fictionalized story of the colonizing of the Washington
County, Utah, community, based upon contemporary diaries and records, and emphasizing the polygynous aspect. Shows the readiness of
the settlers to sacrifice personal pleasure to community welfare.

CHAPTER VIII, "THE CREATION OF NEW COMMUNITIES"

Nordhoff, Charles, *The Communistic Societies of the United States* (New York: Harper & Brothers, 1875). An old book, written when much was expected of communistic communities.

Calverton, V. F., *Where Angels Dared to Tread* (Indianapolis: The Bobbs-Merrill Company, 1941). Descriptions of American communities such as Brook Farm and New Harmony.

Swift, Lindsay, *Brook Farm: Its Members, Scholars and Visitors* (New York: The Macmillan Company, 1900).

Lockwood, George B., *The New Harmony Movement* (New York: D. Appleton-Century Company, Inc., 1905).

Parker, Robert A., *A Yankee Saint: John Humphrey Noyes and the Oneida Community* (New York: G. P. Putnam's Sons, 1935).

Nelson, Lowry, "The Mormon Village: A Study in Social Origins," *Proceedings* of the Utah Academy of Sciences, Vol. VII, 1930. A description of the origin and characteristics of the Mormon type of village community.

Fretz, J. Winfield, "Mutual Aid Among Mennonites," *Mennonite Quarterly Review,* Vol. XIII, No. 1 and No. 3 (January and July, 1939). A brief historical sketch and a description of their co-operative activities.

Fretz, J. Winfield, "Mennonites and Their Economic Problems," *Mennonite Quarterly Review,* Vol. XIV, No. 4 (October, 1940). A continuation of the above subject. The Mennonites probably have an unbroken tradition from prefeudal democracy, and the effectiveness of their co-operation, by means of the vitality of that tradition, is striking.

Dawson, C. A., *Group Settlement: Ethnic Communities in Western Canada* (Toronto: The Macmillan Company of Canada, Ltd., 1936). Describes group settlements of Dukhobors, Mennonites, Mormons, German Catholics, and French Canadians.

Community in a Changing World (Community Service Committee, Dartnell Park, West Byfleet, Surrey, England, 1942). A successor to the book *Community in Britain.* A book by several authors on the theory, the principles, and the practice of community living. Gives an excellent view of the wide range of thought, conviction, and action which enter into community development in England. Emphasizes the religious nature of community and discusses new communities.

The Community Broadsheet, edited by G. M. Faulding, 22 Westbourne Terrace Road, London, W 2. A news sheet describing new community projects in England, largely of religious or idealistic design.

Kollmorgen, Walter M., *The German-Swiss in Franklin County, Tennessee* (Washington: United States Department of Agriculture, Bureau of Agricultural Economics, 1940).

Ragan, Sam, "Carolina Farm Colonies," *Free America,* Vol. V, No. 3 (March, 1941). Tells how Hugh MacRae, Wilmington, North Carolina, agriculturalist, established the Carolina Trucking Development and settled European immigrants—carefully selected—in farm communities which they have helped develop, at St. Helena and Castle Hayne.

Homestead Projects (Washington: United States Department of Agriculture, Farm Security Administration, 1939). A compilation of eight reprinted articles concerning homestead projects of the Farm Security Administration in various sections of the nation, entitled: "Ghost Town Comes Back to Life," "100 Missouri Sharecroppers Move into a Land of Promise," "For the Poor Farmer: A New Lease on Life," "Families of Ashwood Plantation Make Live-at-Home a Reality," "Seek to Make Machinery Servant of the Farmer" (a two-phase experiment by the FSA in Pettis County, Missouri, which attempts to compare results of co-operation among individual farmers with those of a large-scale corporation farm), "You Can't Do Anything with Sharecroppers?," "Homesteaders—New Style," and "Uncle Sam's Co-op for Individualists."

No additional readings are suggested for Chapters IX and X.

CHAPTER XI, "COMMUNITY DESIGN," and
CHAPTER XII, "A STUDY OF THE COMMUNITY"

Sanderson and Polson, *Rural Community Organization* (New York: John Wiley & Sons, Inc., 1939). An excellent guide for persons interested in community organization. The authors are among the foremost authorities in the field. The book is written in clear, simple language.

Sanderson, Dwight, "Criteria of Rural Community Formation," *Rural Sociology*, Vol. III, No. 4 (December, 1938). A discussion of the rural community as an emerging social concept. Discusses the public school as a center for rural community organization.

Brunner, Edmund deS., *Surveying Your Community: A Handbook of Method for the Rural Church* (New York: George H. Doran Company, 1925).

Colcord, Joanna C., *Your Community: Its Provision for Health, Education, Safety, Welfare* (New York: Russell Sage Foundation, 1939). "An excellent monograph to guide the professional or amateur worker in social welfare, education, religion, public health . . . in the effort to acquire a good working knowledge of his community. It can also be used effectively in beginning courses in methods of community surveys."

A Handbook in Community Development (Greenville, South Carolina: The Southeastern Workshop, 1941). Discusses briefly but with valuable practicality the following topics: how to begin a community development program, community health, social agencies, adult education, the church, "40 do's and don't's for community leaders," and many other problems.

Sanderson, Dwight, *School Centralization and the Rural Community*, Cornell Extension *Bulletin 445*. (Ithaca: New York State College of Agriculture at Cornell University, 1940). Declares that the central rural-school district should constitute or have possibilities of becoming a "natural community."

Works and Lesser, *Rural America Today* (Chicago: University of Chicago Press, 1942). See Chapter XV, "What Rural Communities Are Doing to Improve Their Own Situation."

Nelson and Wakefield, *Making Community Surveys*, University of Minnesota Agricultural Extension *Pamphlet 73*, St. Paul, 1941. Discusses factors to consider before making a survey, methods of securing information, and subjects which may be studied.

Heberle, Rudolf, "The Application of Fundamental Concepts in Rural Community Studies," *Rural Sociology,* Vol. VI, No. 3 (September, 1941).

Hanna, Anderson, and Gray, *Centerville* (Chicago: Scott, Foresman & Company, 1938). A "social studies reader for the lower grades. It is also applied rural sociology in story form about business, roads, communication, food, clothes, agriculture, community organization, and the school as a community institution in a small village and its trade area."

Bulletins of the *New Dominion Series,* University of Virginia Extension Division (Charlottesville, Va.): No. 4, "Planning Tomorrow's Community"; No. 10, "Prince William's Five-Point Program"; No. 11, "A Planned Rural Community." These are well written, interesting pamphlets.

CHAPTER XIII, "THE COMMUNITY COUNCIL"

American Youth Commission, *Rallying Resources for Youth* (Washington: American Council on Education, 1940). Describes how three community councils developed and what they have done, in Dowagiac, Michigan; Greenville, South Carolina; and Los Angeles County. Contains bibliography.

Community Cooperation for Social Welfare (New York: National Probation Association, 1937). Contains material by several persons: Lindeman on "New Patterns of Community Organization"; Burgess, Lohmann, and Shaw on "The Chicago Area Project"; Hall on "Administration and Supervision of Community Councils"; Einert on "Qualifications and Training of Coordinating Council Executives"; and Beam, "Report of Coordinating Councils."

Morgan, E. L., *Mobilizing the Rural Community,* Massachusetts Agricultural College Extension *Bulletin 23,* 1918. An original suggestion for community councils, outlining a general form of organization somewhat like that later followed in California and elsewhere. (This is reproduced in Sims' *The Rural Community.*)

Ensminger, Douglas, "The Missouri Standard Community Plan after Thirteen Years," *Rural Sociology,* Vol. IV, No. 1 (March, 1939), pp. 58-66. An account of the working of the community organization plan introduced by E. L. Morgan. A very helpful discussion of causes of success or failure of community organization.

A Guide to Community Coordination (Los Angeles: Coordinating Councils, Inc., 1941). A very useful publication for persons interested in the organization of community councils. The best statement of the Coordinating Council movement.

A Handbook in Community Development (Greenville, South Carolina: The Southeastern Workshop, 1941). Report of the group which attended the "Southeastern Workshop in Community Development" at Greenville during the summer of 1941.

Industrial Areas Foundation (Chicago: Industrial Areas Foundation, 1940). A description of the achievements during five months of the

"Back of the Yards Neighborhood Council" in Chicago's stockyard areas.

Community Coordination, published bimonthly by Coordinating Councils, Inc., 145 West Twelfth Street, Los Angeles. The organ of the Coordinating Council movement; succeeds *Coordinating Council Bulletin*, which ceased publication in December, 1938.

The Coordinator, published monthly by Los Angeles County Coordinating Councils, 139 North Broadway, Los Angeles.

Community Organization News, issued in mimeographed form several times a year; edited by Robert A. Polson of Cornell University.

New Dominion Series, University of Virginia Extension Division, Charlottesville, Va. The leaflets in this series are published monthly January-June and twice monthly July-December, and are distributed free of charge. Series describes experimental approaches to democratic living as practiced in various communities.

CHAPTER XIV, "COMMUNITY LEADERSHIP," and
CHAPTER XV, "COMMUNITY FOLLOWERSHIP"

Sanderson, E. Dwight, *Leadership for Rural Life* (New York: Association Press, 1940). This is an admirable, sane discussion, in simple, non-technical language. An excellent guide for any person who wishes to be useful in his community.

Whitehead, T. N., *Leadership in a Free Society* (Cambridge: Harvard University Press, 1936). An excellent discussion of principles and practice.

Tead, Ordway, *The Art of Leadership* (New York: McGraw-Hill Book Company, Inc., 1935). A very able discussion of the principles and art of leadership in a democracy.

Lindstrom, D. E., *The Rural Community Unit: A Manual for Community Organization Leaders* (Urbana: University of Illinois Extension Service, College of Agriculture, 1941). This manual gives very specific and helpful suggestions for needs, nature, and purpose of organization, as well as procedures, program-planning, activities, co-operation with other groups, etc. Outlines duties of officers, sample meeting plans, a sample constitution and by-laws.

Walser, Frank, *The Art of Conference* (New York: Harper & Brothers, 1933). An excellent discussion of the process of conferring as a way of working in a democracy, with descriptions of a number of cases.

Chancellor, John, *Public Library Discussion Meetings* (Chicago: American Library Association, 1942). Principles and methods of group discussion, with brief bibliography.

Hutchinson, Carl R., *Guide for Discussion Circles* (New York: Co-operative League of the United States of America).

Cooperative Discussion Circles (Columbus: Ohio Farm Bureau). Describes the activities of the Advisory Council groups of the Ohio Farm Bureau, which have been referred to as among the most significant expressions of American democracy.

Schell, Harry, "Experiment in Social Relationships," *Opportunity*, Vol. XIX, No. 2 (February, 1941). Describes the "Fireside Forum" idea in Gary, Indiana, a means through which neighbors of every creed and nationality meet in each other's homes to discuss whatever concerns them in a frank manner, with no thought of formulating a program of action, but with the emphasis on free speech and sincere tolerance.

CHAPTER XVI, "GOVERNMENT AND PUBLIC RELATIONS"

Lancaster, Lane W., *Government in Rural America* (New York: D. Van Nostrand Company, Inc., 1937). Includes a discussion of the origin of New England town government. A realistic description of the various units of local rural government in America as they now function.

Dewey, John, *The Public and Its Problems* (New York: Henry Holt & Company, 1927). See Chapter V, "Search for the Great Community."

Bryce, James, *Modern Democracies* (New York: The Macmillan Company, 1927, 2 vols.). See Vol. I, Chapter XII, and Vol. II, Chapter LXVI. These chapters deal with local government and its importance in relation to central government.

Manny, Theodore B., *Rural Municipalities* (New York: The Century Company, 1930). Discussion of the need for uniting villages and their surrounding tributary territory into single governmental units.

Duncan, Kunigunde, "Town Hall Goes to the Country," *Free America*, Vol. V, No. 7 (July, 1941). More than forty states have enabling acts by which farmers may organize a district, make laws governing land practices therein, and enforce them. This article describes the general working of the plan in Texas.

CHAPTER XVII, "COMMUNITY ECONOMICS"

Kolb and Brunner, *A Study of Rural Society* (Boston: Houghton Mifflin Company, 1940). Chapter XXI, "Rural Merchandising and Industry," is one of the best descriptive treatments of rural economics in America. While most discussions on rural economics are chiefly concerned with agriculture, we read in this chapter that ". . . approximately one village out of every four classified by the United States census as 'rural' has no connection with agriculture, and no dependence on it for livelihood."

Brunner and Lorge, *Rural Trends in Depression Years* (New York: Columbia University Press, 1937). Chapter V, "Business and Industry," and Chapter VI, "Rural Banking," are chiefly informative and statistical.

Cole and Crowe, *Recent Trends in Rural Planning* (New York: Prentice-Hall, Inc., 1937). Chapter II, "The Economic Bases of Rural Planning," is mainly a statistical discussion of agricultural economy.

Colcord, *Your Community* (New York: Russell Sage Foundation, 1939). Chapter VI, "Workers, Wages, Conditions of Employment," is an outline for community surveys on these subjects.

Gutheim, Frederick, "Frank Lloyd Wright: Prophet of Decentralization," *Free America*, Vol. V, No. 4 (April, 1941).

Useem, John, "Does Decentralized Industry Mean Greater Security? The Case of Massachusetts," *Rural Sociology*, Vol. VI, No. 1 (March, 1941). This survey of the situation in Massachusetts concludes that decentralized industry in its present form does not mean greater security either for the workers or for their communities, and, among other indications, the rural industrial worker has much less security than the city industrial worker or the full-time farmer.

How to Discover and Develop the Assets of Small Communities and Thus Insure for Them a More Prosperous Future (Washington: United States Department of Commerce, 1942). This "small-town manual" describes a tested plan for improving business in small towns to meet the needs of communities in war time.

Greenleaf, Walter J., *80 New Books on Occupations, 1939-40* (Washington: United States Federal Security Agency, United States Office of Education, Misc. 2395, 1940). Some of the most useful books in the field are annotated from an occupational viewpoint to aid the counselor, student, or job-seeker, from the hundreds published between January, 1939, and July, 1940. Index helps identify books on particular occupations.

Gregg, Richard B., *The Value of Voluntary Simplicity* (Wallingford, Pennsylvania: Pendle Hill, 1940).

CHAPTER XVIII, "CO-OPERATIVES AS AN EXPRESSION OF COMMUNITY"

Kress, Andrew J., ed., *Introduction to the Cooperative Movement* (New York: Harper & Brothers, 1941). Contains selections from most of the important writings in the field during the last century, including material by Robert Owen, Albert Sonnichsen, Beatrice Webb, Horace Kallen, George W. Russell (A. E.), Dr. James P. Warbasse, Charles Gide, Toyohiko Kagawa, et al. This is supplemented with shorter descriptions of the movement to date.

Sorenson, Helen L., *The Consumer Movement: What It Is and What It Means* (New York: Harper & Brothers, 1941). "A splendid survey of the problems of the consumer and the organizations which have been formed to work toward a solution of these problems."

How to Organize a Cooperative Club (Brooklyn: Eastern Cooperative League, 1939). Full explanation with by-laws, forms and commodity buying lists, shelf construction diagrams for a grocery co-operative. The cover design indicates the growth of a study club into a buying club and finally a co-operative store.

Alanne, V. S., *Manual for Cooperative Directors* (New York: Cooperative League of the United States of America).

Rochdale Institute (New York: Cooperative League House, 1941). The prospectus of the national training school for service and leadership in co-operative business and education. Contains brief list of books on co-operation by Rochdale teachers.

Hoffer, C. R., "Cooperation as a Culture Pattern within a Community," *Rural Sociology,* Vol. III, No. 2 (June, 1938). A description of a long period of co-operative development in Howell, Michigan, a community of about 8300. An unusually successful co-operative history.

Turner, H. Haines, *Case Studies of Consumers' Cooperatives* (New York: Columbia University Press, 1941). An appraisal of consumer co-operatives as a means of storekeeping, with attention to the Finns of the Lake Superior region and of Maynard, Massachusetts.

Fretz, J. Winfield, "Mutual Aid Among Mennonites," *Mennonite Quarterly Review,* Vol. XIII, Nos. 1 and 3 (January and July, 1939). Describes

the habit of co-operation which gives expression to the sense of brotherhood among the Mennonites. (The oldest Mennonite co-operative—fire
insurance—antedates Rochdale by about two centuries). Particularly
describes co-operatives at Mountain Lake, Minnesota.

Coady, M. M., *Masters of Their Own Destiny* (New York: Harper &
Brothers, 1939). "This is the story, as told by the Director of Extension
at St. Francis Xavier University, of the efforts and methods used to
spread the philosophy of economic co-operation through adult education to the Scottish, French, and Irish people of the Maritime Provinces."

Fowler, Bertram B., *The Lord Helps Those* (New York: Vanguard Press,
Inc., 1938). "The story of the Nova Scotia cooperators given hope by
Father Tomkins." A popular account.

Bergengren, Roy F., *Credit Union, North America* (Kingsport, Tennessee:
Southern Publishers, Inc., 1940).

New Plans of Medical Service (New York: Bureau of Cooperative Medicine, 1940).

Woodbury, Lawrence C., "A Neighborhood Cooperative Nursery School,"
Recreation, Vol. XXXV, No. 5 (August, 1941).

Mann, L. B., *Refrigerated Food Lockers: A New Cooperative Service*
(Washington: United States Farm Credit Administration *Circular
C-107,* 1940).

Organization and Management of Cooperative Housing Associations (Washington: United States Department of Labor, Bureau of Labor Statistics, *Bulletin No. 608,* 1934).

Oppenheimer, Franz, *Cooperative Farm Communities* (Athens: University
of Georgia).

Good Neighbor: An Explanation of the Community Services Program
(Washington: United States Department of Agriculture, Farm Security
Administration). The program was designed as a facility to meet the
need for rural rehabilitation borrowers and other low-income farmers.
"When two or more farmers agree to use the same service, equipment,
or property, this is a Community Service." A brief description of the
idea.

CHAPTER XIX, "COMMUNITY HEALTH"

Smillie, Wilson G., *Public Health Administration in the United States*
(New York: The Macmillan Company, 1936). Chapter XXX, "Rural
Health Administration," is a good discussion of the subject.

Mustard, Harry S., *Rural Health Practice* (New York: The Commonwealth
Fund, 1936). A very comprehensive discussion, of value principally to
public health officers.

Halbert, Blanche, *Hospitals for Rural Communities* (Washington: United
States Department of Agriculture, *Farmers' Bulletin No. 1792,* 1937).

Osborn, Frederick, *Preface to Eugenics* (New York: Harper & Brothers,
1940). An outline of the field. Provides a background for thinking in
the field of health and social welfare.

American Red Cross, *First Aid Text-Book* (Philadelphia: Blakiston Company, 1940). Probably the best text for teaching first aid methods.

Lapham, Maxwell E., *Maternity Care in a Rural Community* (New York:

The Commonwealth Fund, 1940). Description of work in Pike County, Mississippi, 1931-36.

Bassett, Clara, *Mental Hygiene in the Community* (New York: The Macmillan Company, 1934).

Community Committees for Dental Health (Washington: National Dental Hygiene Association, 1941). Describes magnitude of dental health problem and offers suggestions for development of specific community programs of control.

Works and Lesser, *Rural America Today* (Chicago: University of Chicago Press, 1942). See Chapter IX, "The Schools and Rural Health."

Goldmann, Franz, *Prepayment Plans for Medical Care* (New York: Joint Committee of the Twentieth Century Fund and the Good Will Fund, and Medical Administration Service, Inc., 1941). Discusses general principles. Then compares five plans of organized medical care for self-supporting people—two consumers' co-operatives, two connected with group clinics operated by private physicians, and one managed by an industrial corporation.

Group Health Cooperative, Incorporated (New York: Group Health Co-operative, Inc.). The prospectus of a "voluntary, non-profit health insurance plan operating under the supervision of the New York State Insurance Department pursuant to Article IX-C of the Insurance Law."

New Plans of Medical Service (New York: Bureau of Cooperative Medicine, 1940). Describes thirty organized local plans for providing or paying for medical services in the United States.

Shadid, Michael A., *A Doctor for the People* (New York: The Vanguard Press, 1939). Autobiography of the doctor who established the first co-operative hospital in the United States, at Elk City, Oklahoma.

CHAPTER XX, "COMMUNITY SOCIAL SERVICES"

Kurtz, Russell H., ed., *Social Work Year Book, 1941* (New York: Russell Sage Foundation, 1941). An encyclopedia of "organized activities in social work and in related fields." Brief authoritative articles, alphabetically arranged, on topics relating to social welfare; also directories of national and state welfare organizations.

Proceedings of the National Conference of Social Work. Issued annually.

Cowgill, Ella Lee, *A Guidebook for Beginners in Public Assistance Work* (New York: Family Welfare Association of America, 1940).

De Schweinitz, Karl, *The Art of Helping People Out of Trouble* (Boston: Houghton Mifflin Company, 1924).

Byington, Margaret F., *What Social Workers Should Know about Their Own Communities* (New York: Russell Sage Foundation, 1929).

Kurtz, Russell H., ed., *The Public Assistance Worker* (New York: Russell Sage Foundation, 1938).

Healy and Bronner, *New Light on Delinquency and Its Treatment* (New Haven: Yale University Press, 1936).

Brown, Josephine C., *The Rural Community and Social Case Work* (New York: Family Welfare Association of America, 1933).

Hayes, Wayland J., "Public Welfare and Family Social Work in Rural Areas," *Rural Sociology*, Vol. VI, No. 1 (March, 1941).

CHAPTER XXI, "SMALL COMMUNITY RECREATION"

Cole and Crowe, *Recent Trends in Rural Planning* (New York: Prentice-Hall, Inc., 1937). Chapter XIII, "Planning for Effective Rural Recreation," is one of the better discussions of rural recreation, especially as related to agricultural and small village conditions.

Recreation: *A Major Community Problem* (New York: National Recreation Association, 1936).

Butler, George D., *Introduction to Community Recreation* (New York: Prepared for the National Recreation Association by McGraw-Hill Book Company, Inc., 1940). "This book deals with forms of recreation which require a large degree of organization and leadership." An authoritative guide and textbook for professional leaders of recreation, especially in large cities. Small-community recreation under volunteer leadership is not emphasized.

Jacks, L. P., *Education Through Recreation* (New York: Harper & Brothers, 1932). A book dealing with the art of living creatively. An excellent general discussion of the place of recreation in normal living.

Patten, Marjorie, *The Arts Workshop of Rural America* (New York: Columbia University Press, 1937). Describes significant rural community programs in drama, art, and music, worked out with the aid and leadership of state college extension services.

Todd, Arthur J., "Recreation and Delinquency," *Youth Leaders Digest*, Vol. IV, No. 6 (March, 1942). "The fact that delinquency is on the increase in spite of the rapid growth of organized recreation programs should make some of us think a little deeper" about the alleged therapeutic value of recreation. The Chicago Recreation Commission's three-year study indicates that the amount of time spent in recreation is much less significant than the selection and quality of the activity. Delinquents actually spend more time in recreation than non-delinquents, but prefer unsupervised, "rough-and-tumble," and less creative activities.

Works and Lesser, *Rural America Today* (Chicago: University of Chicago Press, 1942). See Chapter X, "The Schools and Rural Recreation."

Recreation, published monthly by the National Recreation Association, 315 Fourth Avenue, New York City. A periodical survey of the recreation field, indispensable for persons engaged in recreation as a calling or as a public service. The Association also issues up-to-date information on recreation through its "Recreation Bulletin Service."

The Kit, edited by Lynn Rohrbough, published quarterly by the Cooperative Recreation Service at Delaware, Ohio. Gives up-to-date recreation materials in form of small pamphlets, some of which have been assembled in loose-leaf covers under the titles of "Handy Kits" and "Bargain Kits." They cover such subjects as "Quiet Games," "Outdoor Games," "Mountain Dances," "Family Recreation."

Grey, Viscount, *Recreation* (Boston: Houghton Mifflin Company, 1920). This little book is one of the finest discussions of recreation ever written. Grey, who was a great foreign minister of England during the first World War, was great also as a human being, and his book might well set the ideal of recreation for persons who would have their play an integral part of a well-proportioned life. "We may make the joy of life great as well as the duty of life, and we may find that the joy of life and the duty of life are not things adverse or even to be contrasted, but . . . companions and complements of each other."

Palmer, E. Laurence, "Waterways in Spring," *Cornell Rural School Leaflet* Vol. XXXIII, No. 4 (March, 1940), published by the New York State College of Agriculture at Cornell University, Ithaca, New York. This is one of a series of pamphlets on phases of nature. Excellent for boys and girls who have a spark of love for nature.

"It's Being Done in Nature Recreation," *Recreation* magazine. A department of the magazine edited by "Cap'n Bill." It briefly reviews many activities and projects in nature recreation.

The Living Wilderness, published quarterly by The Wilderness Society, 1840 Mintwood Place, Washington, D. C., in the interest of those who appreciate the unspoiled nature of America.

Van De Wall, Willem, *The Music of the People* (New York: American Association for Adult Education, 1938). A discussion of the place of music in America.

Rodeheaver and Ford, *Song Leadership.*

Zanzig, A. D., *Community and Assembly Singing* (New York: National Recreation Association).

Songs for Informal Singing (New York: National Recreation Association). Folk songs with melodies. Two sets available, about 24 songs in each.

Rohrbough, Lynn, *Musical Kits* (Delaware, Ohio: Cooperative Recreation Service).

Arnold, Alfred G., *The Little Country Theater* (New York: The Macmillan Company, 1921).

Perry, Clarence A., *The Work of the Little Theatres: The Groups They Include, The Plays They Produce, Their Tournaments, and the Handbooks They Use* (New York: Russell Sage Foundation, 1933).

Dean, Alexander, *Little Theatre Organization and Management for Community, University, and School* (New York: D. Appleton-Century Company, Inc., 1926).

Wileden, Rockwell, and Borchers, *Dramatics for Small Groups,* University of Wisconsin Extension Service *Circular 257,* Madison, 1933.

Kozlenko, William, compiler, *One Hundred Non-Royalty One-Act Plays* (New York: Greenberg Publishers, Inc., 1940).

Tolman and Page, *The Country Dance Book* (Weston, Vermont: The Countryman Press, 1937).

Nielsen, Aksel G., *An Evening of Old Time Social Dancing* (Los Angeles: Work Projects Administration, Division of Community Service Programs, 1942). "Descriptions and music for twelve 'popular' old time dances."

Rohrbough, Lynn, ed., *Handy Country Dance Book* (Delaware, Ohio: Cooperative Recreation Service, 1941).

Muller, "Allemande" Al, *All-American Square Dances* (New York: Paull-Pioneer Music Corporation). Contains music, calls, diagrams, directions, and glossary of terms used in square dances, quadrilles, and lancers. Extra music for schottisches, polkas, and waltzes. Practical, with music simply arranged.

Harbin, Elvin O., *The Fun Encyclopedia* (Nashville: Cokesbury Press,

1940). "A single volume covering the entire recreational field. It contains twenty-four hundred game and entertainment ideas for all ages, and will be especially useful in conducting school, church, club, and camp activities."

Smith, Charles F., *Games and Game Leadership* (New York: Dodd, Mead & Company, Inc., 1932). All kinds of indoor and outdoor games most suitable for children.

Handbook for Recreation Leaders (Washington: United States Department of Labor, Children's Bureau *Publication 231*). A collection of games useful for rural groups indoors or outdoors.

Calkins, Ernest E., *The Care and Feeding of Hobby Horses* (New York: Leisure League of America, 1934).

Lampland, Ruth, ed., *Hobbies for Everybody* (New York: Harper & Brothers, 1934).

Leisure League Little Books (New York: Leisure League of America, Inc.). A series of fifteen books on hobbies, including photography, quilting, music, stamp collection, hiking.

Butler, George D., *Playgrounds: Their Administration and Operation* (New York: A. S. Barnes & Company, 1936).

Conduct of Playgrounds (New York: National Recreation Association). Many suggestions will be found here which will be of help to the community-center worker.

Mulac, Margaret E., *The Playleaders' Manual* (New York: Harper & Brothers, 1941).

What Recreation Executives Do (New York: National Recreation Association). Prepared in co-operation with recreation executives, this sheet lists 48 detailed directive and supervisory activities.

Manufacturers and Distributors of Craft Supplies and Equipment (New York: National Recreation Association, 1941).

Home Made Play Apparatus (New York: National Recreation Association, 1940). Contains detailed diagrams for constructing a jump standard, see-saw, balance beam, horizontal bar, three swing set, sand box, basketball goal, horizontal ladder, and baseball backstop, with brief suggestions on construction.

Orsatti, L. A., "First Aid for Recreation Supplies," *Recreation,* Vol. XXXVI, No. 1 (April, 1942). Gives a number of general and specific suggestions for group-recreation leaders for the purchase, proper use and care, and repair of recreational supplies and materials.

The National Recreation Association has booklets on arts and crafts, clay modeling, crafts projects that can be made with inexpensive and discarded materials, cylinder weaving, outline guide in arts and crafts, shadow puppets, simple weaving, etc.

CHAPTER XXII, "SOCIAL AND CULTURAL ASPECTS OF COMMUNITY LIFE"

The literature of general education is so vast and so specialized that it is not touched on in this reading list. Publications of other social and cultural aspects of community life are included in suggested readings for Chapters XVI, XVII, and XXI.

Conduct of Community Centers: A Practical Guide for Community Center Workers (New York: National Recreation Association, 1936). Gives

SUGGESTED READINGS 301

quite specific suggestions, with some examples of existing centers, on organizing the center, its program, facilities and equipment, administrative policies, suggestions to workers, and a short bibliography.

Halbert, Blanche, *Community Buildings for Farm Families* (Washington: United States Department of Agriculture, *Farmers' Bulletin 1804*, 1938). Suggests planning such centers in relation to churches, stores, etc., as many-use buildings which bring people together not only for activities, but to meet the problem of planning and financing the center. Photographs or floor plans are given for about 25 many-use, special-use, and remodeled buildings which illustrate various considerations.

Englehart and Englehart, *Planning the Community School* (New York: American Book Company, 1940). Discusses design and use of school plant to make it available for general community purposes.

Beals and Brody, *The Literature of Adult Education* (New York: American Association for Adult Education, 1941). A very extensive bibliography, with many subheadings. Discusses briefly the various phases of adult education. A good encyclopedia and handbook for persons desiring a general view of the field, and a full bibliography of related literature.

McClusky, Howard Y., "Mobilizing the Community for Adult Education," *Michigan Alumnus Quarterly Review*, Vol. 45, No. 19 (April 29, 1939). Reprints available from the American Library Association, 520 North Michigan Avenue, Chicago. "Probably the clearest, most penetrating, and practical analysis of the need for coordination of a community's efforts for its own improvement."

McClusky, Howard Y., "It's Happening Here!" *Michigan Education Journal*, April, 1939. Reprints available from the American Library Association. "Several Michigan communities—Branch County, Dowagiac, and Hartland—are developing total educational resources through cooperative planning."

The Study Club Way of Adult Learning (Antigonish, Nova Scotia: St. Francis Xavier University Extension Department).

How St. Francis Xavier University Educates for Action (New York: Co-operative League of the United States of America, 1938). Stimulating accounts of adult education for co-operation in Nova Scotia.

American Youth Commission, *Youth and the Future* (Washington: American Council on Education, 1942). A sweeping view of the problems of youth and of society in general, with proposals for meeting those needs in economic life, education, recreation, marriage and the home, health, delinquency, and citizenship.

Chambers, M. M., *Youth-Serving Organizations* (Washington: American Council on Education, 1941). "A descriptive directory, revised and enlarged (from the 1937 edition), supplying essential data on 320 national, non-governmental agencies serving youth."

Folsom, Joseph K., *Youth, Family, and Education* (Washington: American Council on Education, 1941). This report to the American Youth Commission covers the development and contemporary status of the relation and integration of education and family living.

Menefee and Chambers, *American Youth: An Annotated Bibliography*

(Washington: American Youth Commission, 1938). "A basic reference for those working with young people, containing annotations of 2,500 published items on youth problems."

Rural Public Library Service (Chicago: American Library Association, 1941). "Tells what to do about the situation. For the rural leader interested in developing good library service in his own state."

The Equal Chance: Books Help to Make It (Chicago: American Library Association, 1936). "Makes very clear the need for extension of library service."

Humble, Marion, *Rural America Reads* (New York: American Association for Adult Education, 1938). A discussion of reading facilities in rural areas.

Rural Library Service (Washington: United States Department of Agriculture, Bureau of Agricultural Economics, Farmers' *Bulletin 1847*, 1940). This pamphlet describes how the service is started, operated, and led, shows how rural people use library books, and gives suggestions for action and brief sketches of three types of county libraries.

Administration of the Small Public Library (Chicago: American Library Association).

Fargo, Lucile F., *The Library in the School* (Chicago: American Library Association, 1939). "The most comprehensive treatment yet given to the school library."

Works and Lesser, *Rural America Today* (Chicago: University of Chicago Press, 1942). See Chapter VIII, "Library Service in Rural Communities and Schools."

Danton, Emily M., *The Library of Tomorrow* (Chicago: American Library Association, 1939). A symposium on what a library should be.

An Invitation to Read (New York: Municipal Reference Library, 1941). Subtitled *The Use of the Book in Child Guidance*, this is an excellent, carefully prepared list of titles recommended by Mayor LaGuardia's "Committee for the Selection of Suitable Books for Children in the Courts." The 382 titles are annotated, and are grouped according to suitability on the basis of school grade levels: 1-3, 4-5, 6-8, and 9-12.

CHAPTER XXIII, "COMMUNITY ETHICS"

Dewey and Tufts, *Ethics* (New York: Henry Holt & Company, 1926). A general treatment of the field from a critical, open-minded viewpoint. An old book, but still one of the best.

Titus, Harold H., *Ethics for Today* (New York: American Book Company, 1936). A clearly expressed, nontechnical discussion of the nature and development of ethics, written for undergraduate college students, from a scientific approach. A good book for getting a present-day view of the subject.

Kropotkin, P., *Ethics: Origin and Development* (New York: The Dial Press, 1924). In this book, which is a development of his earlier work, *Mutual Aid*, Kropotkin undertakes to show that ethics is a natural outcome of social life, and that it is older than humanity. The book presents an attitude toward ethical problems, rather than a detailed ethical code.

Morgan, Arthur E., *The Long Road* (Washington: National Home Library

Foundation, 1936). See Chapter II, "Specifications for National Character."

Morgan, Arthur E., *My World* (Yellow Springs, Ohio: Kahoe & Company, 1927). The writer's view of the basis and nature of ethical action.

CHAPTER XXIV, "THE CHURCH IN THE COMMUNITY"

Troeltsch, Ernst, *The Social Teaching of the Christian Churches* (New York: The Macmillan Company, 1931, 2 vols.). A classic study of the social attitudes of all branches of the Christian church throughout its history. Incidentally discusses early Christian community life.

The Christian Rural Fellowship Bulletin, published monthly by the Christian Rural Fellowship, 156 Fifth Avenue, New York City. Deals with many rural problems and discusses how the church may contribute to their solution.

Brunner and Lorge, *Rural Trends in Depression Years* (New York: Columbia University Press, 1937). See Chapter XII, "Rural Religion."

Rich, Mark, *The Larger Parish: An Effective Organization for Rural Churches,* Cornell Extension *Bulletin 408* (Ithaca: New York State College of Agriculture at Cornell University, 1939).

Brunner, Edmund deS., *The Larger Parish, A Movement or an Enthusiasm?* (New York: Harper & Brothers, 1934).

"Rural Education," *The Catholic Rural Life Bulletin* (published quarterly by the National Catholic Rural Life Conference, 525 Sixth Avenue, Des Moines, Iowa), May 20, 1941.

Clark, J. Reuben, Jr., *Church Welfare Plan* (Estes Park, Colorado: First Citizen's Conference on Government Management, 1939). A description of mutual aid among the Mormons.

Belfrage, Cedric, *South of God* (New York: Modern Age Books, 1941). The biography of Claude Williams, "a minister of the Gospel who has chosen to adventure on behalf of righteousness, asking few questions as to what might happen to himself. It is the story of what happened to him when he dared to make that venture in the kingdoms of cotton and coal."

Smathers, Eugene, *I Work in the Cumberlands* (Black Mountain, North Carolina: Fellowship of Southern Churchmen). "The remarkable story of prophetic religion at work in an isolated mountain community on the Cumberland Plateau, and how a minister brings the resources of the Christian faith to bear upon the difficult economic and social problems of a hard-pressed rural people."

NOTES FOR QUOTATIONS USED IN THE TEXT

Permission to make quotations from copyrighted books and pamphlets was generously granted by publishers and authors. Numbers used with these references correspond to those used in the text following each quotation.

1. Sims, Newell L., *The Rural Community, Ancient and Modern* (New York, Charles Scribner's Sons, 1920), pp. 120-121, by permission.
2. Baker, O. E.; Borsodi, Ralph; and Wilson, M. L., *Agriculture in Modern Life* (New York, Harper & Brothers, 1939), p. 244, by permission of the publisher.
3. Graubard, Mark, "The Value of Group Work," from *Group Work 1939* (New York, American Association for the Study of Group Work), p. 19, by permission of the publisher.
4. Quoted in Sims, Newell L., *The Rural Community, Ancient and Modern* (New York, Charles Scribner's Sons, 1920), p. 50. Reprinted by permission of the publisher.
5. Hatch, Edwin, *The Organization of the Early Christian Church* (New York, Longmans, Green & Company, 1895), pp. 57, 69-70. Reprinted by permission of the publisher.
6. Smith, Arthur H., *Village Life in China* (New York, Fleming H. Revell Company, 1899), p. 227. Reprinted by permission of the publisher.
7. Liang, Y. K, and Tao, L. K., *Village and Town Life in China* (London, George Allen and Unwin, Ltd, 1923), pp. ix, vii, 4-5, by permission.
8. *Ibid.*, p. 40.
9. *Ibid.*, pp. 11, 45.
10. Altekar, A. S., *A History of Village Communities in Western India* (Calcutta, Oxford University Press, 1927), pp. iii, vii, ix, x, by permission of the publisher.
11. Peake, Harold, *The English Village: The Origin and Decay of Its Community: An Anthropological Interpretation* (London, Benn Brothers, Ltd., 1922), pp. 18, 19, 20, 21, 22. Reprinted by permission of the publisher.
12. Fielding, H., *The Soul of a People* (London, Macmillan & Company, Ltd., 1899), p. 59. Reprinted by permission of the publisher.
13. *Ibid.*, p. 61.
14. *Ibid.*, p. 72.
15. *Ibid.*, pp. 91-92.
16. *Ibid.*, p. 100.
17. Sorokin, P. A.; Zimmerman, Carle C.; and Galpin, Charles J., *A Systematic Source Book in Rural Sociology*, Vol. I, pp. 230-231, by permission of the publisher, The University of Minnesota Press, Minneapolis, Minnesota.

18. Fry, Charles Luther, *American Villagers* (New York, Harper & Brothers, 1926), p. 22. Reprinted by permission of the publisher.
19. Sorokin, Zimmerman, and Galpin, *Systematic Source Book, op. cit.,* Vol. I, pp. 324, 325, by permission of the publisher.
20. Smith, T. Lynn, *The Sociology of Rural Life* (New York, Harper & Brothers, 1940), p. 15. Reprinted by permission of the publisher.
21. North, Cecil, *The Community and Social Welfare* (New York, McGraw-Hill Book Company, Inc., 1931), p. vi, by permission of the publisher.
22. Sanderson, E. Dwight, and Polson, Robert A., *Rural Community Organization* (New York, John Wiley and Sons, Inc., 1939), pp. 73-74. Reprinted by permission.
23. Beam, Kenneth S., *Coordinating Councils in California,* Bulletin of the California State Department of Education, No. 11, September 1, 1938, p. 49. Reprinted by permission of the publisher.
24. Sanderson and Polson, *Rural Community Organization, op. cit.,* p. 234. Reprinted by permission.
25. Hart, Joseph K., *Community Organization* (New York, The Macmillan Company, 1920), p. 210, by permission of the publisher.
26. Sanderson, E. Dwight, *Leadership for Rural Life* (New York, Association Press, 1940), p. 49. Reprinted by permission.
27. Tead, Ordway, *The Art of Leadership* (New York, McGraw-Hill Book Company, Inc., 1935), p. 268. Reprinted by permission.
28. Hart, Joseph K., *Community Organization, op. cit.,* pp. 207-208, by permission of the publisher.
29. Locke, John, "Some Thoughts Concerning Education," from *The Harvard Classics* (New York: P. F. Collier & Son Corporation, 1910), Vol. 37, p. 187. Reprinted by permission of the publisher.
30. Dewey, John, *Democracy and Education: An Introduction to the Philosophy of Education* (New York, The Macmillan Company, 1921), p. 359. Reprinted by permission of the publisher.
31. Overstreet, Harry A., and Overstreet, Bonaro W., *Leaders for Adult Education* (New York, American Association for Adult Education, 1941), p. 26, by permission of the publisher.
32. Inge, Dean W. R., *Christian Ethics and Modern Problems* (New York, G. P. Putnam's Sons, 1930), pp. 5-6, by permission of the publisher.

INDEX

Adams, Herbert B., 41, 287
Adult education, 246; literature of, 248
Advisory Councils, Ohio Farm Bureau, 15, 25, 200-201, 252
Agricultural communiti s in America, 34-35
Alanne, V. S., 295
Alexandria, Ohio, Community Council, 15, 146, 154, 155; voluntary playground construction, 232
Altekar, A. S., 46
Amana, Iowa, 92, 100
Amish, 92
Anderson, G., 292
Antioch College, ix, 273
Archimedes, xvi
Arensberg, Conrad M., 285
Arnold, Alfred G., 299
Art for art's sake, 238, 239
Arts and sciences in community life, 251
Associations, single-purpose, 25
Augustine, 253

Bassett, Clara, 297
Beals, R. A., 301
Beam, Kenneth S., 148, 160
Beauty spots, community, 229
Belfrage, Cedric, 303
Bergengren, Roy F., 296
Berkeley, California, Coordinating Council, 146
Birth rates, rural and urban, 4
Blumenthal, Albert, 288
Boodin, J. E., 283, 284, 285
Brody, Leon, 301
Bronner, A. F., 297

Brook Farm, 101, 133, 265
Brown, Josephine C., 297
Brunner, Edmund DeS., xxi, 16, 283, 284, 286, 287, 291, 294, 303
Bryce James, 286, 294
Burma, British conquest of, 49-53; village autonomy in, 49-53
Butler, George D., 298, 300
Buy-at-home programs, 192
Byington, Margaret F., 297

Calkins, Ernest E., 300
Calverton, V. F., 290
Camping, hunting, and fishing, 231
Cash, W. J., 288
Chambers, M. M., 301
Chancellor, John, 283, 293
Christian ethics, origin of, 254
Christianity, early community life, 44; origins, 253
Churches, 263 ff.; democratic methods in, 92; desirable size of, 266; divisive factor in community, 110, 265-266; number of in U.S., 263; place of, in early America, 263-264; proper place of, in community, 264-268
Cincinnati, Neighborhood Coordinating Councils, 147
Cities, duration of, 4; size of medieval, 4
City, as a community, 87-88; unwholesomeness of life in, 32-33, 110
Clarence, New York, Community Council, 146, 154
Clark, J. Reuben, 303
Coady, M. M., 296

307

307, 762
MOR

CPSIA information can be obtained at www.ICGtesting.com
Printed in the USA
BVOW081534070113

309977BV00005B/19/P